ON METAPHYSICAL NECESSITY

ON METAPHYSICAL NECESSITY

ESSAYS ON GOD, THE WORLD,
MORALITY, AND DEMOCRACY

FRANKLIN I. GAMWELL

Published by State University of New York Press, Albany

© 2020 State University of New York Press

All rights reserved

No part of this book may be used or reproduced in any manner whatsoever without written permission. No part of this book may be stored in a retrieval system or transmitted in any form or by any means including electronic, electrostatic, magnetic tape, mechanical, photocopying, recording, or otherwise without the prior permission in writing of the publisher. For information, contact State University of New York Press, Albany, NY
www.sunypress.edu

Library of Congress Cataloging-in-Publication Data

Names: Gamwell, Franklin I., author.
Title: On metaphysical necessity : essays on God, the world, morality, and democracy / Franklin I. Gamwell.
Description: Albany : State University of New York Press, 2020 | Includes bibliographical references and index.
Identifiers: LCCN 2019030515 | ISBN 9781438479316 (hardcover) | ISBN 9781438479309 (paperback) | ISBN 9781438479323 (ebook)
Subjects: LCSH: Metaphysics. | Philosophical theology. | Ethics. | Religion and politics.
Classification: LCC BD111 .G33 2020 | DDC 110—dc23
LC record available at https://lccn.loc.gov/2019030515

10 9 8 7 6 5 4 3 2 1

for
FRAN
"the last, my love, the final thing"

CONTENTS

INTRODUCTION: ON TRANSCENDENTAL METAPHYSICS		1
Metaphysics		3
Transcendental		8
The Following Chapters		13

PART ONE
GOD AND THE WORLD: METAPHYSICS IN THE STRICT SENSE

1	A DEFENSE OF METAPHYSICAL NECESSITY	21
	Recent Thinkers	25
	The Pragmatic Self-Refutation	29
	Recent Thinkers Revisited	36
	Metaphysical Necessity	40
2	SPEAKING OF GOD AFTER AQUINAS	47
	A Reading of Aquinas	49
	Analogical and Purely Equivocal Names	53
	Theistic Arguments	58
	Burrell's Alternative	62
	The Principle of Prior Actuality	65
3	SCHLEIERMACHER AND TRANSCENDENTAL PHILOSOPHY	71
	Schleiermacher's Introduction to Dogmatics	72
	An Assessment of Schleiermacher's Achievement	80

4	THE SOURCE OF TEMPTATION	87
	Augustine: Through Adam to the Devil	87
	Reinhold Niebuhr: Sin Posits Itself	94
	Another Account: Human Fragmentariness	98
	Conclusion	106

PART TWO

MORALITY AND DEMOCRACY: METAPHYSICS IN THE BROAD SENSE

5	MORAL CREATURES AND THEIR DECISIONS	111
	Neoclassical Metaphysics in the Strict Sense	113
	Moral Understanding	118
	The Strictly Metaphysical Definition of Good	123
	Moral Creatures as Subjects	130
	The Transcendental Moral Principles	134
6	ON THE INTERPRETATION OF RELIGIOUS FREEDOM: A CONVERSATION WITH RONALD DWORKIN	141
	Dworkin's Interpretation	143
	Dworkin's Interpretation: A Critique	150
	Toward an Alternative Interpretation	157
7	ON RELIGIOUS FREEDOM AND ITS FREE EXERCISE	169
	Recent Theories	171
	Politics by the Way of Reason	173
	Free Exercise Exemptions	178
	Convictions and Confessions	184
8	THE REVOLUTION'S PROMISE	193
	Popular Sovereignty	195
	The States' Rights View	202
	The National View	206
	Consequences of the Revolution	213

NOTES	221
WORKS CITED	251
INDEX	257

INTRODUCTION

ON TRANSCENDENTAL METAPHYSICS

The importance of metaphysics to both philosophical theology and moral and political theory has been on my mind for some years, where philosophical theology asks about God and this world, and moral and political theory ask about the principles for our decisions and our decisions together in the political community. I have chosen the chapters collected in this volume with a view to that importance. As a kind of thinking about pervasive conditions, metaphysics is also, on my intention, a kind of critical reflection—where "critical" means simply reflection that seeks not only to formulate but also to validate relevant understandings. "Metaphysics" designates, then, in two systematically related senses. On the one hand, "metaphysics" has a strict sense, which means an explication of all possible reality or existence as such—where "as such" means the character or nature of existence in its most general sense. On the other hand, "metaphysics" has a broad sense and means an explication of all possible subjectivity or subjectivity as such.

The two are united in the most general moral and political principles—because they are themselves metaphysical in the broad sense, even while the good or telos, whose pursuit is what those principles prescribe, is defined metaphysically in the strict sense. Moreover, the metaphysics commended here is transcendental, where this means that both existence as such and subjectivity as such are literally designated, and is neoclassical, where this means that all possible reality and all possible subjectivity are best understood in terms of becoming rather than being (the meaning of both terms is further clarified later in this introduction and, respectively, in chapters 1 and 5).

Several of the chapters that follow have been previously published, although each has been revised in minor ways in order to ensure consistency in the concepts and terms used throughout. The introduction and chapters 5 and 8 appear here for the first time. The common theme throughout is the importance of metaphysical necessity both to philosophical theology and, through it, to moral and political theory. Precisely because this theme persists, I wish to speak of metaphysics in both strict and broad senses. If some thinkers within the current philosophical context allow the metaphysics of subjectivity, most reject or are suspicious of the metaphysics of existence. In this context, surely the first task is to make a case for the latter. Chapter 1, then, is an argument for metaphysics in the strict sense, and the following chapters of part 1 exploit this conclusion for several discussions in philosophical theology: about Thomas Aquinas's concept of theistic analogies, Friedrich Schleiermacher's account of how dogmatics relates to philosophy, and whether either Augustine or Reinhold Niebuhr is convincing in describing the relation between God and the source of temptation to human fault or sin.

The importance of metaphysics to philosophical theology is, then, background for the discussion of morality and democracy, which concerns metaphysics in the broad sense. In part 2, I am especially concerned to clarify what Immanuel Kant called "the supreme moral principle" (although, as I argue, that principle is a comprehensive purpose, not Kant's categorical imperative) and its significance for religious freedom. Chapter 5 includes an argument for a comprehensive purpose, whose telos is defined metaphysically in the strict sense, and serves for part 2 what chapter 1 does for part 1. In other words, chapter 5 seeks to bridge the two senses of metaphysics, so that a supreme moral principle results.

This conclusion is then exploited in chapter 6 through a conversation with Ronald Dworkin, a thinker whose political judgments I have long admired but whose moral and political account of religious freedom, as that of many others, I find problematic. I propose, in contrast, the way of reason as the form of political community constituted by religious freedom and consistent with transcendental metaphysics. The subsequent chapter addresses the problem of religious liberty, that is, claims for exemptions from generally applicable laws, and argues, given transcendental metaphysics, that opposition to the law is not cause for such an exemption. The final chapter seeks to confirm the importance of transcendental metaphysics to historical interpretation by showing how the former provides a resolution to the enduring debate between the so-called states' rights and the so-called national view of the US Constitution's authority.

In sum, then, these chapters have been chosen to commend transcendental metaphysics in its neoclassical mode, and to confirm its importance by application to abiding problems for philosophical theology and human existence—including talk about God and the world and morality and democracy.

I express my gratitude for permission to republish here chapters that have been previously published. Chapter 1 was published in the *Review of Metaphysics* 71, no. 2 (December 2017): 233--64. Reprinted by permission. Chapter 2 was published in the *Journal of Religion* 81, no. 2 (April 2001): 185--210 (© 2001 by the University of Chicago). Reprinted by permission. Chapter 3 was published in *Schleiermacher, the Study of Religion, and the Future of Theology: A Transatlantic Dialogue*, edited by Brent W. Sockness and Wilhelm Grab (Berlin: Walter DeGruyter, 2010), 135--49. Reprinted by permission. Chapter 4 was published in *Augustine Our Contemporary: Examining the Self in Past and Present*, edited by Willemien Otten and Susan E. Schreiner (Notre Dame, IN: University of Notre Dame Press, 2018), 267--91. Reprinted by permission. Chapter 6 was published in the *Journal of Religion* 95, no. 4 (October 2015): 506--33 (© 2015 by the University of Chicago). Reprinted by permission. Chapter 7 was published in the *Journal of Religion* 97, no. 4 (October 2017): 500--523 (© 2017 by the University of Chicago). Reprinted by permission.

I also express my gratitude to Philip Devenish, Brent Sockness, Schubert Ogden, and Alex Vishio—each of whom read some of the essays enclosed herein and gave me the benefit of his critical response. I thank especially the late Schubert M. Ogden, to whom, more than any other single individual, I owe the education I have received—not least, with respect to the following chapters, even if he might disagree with some things I say therein.

METAPHYSICS

If "transcendental metaphysics" designates in both strict and broad senses, we may say of the former that it explicates the features or conditions all possible things have in common, and of the latter that it explicates the features or conditions all possible subjects have in common. I will call metaphysics in the strict sense a set of statements about existential necessities and will also use this term to mean the features or conditions thereby made explicit—and I will sometimes speak of such statements or necessities as strictly metaphysical. Similarly, I will call metaphysics in the broad sense a set of statements about subjective necessities and will also use this term to mean the features or conditions thereby made explicit—and I will sometimes speak of such statements or necessities as broadly metaphysical. The two senses of "metaphysics" are systematically related because, as I will argue (in chapters 1 and 5), broadly metaphysical features include those that are strictly metaphysical; that is, some but not all subjective necessities are existential necessities. Subjects are, in other words, a specific kind of thing among all possible things, so that subjects as such also exemplify specific features or conditions, or subjects are specifications of existence as such.

That metaphysics (as a kind of critical reflection) is properly "transcendental" is something of which I have become convinced more recently—and some brief attention to uses of this term may be useful. On the whole, the scholastic use of "transcendental" designated features or conditions of the possible as such or existence as such, which I have called metaphysical in the strict sense; hence, transcendentals characterize anything real, given the differing senses in which something can be real—and these conditions were said to be either convertible or disjunctive. For instance, the terms "being," "one," "true," "good," and (sometimes) "beautiful" were said to name convertible transcendentals; that is, each designates a feature of anything real in the sense that it is real. On the other hand, the term "necessary or contingent" was said to be a disjunctive transcendental because anything real, in the sense that it is real, was said to be either necessary or contingent.

Transcendental metaphysics was also central to Kant's project, but he redefined the term. For him, the conditions in question were specifically human, that is, features of human reason, theoretical and practical—although these include a moral law that is "valid ... for all *rational creatures generally*" (Kant 1949, 26, see also 42), even if, for Kant, there could be no (theoretical) knowledge of rational creatures other than humans. In any event, critical reflection on the features necessary to human reason did not, for Kant, explicate any that humans share with all possible things, because he denied possible knowledge of things-in-themselves and thus transcendentals in the scholastic sense. For Kant, *all* (theoretical) knowledge of metaphysical conditions was specific to human reason as such.

In this work, "transcendental" will always designate metaphysical necessities. In either its strict or broad sense, then, transcendental metaphysics is here said to consist of statements that are necessarily true or statements that designate a form or forms of necessity. Clarity about why this is so will be aided by attention to the differing ways in which a critical statement may be necessarily true, such that its denial is self-contradictory. In one sense, a statement may be *pragmatically* necessary, and thus its denial may be pragmatically self-contradictory. A statement is pragmatically necessary when it designates a feature or condition implied by the subject in question. For instance, "I am an American" or "some subject is an American" is pragmatically necessary *if* that statement is uttered by an American, and "I am not an American" or "no subject is an American" is pragmatically self-contradictory *if* uttered by the same subject. Among statements that are pragmatically necessary, the important statements for the present discussion are those uttered by any one among all possible subjects because these statements designate conditions implied by subjects as such. If Kant, for instance, is convincing when he argues that all subjects are bound by a moral law, then any one among all possible subjects who states "I am bound by a moral law" or "some subject is bound by a moral law" states a pragmatic necessity, and any one among all possible subjects who states "I am not bound by a moral law" or "some subject is not bound by the moral law" is pragmatically self-contradictory because this subject implies as a feature or condition of all possible subjects what it also denies. A pragmatic necessity is, we may say, external, in the sense that its denial is contradicted by the implication of the act stating the denial—and the pragmatic necessities I will discuss in these chapters are the subjective necessities, those that no possible subject can deny without pragmatic self-contradiction or those that are metaphysical in the broad sense.

In contrast, the necessity may be internal to the statement itself and is so in either a *syntactic* or *semantic* sense. A syntactic necessity occurs in the structure of the statement's signs, independent of its meaning. For instance, "x is p, and therefore x is p" is necessarily true, and "x is p and not-p" is self-contradictory, whatever meaning is given to x and p, stipulating only that p is a predicate of x in the same respect. Alternatively, a semantic necessity is dependent on a statement's meaning. For instance, "something that is a yellow rose is a colored rose" is necessarily true because being yellow implies being colored; hence, "something that is a yellow rose and is colorless" is semantically self-contradictory.

In the chapters that follow, I will confine use of "necessarily true" and "self-contradictory" to their semantic designations and, further, to statements of existential necessities, and pragmatically necessary or pragmatically inconsistent statements of subjective necessities will be called pragmatically self-verifying or pragmatically self-refuting respectively. Focused on transcendental metaphysics, in other words, this book attends to (1) necessarily true statements having the form "something that is x exists" (so that "something" implies the features of any possible existence or features otherwise unspecified), denial of which is always self-contradictory, and (2) self-verifying statements having the form "some subject that is x exists" (so that "some subject" implies the features of all possible subjects or subjective features otherwise unspecified), denial of which is always pragmatically self-refuting. Given this focus, transcendental metaphysics is a form of logic, in distinction from a contingently true or false statement. Here, the latter means a statement at least some denial of which is neither self-contradictory nor self-refuting—although we should note that a certain statement, "some subject that is x exists" (where x designates a subjective necessity), is *not necessarily true*, and in that sense, the statement and its denial are contingently true or false *semantically*, but self-verifying *pragmatically*.

As noted above, transcendental metaphysics is possible, I think, only if it is also neoclassical. Neoclassical metaphysics is explicated at some length in chapter 5 and may be summarily described as including the systematic assertion that becoming rather than being is the basic character of reality; for such metaphysics, in other words, each instance of this basic character is a becoming or event. One neoclassical distinction, which is metaphysical in the strict sense and important to these discussions, is that between individuals (which endure, at least through more than one state and thus through a given length of time) and the momentary states, which I will call actualities, that actualize a given individual or of which they are parts. The actualities, each of which is fully concrete or particular, belong to an individual when they occur sequentially and when the individual is defined genetically. In other words, no two actualities are contemporaries, and both earlier and later actualities exemplify in common a distinguishing identity (or distinguishing characteristic) of the individual in question through internal relation of the later to the earlier. Moreover, the most extended sequence of actualities distinguished by an identity defines, at least for present purposes, the individual in question. Hence, relevant states both actualize the individual and exemplify an identity that is abstract, and the individual exists as long as it is exemplified somehow.

Unlike some who consider themselves neoclassical thinkers, however, I will use "neoclassical metaphysics" to mean an account in both the strict and broad senses of "metaphysics," that is, of the possible as such (or existence as such) and of subjectivity as such. Most neoclassical thinkers affirm a divine reality, although its nature has been controversial among them. To the best of my reasoning, however, the basic character of reality entails that God is rightly understood as an eminently temporal individual. This individual unifies again and again, without loss of any detail, the whole of what has happened in the world and is, therefore, both unsurpassable by any other individual and also self-surpassing—in distinction from the entirely unsurpassable (even by self) because completely eternal reality characteristic of classical metaphysics.

For neoclassical thought, again on my accounting, a difference between worldly and divine actualities as such is a metaphysical (in the strict sense) self-differentiation or disjunction—namely, between actualities fragmentarily related to other actualities and possibilities and actualities all-inclusively related (that is, related in all detail) to all other actualities and possibilities. The divine or all-inclusive actualities are sequentially ordered because any two could be contemporaries only if they could also be, *per impossible*, identical. Also, there can be only one divine individual, whose identity is all-inclusiveness, because two or more such individuals would have the same identity. This divine identity or nature can be distinguished metaphysically in the strict sense, so that statements about it are about existential necessities, and this follows because the difference between worldly and divine actualities is itself a *metaphysical* self-differentiation or disjunction. Worldly individuals, then, must be fragmentary because they must be different than the all-inclusive individual; in other words, they cannot be distinguished metaphysically in the strict sense. Accordingly, the identity of any given worldly individual must be existentially contingent, even if the distinction between existential necessities and existential contingencies is itself the statement of an existential necessity because actualities as such (even divine actualities) exemplify various contingent features.

When an actuality is subjective, I will call it an activity. Subjectivity characterizes a specific kind of actuality, namely, one that occurs (1) with understanding, and (2) understands itself as a state of the contingent individual thereby actualized. As a consequence, I will also use the term "subject" in a systematically ambiguous sense. On the one hand, "subject" designates a kind of actuality and, on the other, the kind of individual actualized. I mean to assert, then, that individuals and their states do not necessarily exist with understanding (for instance, in the inorganic world) and individuals whose actualities do exist with understanding are not necessarily subjective (possibly, for instance, in some nonhuman animals). Still, I do not limit subjects to human individuals, although human individuals are the most apparent examples of subjectivity. Perhaps certain other (higher) animals or certain individuals elsewhere in the universe, who do not depend on a human body, are also subjects.

If the difference between a given subjective activity and the individual it actualizes is important to the discussion, I will speak of a subjective activity in distinction from a subjective individual. "Subject as such" or "subjectivity as such" will designate what the identities of all possible subjective individuals have in common (and thus what all possible subjective activities exemplify)—and the distinction between subjective individuals and subjective activities is systematic precisely because a subjective individual is a series of subjective activities. This systematic ambiguity is important—again on my accounting—because a creature is moral in distinction from nonmoral (and thus decides between the moral and the immoral) only when it is a subject, that is, when the individual's activities understand themselves to actualize, and thus to exemplify the identity of, the given individual.

As far as I can see, activities that occur with understanding are not necessarily moral in distinction from nonmoral because the moral question is about the future to be pursued insofar as it is understood. Only an understanding of the individual in question opens futures competitive with the future as such (that is, the future without concern for any aspect thereof) in its strictly metaphysical respect.[1] Accordingly, the moral question is this: Is the good to be pursued defined by the future as such in its strictly metaphysical respect (chapter 5 will argue why the good is rightly defined metaphysically in the strict sense), so that this good ought to be maximized; or, alternatively, is the good defined, in some other respect or in some undue measure, or both, by the individual's own future or that of some specific group or community to which the individual is attached? At least as far as we know, a given actuality becomes an activity (that is, not only occurs with understanding but also understands the individual it exemplifies) only if that individual participates in the communication of a more developed linguistic community. Doing so allows an actuality to understand the contingent individual thereby actualized, to remember and envision that individual's own past and future in dramatic measure, and to distinguish contingent other futures from the future as such. In that sense, I will say that subjectivity occurs when its activities actualize existence with *developed* understanding. Hence, learning—specifically, the learning that one's states do actualize the individual in question—is a necessary condition of being a subject and thus a moral creature.

TRANSCENDENTAL

The mark of transcendental metaphysics, in distinction from any other supposed metaphysical statement, is literal formulation—an essential characteristic because metaphysics is a kind of logic. Absent literal formulation, metaphysical reflection cannot be critical: so to explicate existence as such and subjectivity as such as to validate one's statements about them is to demonstrate that denial of such statements is either (semantically) self-contradictory, in the case of statements about existential necessities, or pragmatically self-refuting, in the case of statements about subjective necessities. Moreover, literal concepts for metaphysical features are possible precisely because, as I will mention below, all subjects understand, if only implicitly, both the subjective and thus the existential necessities. Given that every subjective activity understands itself and the individual thereby actualized, literal designation of both kinds of necessity, that is, literal terms in which they are explicated, is a semantic possibility.

Existential necessities are designated in the literal existential statements of transcendental metaphysics in the strict sense—where every such statement, as mentioned above, has the form "something that is x exists." Such statements are necessarily true when x is a feature or condition of the possible as such. To be sure, the terms with which those features or conditions are designated may also have another, contingent meaning. If "relative" has a strictly metaphysical meaning, for instance, the same term may be used to mean another human to which there is a family tie—and if "decision" or "self-determination" has a strictly metaphysical meaning (namely, actual creativity within some given range of possibility, or unification of internal relations [see Whitehead 1978, 43; Hartshorne 1970, 2]), the same word may be used to mean an exercise of freedom that is distinctive to subjects on earth. But the literal meanings of strictly metaphysical terms having also a contingent designation are independent of the latter, save that all contingent meanings imply the metaphysical meanings. Beyond that implication, using the same term for two designations is, in Aristotle's sense, equivocal by chance: "they merely happen to have the same name" (Aristotle 1962, 1096b27)—although each meaning is a literal designation of some feature, and thus neither meaning is completely negative.

The two meanings are different because features of the possible as such are the most general possible features, and designation of any one cannot, as is the case with a contingent feature, be a specification of some greater abstraction. "Relative" as designating a family tie, for instance, is rightly explicated as specifying a greater abstraction, namely, ties to humans more generally, with designation of "family" being the specific differentia. Again, "decision" or "self-determination" as designating a choice specific to subjects on earth specifies a greater abstraction, namely, the self-determination of animals generally, with "subject" being the specific differentia. But strictly metaphysical features are designated in statements of the greatest possible abstraction, and therefore literal statements of existential necessities are, as Alfred North Whitehead says, "incapable of analysis in terms of factors more far reaching than themselves" (Whitehead 1938, 1). The literal meaning can be explicated only by designating its relation to other meanings (or features) of the same, most general measure of abstraction. This, I assume, is why Whitehead says: "the fundamental ideas . . . presuppose each other so that in isolation they are meaningless" (Whitehead 1978, 3).

The difference in meaning can also be clarified as follows: as necessarily true, the meaning of a statement designating some strictly metaphysical feature is infinitely different from the meaning of any statement designating a contingent feature. This is because statements about existential necessities designate features exemplified in the infinite past and the infinite future, and thus the application of each feature is infinite—while the designation of a contingent feature is necessarily finite as the specification of a greater abstraction, that is, necessarily finite by virtue of what it excludes. The infinite is infinitely different than the finite, although a finite feature, to be repetitious, specifies and thus implies features that are infinite. Alternatively stated, there is an infinite hierarchy of contingent features. Hence, generalizing any given such feature can never escape the contingency of the generalized feature.

That all transcendental statements in the strict sense are necessarily true entails their mutual implication; each is implied by all of its implications. This is what makes such metaphysics a form of semantic logic, in distinction from both syntactic and pragmatic logic, and may be called coherence in an emphatic sense. Such coherence is distinguished from a coherent set of statements, each of which implies others that imply it but also implies more abstract statements that do not imply it. Metaphysical features in the broad sense, for instance, include those specific to subjective activities as such (for instance, self-consciousness, understanding, understanding of the individual thereby exemplified, and so forth)—whereby a statement of each such feature implies and is implied by statements of every other such feature, so that these statements form a mutually implicative set. But statements of those specific features also imply statements of metaphysical features in the strict sense, and the latter *do not* imply the former. Hence, it is not the case that *all* implications of any given statement in this set imply it, and statements of the features of subjectivity are not coherent in the emphatic sense. On my reading, the emphatic meaning of "coherence" is what Whitehead intends when he writes that a metaphysical system (in the strict sense) "should be 'necessary' in the sense of *bearing in itself its own warrant of universality* through all experience" (Whitehead 1978, 4, emphasis added); that is, all statements in that metaphysical system are necessarily true.

Transcendental metaphysics is an aspect of philosophy. The former is but a part of the latter because, as mentioned earlier, the subjective necessities are not necessarily the same as those of *humans* as such—and philosophy, on my accounting, is critical reflection on the most general understanding of existence as such and its importance for distinctively human subjects. Kant rightly says of the transcendental moral law, as mentioned earlier, that it "must be valid, not merely for men, but for all *rational creatures* [in my term, 'subjects'] *generally*" (Kant 1949, 26), although, as far as I can see, he was wrong to believe that humans can have no (theoretical) knowledge about rational creatures other than humans. To the contrary, the subjective necessities, inclusive of but not exhausted by metaphysical features in the strict sense, can be known, even if distinctively human subjects are but one way in which those necessities are exemplified.

In the broad sense, then, transcendental metaphysics is a literal formulation and validation of the features, including metaphysical features in the strict sense, that every possible subject exemplifies. As mentioned earlier, subjective necessities are designated in pragmatically self-verifying existential statements, where every such statement has the form "some subject that is *x* exists," and such statements are pragmatically self-verifying because *x* is a feature or condition of subjects as such. I will argue (in chapter 5), moreover, that an understanding of the subjective necessities characterizes subjects as such. Hence, these necessities not only *can be* but also *are* understood. To be sure, understanding the subjective necessities depends on the learning through which actualities become activities, that is, each understands itself as actualizing the contingent individual in question—but so, too, does being a subject depend on that learning. Given subjectivity, I mean to assert, understanding the subjective necessities as such is itself a subjective necessity.

Indeed, an understanding of those necessities is confirmed by showing why the moral law is among them. A moral law cannot be transcendental to subjects unless they are aware of the obligation, that is, unless every subject can decide in accord with it *because* she or he ought to do so.[2] Immorality, in other words, is a kind of duplicity; that is, the individual decides against a moral prescription even while aware of what ought to be chosen. Although rarely the focus of attention and thus not readily apparent, subjective necessities include, I will argue, an activity's self-understanding (that is, an understanding of both the given activity and, through learning, the given individual thereby actualized) as exemplifying subjectivity as such in relation to the world as such and to the whole as such or all-inclusive individual. With Whitehead, "the primitive stage of discrimination is the vague grasp of reality, dissecting it into a threefold scheme, namely, the Whole, that Other, and This-My-Self" (Whitehead 1938, 150).

On my accounting, moreover, this self-understanding is metaphysical in the broad sense because it implies and is implied by an understanding of the moral law. Still, I question whether the psychic features phenomenologically so apparent in human life are, in fact, subjective necessities. That we feel the world around us in various ways is readily confirmed—but since all subjects are not necessarily human, whether all subjects feel the world may be less credible. Hence, the moral character of subjective activities (that is, choice among moral and immoral alternatives given by the past even while aware of the moral law, including whatever other understandings are necessary to that awareness) may exhaust the subjective necessities whose every denial is self-refuting. In any event, a self-understanding includes an awareness of subjectivity as such in relation to the world as such and to the whole as such of which subjects and the world are parts. This self-understanding is, as mentioned above, precisely what makes semantically possible a literal designation of the metaphysical necessities—existential and subjective.

If subjective necessities are understood by subjects as such, it is important to clarify that understandings can be implicit or inchoate as well as explicit in a subject, that is, can be in the dim background of consciousness rather than the focus or center of attention. At least with respect to human life, I take this distinction to be noncontroversial. Whitehead is, I think, phenomenologically correct when he says of human consciousness: "even at its brightest, there is a small focal region of clear illumination, and a large penumbral region of experience which tells of intense experience in dim apprehension" (Whitehead 1978, 267; see also 1958, 78). Moreover, I take the difference between explicit and implicit understanding to be itself a subjective necessity and, thereby, implied by every moral creature. This is because the only alternative account is that implicit understandings are acquired through learning. But learning cannot account for one's self-understanding or for understandings of subjectivity as such in relation to the world as such and the all-inclusive individual—because these are presupposed by learning anything at all, and thus "the primitive stage of discrimination" must be implicitly present as a subjective necessity. Because nondivine individuals are necessarily fragmentary, explicit consciousness, the focus or center of attention, is then a fragment of a fragmentary understanding.

THE FOLLOWING CHAPTERS

The following chapters are divided into two parts. At least roughly speaking, part 1 attends to God and the world or to transcendental metaphysics in the strict sense, and part 2 attends to morality and democracy or transcendental metaphysics in the broad sense. In putting these chapters together, I have sought to minimize needless repetition. Still, I also intend that each chapter might be read independently, such that its argument is relatively complete and can be understood by a reader without consulting any other chapter in the book—and given this intent, some repetition is unavoidable.

Chapter 1 argues, against Kant and a wide range of contemporary philosophy, for the validity of transcendental metaphysics in the strict sense. No assumption is more widely accepted in philosophy today, I judge, than the dictum that all existential statements can be denied without self-contradiction, and thus every existential statement, if true, is contingently true. On this dictum, "nothing exists" is possibly true because "something exists" (where "something" implies the features of all possible existence or features otherwise unspecified) is also an existential statement. The dictum does not mean that necessary statements about existence are widely denied but, rather, that every such statement is conditional, as in the statement "if some subject exists, something that is self-conscious exists." What is widely denied, then, are unconditionally necessary existential statements or all necessarily true statements of the form "something that is x exists." Against the dictum, the chapter argues that "nothing exists" is not possibly true or is impossible—and thus "something exists" (where "something" has the above stated meaning) is necessarily true. Accordingly, whatever statements about features of the possible as such are implied by "something exists" are themselves true and constitute metaphysical necessity in the strict sense.

As mentioned previously, the remaining chapters of part 1 seek to exploit this conclusion through conversations with some prominent theologians about some or other issue central to the thought of each. Together, these chapters intend to confirm that neoclassical metaphysics, for which the divine whole is itself temporal or forever self-surpassing, provides a more coherent account of God and the world than does classical metaphysics, for which the divine whole is in all respects eternal. Chapter 2 is concerned to criticize Thomas Aquinas's theory of analogical predication (on a traditional reading of it) between God and creatures. In the history of Western thought, many thinkers have asserted the existence of both a world and a divine reality but positive speaking of God is impossible, and thus literal (or univocal) designation of God positively must be solely metaphorical or symbolic or analogical or mythological. Indeed, contemporary thinkers also assert this view, and Aquinas's theory is sometimes central to their argument. But transcendental metaphysics, if it speaks of God, must speak literally. This chapter, then, assesses Aquinas's theory—and it cannot, I argue, be sustained. Application to God that is, in his sense, solely analogical cannot clarify what the analogical name means and, therefore, cannot be distinguished from what is, in Aquinas's sense, pure equivocation, so that speaking of God cannot be distinguished from designations that have no meaning at all. At the same time, Aquinas's "principle of prior actuality" is, in effect, his agreement that "nothing exists" is impossible, and the chapter proposes that neoclassical metaphysics is required to speak literally of God.

Chapter 3 is a conversation with Friedrich Schleiermacher and, specifically, about the relation he asserts between Christian theology and philosophy. On his account, Christian dogmatics is separated from philosophy, even while the latter provides an introduction to the former. This view, I argue, asserts that all speaking about God in relation to the world occurs in the symbolism of some or other religion or some or other dogmatics—or what comes to the same thing in Schleiermacher's thought, asserts how the self-consciousness of absolute dependence is united with the sensible self-consciousness or consciousness of the world. This chapter criticizes Schleiermacher's denial of God in relation to the world because it implies a completely negative designation of the divine reality, and thereby violates the transcendental conclusion that features of "something" in its most general sense are necessarily true. The chapter then briefly defends neoclassical metaphysics as a more convincing account of how Christian theology relates to philosophy.

Chapter 4 seeks an understanding of human fault, that is, why at least most human activities, aware of God and the divine good, are nonetheless idolatrous or immoral. With Augustine and Reinhold Niebuhr, this is not a question of why humans sin (all human fault being a decision among alternatives) but, rather, why humans are *tempted* to sin. Augustine's question about the source of temptation is, I argue, answered credibly by neither himself nor Niebuhr. Against both, the chapter proposes a neoclassical understanding of transcendental metaphysics in the strict sense, which denies the traditional view of divine omnipotence and asserts the necessity of a world in which individuals are fragmentary. Such neoclassical metaphysics, I argue, provides a more convincing response to the question about temptation's source. Perhaps this chapter could have been placed in part 2 because it argues from the necessary fragmentariness of human individuals. But part 1 seems the more appropriate setting because the fragmentary character of humans only specifies the necessary fragmentariness of worldly individuals as such—necessary in the sense that both worldly individuals and a divine individual are implied by "something exists."

Part 2 attends to morality and democracy or to transcendental metaphysics in the broad sense and, specifically, to the moral and political opportunity we humans are presented. Chapter 5, as mentioned earlier, serves for this part rather like chapter 1 serves for part 1. Exploited in subsequent chapters, chapter 5 seeks to clarify the conditions under which a creature is moral rather than nonmoral and to show how this difference implies the moral law and thus the difference between moral and immoral. Moral individuals and the activities by which they are exemplified are called subjects or examples of subjectivity, and creatures are, I argue, moral rather than nonmoral only when they exist with understanding and their activities include an understanding of the individual they actualize or to which they belong. This is because the moral question asks: What future is good and thus ought to be maximized? The moral law, I hold, depends on a comprehensive good, that is, a good defined metaphysically in the strict sense, so that the future as such in its strictly metaphysical aspect ought to be maximized. Hence, the moral law, which is broadly metaphysical, is a transcendental teleology, where good is defined as a strictly metaphysical feature.

Chapters 6 and 7 pursue the relation between transcendental metaphysics in the broad sense and the meaning of religious freedom. Chapter 6, as mentioned, is a conversation with Ronald Dworkin, who persistently defended the democratic project and, in the final years of his life, turned especially to the question of democracy in relation to religion. On his answer to this question, Dworkin joins many other theorists who separate justice from the convictions protected by religious freedom, and that account is, I believe, incoherent. Still, Dworkin asserts—rightly, I think—that human subjects as such inescapably live with some view of morality, even while he also holds that no moral principle is thereby implied. On my accounting, then, he asserts that morality itself is transcendental to human life notwithstanding the absence of a transcendental moral principle. Against that view, I argue for Kant's statement, namely, the metaphysics of morals is "nothing more than the investigation and establishment of *the supreme principle of morality*" (Kant 1949, 8)—although the supreme principle is, contrary to Kant, a comprehensive purpose. Accordingly, I contend that religious freedom cannot be rightly understood unless the moral law is transcendental and teleological, prescribing pursuit of a good defined as a strictly metaphysical feature—and, in that context, constitutes the way of reason.

Chapter 7 applies the way of reason to whether and, if so, when religious activities are properly exempted from generally applicable laws. Because the moral law is transcendental, it is an aspect of common human experience, and both religious (in the conventional sense) and secularistic convictions, which typically include or imply some or other conviction about the ultimate terms of evaluation, can be objects of public reason. Exemptions from generally applicable laws, I propose, should be sanctioned democratically only by statutory law because a democratic constitution rightly constitutes politics consistent with popular sovereignty. The chapter then offers a distinction between convictions and confessions, where the former designates the content of a comprehensive view, and the latter refers to symbolic activities derived from some historically specific event or events through which a comprehensive conviction is re-presented and cultivated. Given this distinction, I argue, exemptions should not be permitted for simply any activity said to depend on any such conviction but are, rather, properly confined to activities prescribed only for adherents of the confession in question. In other words, exemptions from generally applicable law should never be granted because a given religion (in the conventional sense) or secularistic conviction prescribes opposition to the law. Moreover, this account is confirmed by any claim to such an exemption, which does not thereby contest the general applicability of the law.

Chapter 8 applies a transcendental account of the moral law to the enduring debate between so-called states' rights and so-called national views of the US Constitution's authority. Both views are and have been, on my perception, committed to government by "consent of the governed" or to popular sovereignty. That commitment, I argue, implies that all political claims are or include claims to moral validity, and thus constitutional ratification cannot be the creation of but, rather, presupposes the prior presence of a national public or "we the people"—because a moral claim for the new federated Union means, given the agreement on popular sovereignty, a public discourse to which that claim is addressed. To be sure the states' rights view might assert that no claim to moral validity is included, even if this assertion is inconsistent with its affirmation of popular sovereignty, because the view then implies that public reason cannot discourse about the moral validity of constitutional or statutory law. In response, I argue briefly that a denial of claims to moral validity implies subjectivism about (supposedly) moral utterances and that subjectivism cannot be decisively defeated except by a transcendental understanding of morality.

Throughout part 2, I propose that religious freedom is essential to democracy. If one allows that popular sovereignty is a political form (which gives a democratic constitution the responsibility to institutionalize the way of reason), one can say that democracy is nothing other than the discourse among convictions about the ultimate terms of political evaluation in their pertinence to politics.

PART ONE

GOD AND THE WORLD: METAPHYSICS IN THE STRICT SENSE

❦ I ❧
A DEFENSE OF METAPHYSICAL NECESSITY

Having modern empirical science in mind, John Dewey once wrote: "The theory of empirical method in philosophy does for experienced subject matter on a liberal scale what it does for special sciences on a technical scale," so that philosophy is scientific "thinking at large" and "has its distinctive position in its generality" (Dewey 1958, 2, 27, 398). To the best of my knowledge, something like this view is today widely endorsed, at least if Dewey's statement is understood to mean the following dictum: "all existential statements can be denied without self-contradiction" (that is, contradiction internal to the statement's semantics). On my reading, the supposed truth of that statement about existential statements marks something like a dominant consensus in recent Western philosophy—and, indeed, is often so assumed as no longer to need critical assessment. Perhaps the dictum can be expressed in another formulation, for instance, "all existential statements are logically (here meaning semantically) contingent," or again, "all existential statements can be false"—but if so, I will understand these formulations as synonymous with "all existential statements can be denied without self-contradiction." Given the dictum, metaphysics, if credited at all, can only speculate about features that can themselves be denied without self-contradiction, namely, those common to all things, in distinction from the features common to some specific kind of thing, which one or another special science explicates. Metaphysics is, at best, science writ large.

As mentioned above parenthetically, the relevant meaning of "self-contradiction" is semantic and thus designates a self-contradiction that occurs within the meaning of a statement. Different from a syntactic self-contradiction, which occurs in the structure of a statement's signs independent of its meaning (for instance, "*x* is *p* and *not-p*"), a statement's semantic inconsistency is also distinguished from what is often called a pragmatic self-contradiction. Although any statement about oneself may be pragmatically self-contradictory if uttered by a relevant subject (for instance, "I am not an American" is pragmatically self-contradictory *if* uttered by an American), the important statements here are those that cannot be consistently asserted because their meaning denies a feature or features of subjectivity as such. In this discussion, "subjectivity" will designate an individual's existence with developed understanding, such that a subjective act includes a self-understanding of both the act and the individual in question—where that individual is the most extended sequence of acts or activities distinguished by an identity later acts inherit from earlier ones.[1] This chapter, then, will focus on the pragmatic inconsistencies occurring when the meaning of a statement denies features of self-understanding every subjective act implies.

In what follows, I will have occasion to speak of such pragmatic inconsistency; for the sake of clarity, however, I will not use the term "pragmatic self-contradiction" and, instead, will speak of a pragmatic self-refutation. In contrast to both syntactic inconsistencies and pragmatic self-refutations, then, the terms "impossible or self-contradictory," "possibly true," and "necessarily true" will here be used to characterize only the semantics of statements. "Possibly true," let us note, includes both "can be true or false" (or "if true, then contingently true") and "necessarily true." If a possibly true existential statement is not necessarily true, it is merely possibly true, which implies that its denial is not self-contradictory.

I will use "existential statement" to mean any possibly true statement of the form "something that is *x* exists" (that is, "something that is *x* is existentially present, rather than absent, or is actualized")—for instance, "something that is alive exists."[2] As noted above, a statement of this form may be possibly true without being true; for instance, "something that is alive exists" may, in fact, be false. If, as the dictum asserts, "all existential statements can be denied without self-contradiction," the statement, "nothing exists"—meaning thereby that no thing exists or all things are absent—is also possibly true. This is because "something exists"—where, throughout the chapter, this statement means "something that is otherwise unspecified exists" or "something in the most general sense exists"—is itself an existential statement. Those who assert the dictum certainly affirm that some existential statements are possibly true because some existential statements, including "something that is a subject exists," are, in fact, true (and I will subsequently argue for knowledge of their truth). It is transparent, in other words, that "'nothing exists' is possibly true" does *not* mean "'nothing exists' is necessarily true" but, rather, means "'nothing exists' is merely possibly true." Hence, the dictum's point is its implied denial that something *must* exist, that is, no existential statement is necessarily true.

In order to discuss the dictum, I will distinguish the statement "nothing exists" from positive existential statements, that is, those that designate or imply a designation of something (either a thing or a kind of thing or thing as such) in terms of its features—for instance, "something that is alive exists" or "something that understands exists" or "something that is temporal exists." In the end, however, I will argue that only positive existential statements are possibly true. In other words, this chapter seeks to establish the following: "nothing exists" is not possibly true but is, rather, impossible because self-contradictory,[3] and thus "something exists," where "something that is otherwise unspecified exists" implies "something that is designated in terms of the most general features exists," is necessarily true. The necessarily true statements for which this chapter argues are always and everywhere true because they explicate the features of the possible as such. These statements are implied by any existential statement and its denial[4]—and, therefore, the denial of a necessarily true existential statement is, against the dictum, self-contradictory.

In seeking to establish this conclusion, I intend to redeem transcendental metaphysics in the strict sense. Here, "metaphysics" means an explication of features necessary to either subjective existence as such or existence as such. As implied by this definition, metaphysics has both a broad and a strict sense. Explication of subjective existence as such (metaphysics in the broad sense) may be distinguished from explication of existence as such (metaphysics in the strict sense). Although Immanuel Kant famously pursued a metaphysics of subjectivity (at least with respect to human subjectivity or human reason) independently of a metaphysics of existence, the former, on my accounting, includes the latter: every denial of a (true) metaphysical statement in the broad sense is pragmatically self-refuting, and some of these, denials of (true) metaphysical statements in the strict sense, are (semantically) self-contradictory. "Transcendental" metaphysics, then, explicates metaphysical features, either broad or strict, in literal terms.

To be sure, such features may also be designated symbolically, that is, through images or metaphors, as is typically the case in religious expressions that speak of God's love for humans or otherwise designate God in psychic terms. Unless the meaning of these symbolic expressions can be formulated literally, however, one cannot know of what the symbols are symbolic or the metaphors are metaphorical designations. Absent transcendental formulation, moreover, one cannot properly call a metaphysical statement necessarily true—because doing so implies successful argument for the self-refutation or, in some cases, self-contradiction present when the statement is denied. Notwithstanding the broad and strict senses of "metaphysics," and the possibility of both symbolic and literal formulations, the term's use in what follows will be confined to explicating literally existence as such, that is, "something" in its most general sense, and thus to literal existential statements that are necessarily true. "Metaphysics" will henceforth be used to mean transcendental metaphysics in the strict sense.

The first section below will review briefly three thinkers who illustrate how recent Western philosophy asserts or assumes that all existential statements can be denied without self-contradiction. The second section will argue the following: if "nothing exists" is possibly true, no subject can know any existential statement; that is, knowing what exists and, indeed, knowing whether anything exists are impossible[5]—where knowing a statement consists in having reasons sufficient to the truth of that statement. On its face, I recognize, this conclusion may seem nonsensical and thus reached deceptively or, at least, without warrant. Still, a defense of metaphysical necessity in the sense described above is, in fact, logically bound to that conclusion: if necessarily true, metaphysical statements are implied by any existential statement and its denial; hence, one could not deny metaphysics (in the strict sense) and consistently claim to know any existential statement.

Given the dictum, in any event, the second section will argue that every supposed claim to truth for an existential statement, including statements about the existence of any subject who makes the statement, is, for all we can know, the mere assertion of its proposer and those people who agree with her or him. Further, this section will show why that conclusion may seem nonsensical, namely, because the statement "knowing what exists is impossible" is pragmatically self-refuting. One condition of subjectivity as such is that some (necessarily positive) existential statements are known. If the argument in that section is sound, it follows that "'nothing exists' is possibly true"—not the statement, "nothing exists," but, rather, the statement, "'nothing exists' is possibly true"—is also pragmatically self-refuting, because this statement implies that knowing what exists is impossible.

The third section will revisit the thinkers previously reviewed as illustrations of recent thought in order to review, again briefly, how the pragmatic self-refutation appears in their thought. The fourth and final section will argue the following: because "'nothing exists' is possibly true" is pragmatically self-refuting, the statement is not true. It then follows that "something exists" is necessarily true, and the task of transcendental metaphysics is to explicate in literal terms the features implied by "something exists."

This summary review of what follows is, I recognize, far too terse. I seek to support it in the subsequent discussion. Still, it may be useful to summarize the argument again, now in something like a schematic way:

1. All existential statements can be denied without self-contradiction.
   Dictum to be critically assessed.
2. "Nothing exists" is possibly true.
   Implication of 1.
3. The statement "'nothing exists' is possibly true" is pragmatically self-refuting.
   "Nothing exists" implies that no existential statements can be known, but subjectivity as such implies that some existential statements are known.
4. "Nothing exists" is not possibly true.
   Implication of 3.
5. "Something exists" and its implied existential statements are necessarily true.
   Implication of 4.

Section 2 below argues for statements 2 and 3 above; section 4 below argues for statements 4 and 5 above.

RECENT THINKERS

The late moral and political theorist Ronald Dworkin accepts what he calls "Hume's principle"—which "describes the independence of morality from science and metaphysics" (Dworkin 2011, 19). This principle, Dworkin says, "seems to me obviously true" (Dworkin 2011, 44). He thereby affirms without qualification the fallacy of any so-called moral naturalism: "No series of propositions about how the world is, as a matter of scientific or metaphysical fact, can provide a successful case on its own—without some value judgment hidden in the interstices—for any conclusion about what ought to be the case" (Dworkin 2011, 44). Accordingly, "religions commonly have two parts: cosmological and evaluative" (Dworkin 2011, 340) or "a science part and a value part"—but "the science part... cannot ground the value part because... these are conceptually different" (Dworkin 2013, 23, 24). Dworkin nonetheless affirms moral and political thought because, on his reading, Hume's principle is "itself a moral principle" or "a thesis about moral responsibility," such that science, on the one hand, and evaluative interpretation, on the other, are two independent "domains of intellectual activity... in an embracing dualism of understanding" (Dworkin 2011, 99, 122, 123). Given this dualism, evaluative interpretation is "holistic" or "interpretive... all the way down" (Dworkin 2011, 134, 131).

That all existential statements can be denied without self-contradiction follows from Dworkin's affirmation of Hume's principle—because Hume's separation of existential statements and evaluative statements derives from his view of the former as entirely a posteriori, always dependent on a relevant particular experience (or, perhaps, specific possible experience) and thus experience of some or other contingent existent.[6] In contrast, the supposed fallacy of all moral naturalism becomes problematic if one or more existential statements are necessarily true and thus metaphysical. Given that condition, perhaps some statement about the good is also metaphysical, whereby our relation to what is the case metaphysically and our relation to the good are mutually implicative. At the least, an independent argument for the fallacy of moral naturalism that is metaphysical would be required. Thus, Dworkin's dualism of science and interpretation expresses his commitment to Hume's view of existential statements. It is to the point, then, that many religions would not recognize Dworkin's description of them. Whatever his own philosophical convictions, Clifford Geertz, I expect, better captures the self-understanding typical of religious adherents:

> Never merely metaphysics, religion is never merely ethics either. The source of its moral vitality is conceived to lie in the fidelity with which it expresses the fundamental nature of reality. The powerfully coercive "ought" is felt to grow out of a comprehensive factual "is" and in such a way religion grounds the most specific requirements of human action in the most general contexts of human existence. (Geertz 1973, 126)

By implication, in other words, religions typically deny that moral naturalism is always fallacious.

The dictum about existential statements fundamental to Dworkin's proposal is also embraced by Karl-Otto Apel's notable Kantian explication of transcendental subjectivity. For Apel, moral and political principles are accountable to a "meta-norm for communicatively generating material norms" (Apel 1979, 335). Unlike Dworkin, in other words, Apel argues, with Kant, for a transcendental principle of practical reason, even if, against Kant, Apel defends the intersubjective and thus pragmatic character of the subject. On his view, transcendental analysis explicates, not solely individual understanding but, rather, a "communication community" and thus "transcendental semiotics" (Apel 1994, 84, 78). But his explication of transcendental thought confines its content to subjects, so that traditional ontology, seeking knowledge of existence or reality as such, cannot succeed. "From the critical point of view of Kantianism, any kind of metaphysical ontology, that is, any attempt to comprehend being as a whole (hence also the mind as a part of being), without reflecting on the transcendental subject-object relation as a precondition of the possible objectivity of being, had to be rejected as 'dogmatic metaphysics'" (Apel 1994, 208).

"Ethical rationality" is, then, one aspect of Apel's "self-differentiation" of reason (Apel 1979, 329, 307). Another is "scientific-technological rationality," which includes "formal-logical and mathematical thinking," even while such thinking has "no cognitive or technical commitment ... to the real world, but only, so to speak, to the mind itself" (Apel 1979, 318, emphasis deleted, 319). If I understand him rightly, Apel's transformation of Kant agrees with Kant in this: all existential statements are synthetic in Kant's sense, that is, can be denied without self-contradiction. In addition to ethical rationality and "explanatory science," the self-differentiations of reason include the "empirical-hermeneutical rationality of communicative understanding within the real community of investigators"—and the formal character of all such self-differentiations presupposes "philosophical rationality" just as it implies them (Apel 1979, 319, emphasis deleted, 317, emphasis deleted).[7] But transcendental statements about the existence of subjects in the communication community are themselves merely possibly true; "something that is x exists," where x is a subject, is not necessarily true. Consistently, then, Apel also affirms, in his own way, the fallacy of all moral naturalism. "Concrete material norms" validated by ethical rationality are not derived from any existential statement but, rather, "take into account the compatibility of the interests of all people who are potentially affected by the question under discussion" (Apel 1979, 335, emphasis deleted)—where those interests are given prior to (such that no inclusive telos for them is implied by) the transcendental form of reasoning by which valid norms are generated. In any event, reason as such excludes any necessarily true existential statement.

That exclusion is also basic to the thought of Thomas Nagel. For this reason, he writes: "the possibility of skepticism is built into our ordinary thoughts, in virtue of the realism that they automatically assume"—where "realism" means "the idea that there is a world in which we are contained," and "skeptical possibilities" means "those according to which the world is completely different from how it appears to us, and there is no way to detect this" (Nagel 1986, 73, 70, 71). Whether skeptical possibilities obtain is, moreover, *forever* beyond human detection; that is, Nagel means a possible reality that "*no* finite mind could ever form a conception of," and thus "anything we come to believe must remain suspended in a cavern of skeptical darkness" (Nagel 1986, 98, 73). To be sure, Nagel affirms the pursuit of objectivity because "we can't cure our appetite for belief" (Nagel 1986, 88). Accordingly, "The best we can do is to construct a picture that might be correct. Skepticism is really a way of recognizing our situation, though it will not prevent us from continuing to pursue something like knowledge, for our natural realism makes it impossible for us to be content with a purely subjective view" (Nagel 1986, 74).

Nagel concedes that skepticism uses "general ideas of something existing . . . or something being the case" but, he argues, "merely believing there might be something" we are incapable of understanding "is not yet a conception of it" (Nagel 1986, 93, 97), that is (in my terms), does not purport to designate its features. "The general concept of *everything*" or "of reality" (Nagel 1986, 98) is sufficient to limit what can be positively conceived.

> The general point I wish to make against restrictive theories of what is thinkable is this. Every concept that we have contains potentially the idea of its own complement—the idea of what the concept doesn't apply to. Unless it has been shown positively that there cannot be such things . . . we are entitled to assume that it makes sense even if we can say nothing more about the members of the class. (Nagel 1986, 97–98)

On my reading, then, realism and skepticism are inseparable because all existential statements can be denied without self-contradiction. Although such statements may designate something in terms of its features, so that insofar we can have "objective knowledge" and, thereby, "fill out the pure idea of realism with more or less definite conceptions of the world" (Nagel 1986, 71), the possibly true denial of all existential statements implies our possible incompetence to form a conception of that reality, so that realism includes skepticism.

Some readers of these three philosophers may find one or more of my brief reviews to be in some way mistaken, although the dictum "all existential statements can be denied without self-contradiction" is, I think, more or less obviously asserted or assumed by each thinker. Be that as it may, if recent philosophy has indeed been widely committed to this dictum, Kant's influence on all philosophy subsequent to him is underscored. For many subsequent thinkers, the long Western metaphysical adventure came to an end with Kant, for whom the pursuit of knowledge about things-in-themselves is futile. In any event, the implications of this dictum for our pursuit of knowledge about ourselves and the world is what I wish now to explore.

THE PRAGMATIC SELF-REFUTATION

If all existential statements can be denied without self-contradiction, one implication is this: "nothing exists," meaning thereby that all things are absent, is possibly true. This is because "something exists" (where this means, as mentioned earlier, "something that is otherwise unspecified exists" or "something in its most general sense exists") is itself an existential statement, and its negation, "no thing exists," is, on the dictum, without self-contradiction. What is implied, then, is the denial that some existential statement or set of statements is necessarily true. The following discussion will focus on the further implications of the statement "'nothing exists' is possibly true."

In Western history, some thinkers have distinguished the statement that all things are absent or no thing exists from the statement that what does exist includes a thing or kind of thing designated only by negation; that is, "something that is completely negative exists."[8] Thomas Aquinas, for instance, argues for God's existence, even though he asserts that God, absent God's special revelation, is designated in univocal or literal terms only by negation because natural reason cannot know God's nature or essence.

> By means of a demonstration many things are removed from Him, so that in consequence we understand Him as something apart from other things. For demonstration proves that God is immovable, eternal, incorporeal, utterly simple, one, and the like. . . .
> Now we arrive at the proper knowledge of a thing not only by affirmations, but also by negations. For just as it is proper to man to be a rational animal, so it is proper to him not to be inanimate or irrational. Yet there is this difference between these two modes of proper knowledge, that when we have proper knowledge of a thing by affirmations we know what a thing is, and how it is distinguished from others; whereas

when we have proper knowledge of a thing by negations, we know that it is distinct from others, but remain ignorant of what it is. Such is the proper knowledge of God that can be obtained from demonstrations. (S.C.G. 3, part I. 39. 1)[9]

Similarly, Kant asserts a possible difference between noumena and phenomena. Notwithstanding that, for him, any attempt to know things-in-themselves or existence as such is futile, he argues for the validity of an a priori synthetic understanding of things-as-they-appear and thus of appearing object-as-such: intuitions or sense data caused by noumena are received by humans within a priori forms of human sensibility—namely, space and time—and a world of appearances is understood when consciousness of that reception occurs through a priori but otherwise empty categories. On the best (or, at least, most charitable) reading of Kant, perhaps, he does not assert that noumena *do* differ from phenomena; rather, noumena *may* not exist in space and time—and whether this difference is present is forever inaccessible to human knowledge. Still, noumena are surely things, the more so because they somehow cause the intuitions or sense data given which phenomena are understood. As far as we can know, then, things-in-themselves can be designated only as not-phenomena, that is, only by negation.

To first appearances, perhaps, the possible truth of "no thing exists" and the possible truth of "something that is completely negative exists" seem to be different. But these statements cannot be distinguished. This is because, in each case, the same predicate ("exists") is attached to a grammatical subject ("no thing," in the one case, "a thing or kind of thing," in the other) said to be designated only by negation. A distinction between the two statements is impossible because difference requires a positive comparison, and thus at least one of the two grammatical subjects said to be different must be explicated in positive terms, that is, in terms of its features. The point may be formulated another way: *complete negation cannot be distinguished from complete negation.* A supposed statement, the content of which is the absence of all things, and a supposed statement, the content of which is the presence of a thing or kind of thing designated only by negation, are identical in content, and identity does not allow difference.

This conclusion is not challenged if the second and not the first is said to state a presence rather than the absence thereof. That supposed difference is precisely what cannot be distinguished without a positive designation of the supposed presence. Perhaps some will reply: once the presence of something is asserted, "presence" or "existence," in distinction from absence or nonexistence, must, regardless of what is said to be present or to exist, have a common meaning. But if some presence is designated only by negation (for instance, Aquinas's God or Kant's noumena), it can have nothing in common with things designated by their features—precisely because a completely negative presence cannot be distinguished from its absence and, indeed, the absence of all things. Hence, "presence" or "existence" as such can be distinguished from absence or nonexistence only if the term's meaning designates one or more features and thus designates positively, and this condition is contradicted by implications of the dictum "all existential statements can be denied without self-contradiction." In other words, (1) "no thing exists" and (2) "something that is completely negative exists" are two indistinguishable ways to state "nothing exists."

Because complete negation cannot be distinguished from complete negation, we can also say the following: if "nothing exists" is possibly true, a distinction between a thing or kind of thing designated only by negation and every possible thing designated only by negation is impossible. If a statement of the former is possibly true, a statement of the latter is possibly true—as I will now argue.

Let us posit a difference between the presence of something and the absence of all things and, further, a statement that some thing or kind of thing is designated only by negation. Aquinas, for instance, asserts that God and the world both exist. Indeed, for him, the absence of all things ("no thing exists") is impossible because God's existence is "self-evident in itself" (S.T. I. 2. I); that is, "something that is God exists" or "God exists" is necessarily true given God's essence.[10] At the same time, God's essence cannot be demonstrated, and thus God is, for natural reason, designated univocally only by negation—in contrast to designation of things in the world, which occurs in terms of their features. Similarly, Kant claims to know the presence, not the absence, of things-in-themselves (that is, "something that is noumenal exists" or "noumena exist"), which somehow cause the intuitions or sense data through which a phenomenal world is designated in positive terms, even while the designation of noumena is, for all we can know, only by negation.

But (a) "something that is completely negative exists," where "something" means a thing or kind of thing, and (b) "something that is completely negative exists," where "something" is otherwise unspecified or means every possible thing, cannot be distinguished. Again, this is because difference requires a positive comparison, and thus at least one of the two grammatical subjects said to be different must be designated in positive terms—and in both (a) and

(b) above, the something in question is said to be designated only by negation. Complete negation, to repeat, cannot be distinguished from complete negation. Hence, if the statement that some thing or kind of thing is designated only by negation is possibly true, the statement that every possible thing is designated only by negation is possibly true.

That a difference between those two meanings of "something" is impossible may also be inferred from the previous argument, namely, that "no thing exists" (or "all things are absent") and "something (a thing or kind of thing) that is completely negative exists" are two indistinguishable ways to state "nothing exists." If that argument is sound, the first statement ("no thing exists) may be used to restate the second ("something [a thing or kind of thing] that is completely negative exists"). Given its function as this restatement, "no thing exists" could only mean that no thing designated in positive terms exists. Hence, if "something designated only by negation exists" is possibly true, where "something" means a thing or kind of thing, "something that is completely negative exists" is possibly true, where "something" means anything you please or every possible thing. For this reason, Charles Hartshorne asks rhetorically: "If one purely negative fact is admitted, why could not all facts be purely negative?" (Hartshorne 1970, 160).

It would not follow that no thing exists—or, indeed, that no thing designated in terms of its features exists. One might formulate a statement about some thing or things and, thereby, tell the truth. But if "nothing exists" is possibly true, we simply cannot distinguish (1) "no thing exists," (2a) "something (a thing or kind of thing) that is completely negative exists," and (2b) "something (otherwise unspecified and thus every possible thing) that is completely negative exists." These are three alternative formulations of what is possibly true. Given that "nothing exists" with this threefold formulation could be true, moreover, we should ask whether any subject could know any existential statement. Could any subject have any knowledge of what exists or know that something is present rather than absent?

Let us propose summarily that knowing a statement means, as previously suggested, having reasons sufficient to its truth. If we posit that "nothing exists" is possibly true, we can at least say this much: no subject could know a statement that something (a given thing or kind of thing or thing as such) is designated only by negation because any such something is indistinguishable from the absence of all things; that is, the statement cannot be distinguished from "no thing exists." Hence, knowing what exists can only be positive—and our question may be reformulated: Could any subject have reasons sufficient to the truth of a positive existential statement if a statement designating the same something (a thing or kind of thing or thing as such) only by negation is possibly true?

But the point of our thinking, some may assert, is not to *have* knowledge; rather, we *pursue* it—and in this pursuit, it is sufficient to reach plausible existential statements, those conducive to the truth and thus more probably true than statements on which the things in question are designated only by negation. Notwithstanding that all existential statements can be denied without self-contradiction, in other words, the quest for knowing what exists is, on this account, affirmed. In fact, however, speaking of such probability is not credible. A comparison of two items, such that one is more and the other less in some given respect, requires, by definition, a common (or similar) respect each exemplifies. Two humans, for instance, can be compared with respect to their height, or two roses with respect to their color. If more or less probably true, two comparable statements about the designation of something must likewise exemplify some common respect, namely, whatever respect greater and lesser adequacy to the something in question requires. To the contrary, two statements, on one of which something is designated in terms of its features and, on the other, is designated only by negation, exemplify *nothing* in common.

This follows because designation only by negation *is* designation by nothing. Indeed, the recognition that something completely negative cannot be distinguished from the absence of all things confirms (or simply repeats) that a positive existential statement and one on which designation of the same thing is completely negative have nothing in common. However apt the pursuit of knowledge may be in certain contexts, the phrase "more probably true" has no credible application to positive existential statements in comparison with those on which the same things are designated only by negation. For all we can know, any positive existential statement can be only the mere assertion of the subject or subjects who assert it.

When Aquinas asserts that God is univocally designated, at least absent God's special revelation, only by negation, he thereby implies that we cannot know the world's features—cannot have the supposed knowledge from which he demonstrates God's existence. For all he or anyone can know, all worldly things are designated only by negation and, in fact, cannot be distinguished from their absence. Hence, the most Aquinas can consistently assert is the following: for those who agree to posit a world (including subjects) with the features he proposes, it follows that God's existence can be demonstrated.[11] Kant, having conceded that things-in-themselves can be designated only by negation, is indeed bound to say of noumena that we cannot know their features; but he errs, I think, in claiming to know how the world appears to all humans. For all he or anyone can know, his own intuitions or sense data and thus things-as-they-appear to him are themselves designated only by negation—and, in fact, neither things nor humans can be distinguished from their absence. In other words, both things-as-they-appear and the subject to whom they appear depend entirely on what that subject posits or stipulates. Hence, the most Kant can consistently assert is the following: for those agreeing to posit themselves as rational beings who, as he proposes, have intuitions or sense data and understand objects within space and time, it follows that objects as they appear have the features he describes.

If "nothing exists" is possibly true, a subject who asserts any positive existential statement or statements, including about the subject in question, can express nothing more than how things appear to her or him and to subjects who happen to agree, that is, nothing more than how that subject or group posits itself and stipulates the features of some other thing or things said to appear. This follows even if the given group is said to be historically extended because it includes those within a given linguistic or lifeworld tradition. That such a historical group, circumscribed by the language or lifeworld in question, does exist can be, given the premise that "nothing exists" is possibly true, only posited—along with the world as it appears to that specific historical community.[12]

Assuming that all existential statements can be denied without self-contradiction, we reach, to the best of my reasoning, this conclusion: no existential statements can be known, that is, knowing what exists and, moreover, knowing whether anything exists are impossible. We cannot know that one or more things exist because any proposed statement about them can be only the mere stipulation of its proposer and those people who agree with her or him, including stipulation by the proposer and any who agree of their own existence as subjects. The conclusion is entailed precisely because a statement that some thing or things are designated only by negation could be true and cannot be distinguished from the possible truth of "no thing exists"—and thus there is no way to compare with respect to truth statements that a thing or kind of thing or thing as such exists and is designated positively, on the one hand, and on the other, is designated only by negation or is absent. Knowing what exists and, indeed, whether anything exists is, given the dictum in question, forever denied to us.

On its face, this conclusion may seem nonsensical; that subjects can and do know some existential statement or statements may not be contested. Still, if this fact is questioned, the statement "no existential statements can be known" is, we can note, pragmatically self-refuting. On my intention here, the relevant kind of pragmatic self-refutation occurs when the meaning of a statement denies a feature or features of subjectivity as such or denies what every subjective act implies. For instance, if one such feature is (as Kant, among others, argues) a moral law, the statement "some subject is not bound by the moral law" is pragmatically self-refuting because it denies what every subjective act implies, namely, the moral law. The statement "no existential statements can be known" can be similarly self-refuting, then, only if every subjective act implies knowledge (that is, the subject has reasons sufficient to the truth) of some existential statements.

Every subjective act does indeed imply such knowledge because a subjective act both implies the presence of the subject in question and occurs by way of a self-understanding. Hence, the subject understands its own existence and, further, knows that it exists, that is, has reasons sufficient to the truth of the existential statement: "something that understands exists" or "something that is a subject exists" (the reasons being one's self-understanding as a subjective act belonging to a subjective individual). Moreover, the subject must also understand something else; a self-understanding cannot merely understand this very understanding because something else must constitute the self to be understood. Accordingly, the subject that understands itself must know that it relates to a world—where "world" here means only "something that is other than the self." To be sure, subjects are also marked by fallibility and thus can be mistaken about the world. But such mistakes are false about something, namely, that to which the existing subjective act relates.[13] Thus, every subject has reasons sufficient to the truth of the existential statement "something that is the world exists"—and the statement "no existential statement can be known" is pragmatically self-refuting because any subject who asserts it simultaneously knows its own existence in relation to the world. The statement "no existential statement can be known" contradicts a feature of subjectivity as such.

The statement "'nothing exists' is possibly true" and the dictum "all existential statements can be denied without self-contradiction" are, it now follows, also pragmatically self-refuting because they imply "no existential statements can be known." Still, some thinkers may conclude to the contrary: precisely because knowing some existential statements is implied by every subjective act, the argument goes, knowing what exists is possible notwithstanding that all existential statements can be denied without self-contradiction. But this argument, if the above analysis is correct, is thoroughly unconvincing. The analysis in this section has sought to establish that, given the dictum "all existential statements can be denied without self-contradiction," knowing what exists and, indeed, whether anything exists is impossible—and because every subjective act implies knowledge of certain existential statements, the dictum is pragmatically self-refuting. In other words, this analysis seeks to be a reduction ad absurdum.

RECENT THINKERS REVISITED

An earlier section reviewed briefly three thinkers who illustrate how recent thought has affirmed or assumed the dictum "all existential statements can be denied without self-contradiction." If this dictum implies "'nothing exists' is possibly true" and both statements are pragmatically self-refuting, the inconsistency should be present in each of the three projects reviewed. This section will seek briefly to confirm this presence.

For Dworkin, Hume's separation of "is" and "ought" is itself a moral statement. This allows Dworkin to pursue nonempirical moral and political principles as a kind of evaluative reasoning, such that truth about such principles is articulated as a genre of interpretation, and interpretation is, he says, "interpretive... all the way down" (Dworkin 2011, 31). Because he finds Kant's arguments for a priori practical principles "comparatively weak" and Kant's "theories of freedom and reason... opaque" (Dworkin 2011, 265), Dworkin never says that practical reasoning or interpretation is bound by a necessary principle. Indeed, his conviction to the contrary becomes apparent when he considers "someone who holds moral opinions radically different from my own," and Dworkin responds: "I cannot count on finding anything in my set of reasons and arguments that he would be irrational not to accept. I cannot *demonstrate* to him that my opinions are true and his false" (Dworkin 2011, 100).

Accordingly, an interpretation with integrity cannot avoid "a kind of circularity" (Dworkin 2011, 100, see 101). This circularity, we have every reason to understand, obtains among contingently held beliefs, such that no belief can be successfully defended without merely positing others. Nonetheless, Dworkin formulates a criterion for interpretive success: "A particular interpretation succeeds—it achieves truth about some object's meaning—when it best realizes, for that object, the purposes properly assigned to the interpretive practice [that is, practice of the interpretive genre] properly identified as pertinent" (Dworkin 2011, 131). But this criterion defines interpretive success in terms of itself because "best" and "properly" can only be defined in terms of a successful interpretation. Hence, the criterion may be restated:

"a particular interpretation succeeds—it achieves truth about some object's meaning—when it successfully interprets, for that object, the purposes successfully interpreted as proper for the interpretive practice that is successfully interpreted as proper to that object." In other words, the criterion for successful interpretation assumes itself as a prior criterion for successful interpretation—and thus this criterion, too, can only be an aspect of Dworkin's circular integration of contingently held beliefs. But, then, the criterion is simply posited, and neither he nor any other subject can have reasons sufficient to the truth of his evaluative principles. Dworkin's commitment to Hume's view of existential statements is inconsistent with Dworkin's claim to achieve moral and political truth.

Moreover, Dworkin's "embracing dualism of understanding" (Dworkin 2011, 123), which consists of science and interpretation, must itself be an interpretation of science and interpretation—precisely because Hume's principle is said to be a moral one and is, therefore, an evaluative conclusion. But that recognition, I submit, implies that Dworkin's entire project is nothing more than the mere assertion of its proposer and those people who agree with him. I do not say that Dworkin's moral and political principles and, especially, his application of them to contemporary political and judicial issues are discredited; to the contrary, I think, his analyses are in many respects instructive, even while I intend to set their merits in a metaphysical context. On his appropriation of Hume's principle, however, Dworkin's implied assertions that "nothing exists" is possibly true and thus all existential statements can be denied without self-contradiction are pragmatically self-refuting because inconsistent not only with a claim to know moral and political principles but also any claim to scientific knowledge as well.

Apel, it might be said, stands to Dworkin something like Kant stands to Hume—at least in the sense that Apel, with Kant, argues for a transcendental account of subjectivity that Dworkin, with Hume, refuses. In any event, Apel defends his transcendental pragmatics or transcendental semiotics by exposing the pragmatic self-refutation involved whenever such transcendental thought is explicitly or implicitly denied. In response to all forms of relativism, he writes:

> Thus, for example, in the sentence, "In principle, we cannot abstract from the fact that we are individuals conditioned by different forms of life," the first part contradicts the second on the level of philosophic discourse. The first part implicitly views the "we" as the subject of the intersubjectively valid insight into the limits of the possibility of the

abstraction; hence, it attributes to the "we" precisely the transcendental function disputed by the second part. (Apel 1984, 238)

Or again, in response specifically to what he takes as the later Heideggerian position, Apel writes: "Whoever seriously speaks of the conceptual meaning of 'meaning' and 'truth' as being in the last instance dependent on events or fate—that is, [asserts] that the *logos* of our discursive claim to meaning and truth is in principle subordinate to *time*—thereby cancels the claim to the meaning and truth of their discourse" (Apel 1996, 178). Reason cannot function, he says more tersely, "merely as object and no longer as subject of critique" (Apel 1998, 164).

But Apel's embrace of the dictum in question introduces into his proposal its own pragmatic self-refutation. If "nothing exists" is possibly true, the previous section of this paper concluded, he cannot know any existential statement, including statements about the presence and character of subjectivity and thus about the supposedly transcendental character of subjects as members of the communication community. Such statements are, then, merely his own assertions, along with those of any other people who agree with him. Arguing for his proposal, Apel implies a claim to know the presence and features of existence with developed understanding as such, but given the dictum, knowing what exists or, indeed, knowing whether anything exists is impossible. Whoever claims truth for the dictum thereby cancels the claim to know any existential statement, and for all Apel can know, subjectivity may be designated only by negation and, further, cannot be distinguished, except by stipulation, from its absence.

The self-refutation becomes apparent when Apel affirms, in his own way, the fallacy of all moral naturalism. On his proposal, recall, "concrete material norms" are not derived from any existential statement because they take "into account the compatibility of the interests of all people who are potentially affected by the question under discussion" (Apel 1979, 335)—where those interests are given prior to the transcendental form of reasoning by which valid norms are generated. It follows that all interests are inescapably relative in all respects to lifeworld or historical context. But, then, Apel's transcendental "meta-norm for communicatively generating material norms" (Apel, 1979, 335, emphasis deleted) must imply the following transcendental (and existential) statement: all interests are in all respects relative to lifeworld or historical context. This statement implies a transcendental comparison of strictly all possible objects of interest—and moreover, a comparison that is or includes a moral one because it allows the material norms that ethical rationality generates to determine what and how interests are compatible (that is, good). I do not say that a transcendental self-differentiation of reason is impossible; to the contrary, Apel's pursuit of it is instructive, even while I intend to set that pursuit in a metaphysical context. Rather, his project becomes pragmatically self-refuting when he also denies metaphysics, that is, denies a transcendental analysis of the objects subjects can understand and in which they might have interest because he claims truth, at least by implication, for the dictum "all existential statements can be denied without self-contradiction."

As earlier comments suggest, Nagel affirms the pursuit of "something like knowledge" and thus seeks to encourage our incurable "appetite for belief" notwithstanding the possibility of skepticism (Nagel 1986, 74, 88). In doing so, he explicates what he takes to be a distinction constitutive of human understanding, namely, between "two standpoints, the subjective and the objective" and thus between "the perspective of a particular person inside the world" and "an objective view of that same world" (Nagel 1986, 4, 3). Although neither can be pursued without the other, the latter allows us nonetheless to correct mistaken appearances. For instance, we can correct the first appearance of the world as inclusive of secondary properties (colors, tastes, smells, and so forth) by objectively accounting for them in terms of how we perceive things, even while the primary qualities (for instance, shape and size) are inescapably features of things we experience (see Nagel 1986, 75--76). Or, again: the first appearance of "unqualified temporal and spatial relations between events, things, and processes" is corrected by Einstein's more objective "special theory of relativity . . . according to which events are not without qualification simultaneous or successive, objects without qualification are not equal or unequal in size" (Nagel 1986, 76). Accordingly, the pursuit of objectivity can be itself the pursuit of knowledge: "our knowledge of the phenomenal world is partial knowledge of the world as it is in itself" (Nagel 1986, 101).

But the argument above—from the premise "'nothing exists' is possibly true" to the conclusion that knowing what exists and, indeed, knowing whether anything exists is impossible—intends to show that a positive distinction between supposed appearances and subsequent objective corrections is, given the premise, itself the mere assertion of its proposer and those people who agree with her or him, all of whom, including the proposer, must also stipulate their own existence. Hence, a modern distinction between secondary and primary qualities or between unqualified temporal and spatial relations and Einstein's theory of special relativity cannot be "partial knowledge of things-in-themselves" (or even, as Nagel says elsewhere, "something like knowledge") (Nagel 1986, 101, 74)—if, for all we can know, all things can be designated only by negation and, indeed, cannot be distinguished from their absence. Our incurable "appetite for belief" is entirely futile given the dictum about existential statements. Naturally, I do not assert this futility and, therefore, do not mean that partial knowledge of what exists is impossible or that our capacity for objectivity does not correct more narrow appearances, much less that modern science is impossible. To the contrary, I intend to credit the pursuit of knowing what exists and, further, to affirm knowledge of existence as such, and Nagel's analysis of what exists is, in significant respects, instructive. But he cannot consistently assert or assume that all existential statements can be denied without self-contradiction, and thus "nothing exists" is possibly true, because these assertions or assumptions are inconsistent with knowing what exists.[14]

Unless I misunderstand him, moreover, Nagel himself reaches a similar conclusion: "We can't fully take on skepticism . . . because we can't cure our appetite for belief" (Nagel 1986, 88). Or again: "What should be the relation between the beliefs we form about the world, with their aspirations to objectivity, and the admission that the world might be completely different from the way we think it is, in unimaginable ways? I believe that we have no satisfactory way of combining these outlooks" (Nagel 1986, 88). On my accounting, the realism and skepticism Nagel asserts, far from being inseparable, are inconsistent with each other—because his acceptance of the dictum I take to be widespread among his contemporaries is pragmatically self-refuting.

METAPHYSICAL NECESSITY

At least given a subject or subjects, the statement "'nothing exists' is possibly true" is not true because its implications deny a feature of subjectivity as such, and therefore the statement is pragmatically self-refuting. Still, some who affirm the dictum "all existential statements can be denied without self-contradiction," and who thereby imply "'nothing exists' is possibly true" may not be troubled by this pragmatic self-refutation. It remains, they may argue, that "nothing exists" could be true; were all things absent, the argument goes, there would be no subjects and hence no pragmatic self-refutation.

But any thinker who so defends the dictum is insufficiently mindful of *what* statement the above argument has shown to be pragmatically self-refuting—not "nothing exists" but, rather, "'nothing exists' is possibly true." To be sure, "nothing exists" is also pragmatically self-refuting because any subject who asserts it implies "I exist" or "something that understands exists." But this inconsistency alone means: *if* one or more subjects exist, *then* "nothing exists" is not true—and the conditional necessity of that statement, as those who affirm the dictum may insist, does not refute the possible truth of "nothing exists." Given that a subject does, in fact, exist and, indeed, must exist in order to assert "nothing exists," this fact alone seemingly begs the question of whether "nothing exists" *could* be true.[15] On the argument above, however, a pragmatic self-refutation also occurs when the statement "'nothing exists' could be true" is itself asserted. What is now at issue is not the statement, "nothing exists," but, rather, a statement about that very statement, namely, that it could be or is possibly true. Accordingly, the self-refutation that occurs does not beg the question and, to the contrary, implies that "nothing exists" is not possibly true—neither "can be true or false" nor, transparently, "is necessarily true." It then follows that "nothing exists" is impossible.

In other words, this conclusion does not mean the conditional truth: *if* one or more subjects exist, *then* the statement "'nothing exists' is possibly true" is not true—such that, absent subjects, "nothing exists" could be true. On that interpretation, "'nothing exists' is possibly true" is simply reasserted. But precisely this statement is itself pragmatically self-refuting, whereby a conclusion about "nothing exists" is implied, namely, it is *not* possibly true and, therefore, is impossible because self-contradictory.[16] That conclusion may be confirmed in the following way: a statement assigning to another statement its merely possible or necessary truth is necessarily true, that is, true independent of conditions.[17] But "'nothing exists' is possibly true" is not true independent of conditions because, on conditions in which one or more subjects exist, it is pragmatically self-refuting. "'Nothing exists' is possibly true" is not what it would be were it true (that is, this statement about the statement "nothing exists" is necessarily true) and thus is not true. Because "possibly true" and "impossible or self-contradictory" exhaust the options for a statement's truth status, "nothing exists" has the latter status.[18]

It now follows that "something exists" (that is, something otherwise unspecified and designated positively) is necessarily true. The contradictory of a self-contradictory statement is necessarily true. We might put the point this way: a subject who denies any existential statement designating a feature or features of *subjective existence as such* (or subjectivity as such) is pragmatically self-refuting, and some (but not all) of those denials are (semantically) self-contradictory because they deny one or more existential statements designating a feature or features of *existence as such* (which are also features of subjective existence as such), that is, one or more necessarily true existential statements. Accordingly, metaphysics may be defined as the literal explication of what must be the case because "nothing exists" is impossible. Or, again: metaphysics is the literal explication of features implied by every existential statement and its denial, the possible as such, and thus every denial of a (true) metaphysical statement is self-contradictory.

If, for Nagel, "every concept that we have contains potentially the idea . . . of what the concept doesn't apply to . . . even if we [that is, finite minds as such] can say nothing more about the members of the class" (Nagel 1986, 97--98), this cannot be the case with the concept "something" in its most general sense. If finite minds as such "can say nothing more" about "what the concept doesn't apply to," members of that class could be designated only by negation, and to designate only by negation is not to designate. Hence, the concept "something" in its most general sense must imply features, that is, must be positive. For the same reason, "something that is x exists" can be distinguished from another instance of "something that is x exists" only if both values of x are marked in terms of their features, that is, only if both designations of x are positive; were a value of x marked only by the absence of some feature or features, this value of x would be designated only by negation.[19] Moreover, every possibly true statement, even a statement that is not explicitly about existence (for instance, a mathematical statement or, alternatively, a statement about statements) implies existential statements. Were this not the case, some possibly true statement or statements would imply that "nothing exists" is also possibly true.

Given that "nothing exists" is impossible, we can also conclude that every existential negation is at least partially positive. A possibly true statement in the form "something that is x exists" can be consistently denied only if the negation implies some other (positive) statement in the form "something that is x exists"—or again: every possibly true statement that a certain thing or kind of thing is absent is, by implication, the statement that something else, exclusive of the first, is present. "Dinosaurs do not exist," for instance, implies that something other than dinosaurs and incompatible with their existence is present under whatever conditions dinosaurs are said to be absent. "After the next federal election, a Democratic Congress may not exist" implies, to illustrate further, that future conditions may be incompatible with Democratic control of the next Congress. Indeed, as Hartshorne has insisted, our awareness of absence depends on our awareness of presence (see Hartshorne 1970, 160): we can deny the existence of some given thing because we are conscious of features incompatible with it, and we are aware that some decision is immoral because we experience the moral law.

As the foregoing has said, the features common to all possible things are implied by "something exists," and the clarification of those implications is the task of explicating literally what must be the case because "nothing exists" is impossible. Because they, too, are, like "something exists," necessarily true, all other metaphysical statements are not only implied by but also imply "something exists." In other words, all metaphysical statements imply all others. This is one way to read Alfred North Whitehead's metaphysical use of "coherence": the "fundamental ideas" of a metaphysical system or scheme, he says, "presuppose each other" (Whitehead 1978, 3), so that "each must be displayed as necessary to the various meanings of groups of notions, of equal depth with itself" (Whitehead 1938, 1). The coherence of metaphysical statements then, is not exhausted by logical consistency, because the latter may occur when some statements imply others but are not implied by them.[20] A metaphysical system is coherent when all of the implications of any given statement also imply it—because all of the statements are necessarily true. Thus, Hartshorne writes:

> It is arguable that strictly speaking there is but *one* metaphysical, innate or strictly universal and necessary idea or principle ... so that to speak of innate ideas in the plural is really to slur over the distinction between our formulations of metaphysical truth and the truth itself, or the necessary non-restrictive aspect of reality. The former, the ideas in the plural, are our contingent ways of trying to become conscious of the non-contingent ground of all contingency. (Hartshorne 1970, 32)

To be sure, Whitehead also asserts that metaphysics should be "adequate," not merely applicable to "such items as happen to have been considered" but also to "all related experience" (Whitehead 1978, 3–4)—and if "all related experience" is understood to mean experience of the possible as such, being adequate entails being applicable to strictly any conceivable item of experience and thus anything about which any subject might think. As criteria for metaphysics, then, "coherent" and "adequate" are finally two ways of defining the same system of necessarily true existential statements: a coherent system of such statements *is* applicable to any conceivable item of experience, and all statements within an adequate such system *are* mutually implicative. So understood, the system "should be 'necessary' in the sense of *bearing in itself its own warrant of universality* throughout all experience" (Whitehead 1978, 4, emphasis added).

Metaphysics so defined is properly transcendental, that is, consists in a literal explication of necessarily true existential statements and, thereby, an explication that permits sound argument for the self-contradiction present whenever a necessarily true existential statement is denied.[21] Among other reasons, literal designation is required because the meaning of metaphysical or necessary existential statements, which are nonrestrictive of existential possibilities, differs from the meaning of nonmetaphysical existential statements, which are restricted to or contingent on some existential possibilities.[22] The meaning of a metaphysical or necessary existential statement can be explicated only by way of its coherence with (that is, the statement is implied by) all of its implications, while the meaning of a nonmetaphysical or contingent existential statement can be explicated by way of differentia that distinguish its designated thing or things from other specifications of some greater abstraction (that does not imply the given nonmetaphysical statement)—or, alternatively stated, explicated by way of existential possibilities it excludes.

To be sure, one may, as mentioned earlier, designate the necessary features of all things symbolically, that is, designate them in statements whose literal meaning designates some nonmetaphysical possibility—as religions seek to do when, for their purposes, they assert, say, that certain psychic qualities are features of ultimate reality and thus God loves all of the world. But any symbolically formulated statement will, precisely because of the difference in meaning, require literal restatement for the purpose of critically assessing its truth. As formulated in transcendental statements, metaphysics is not empirical scientific "thinking at large" but, rather, explicates the (semantic) logic of existence.

Naturally, nothing said above implies that *all* true existential statements are necessarily true. Were that so, the coherence of metaphysical statements would entail that all existential statements, because all are implied by each, designate one thing—and as far I can see, this designation of it could be only by negation because that single thing would be in all respects nontemporal. In any event, metaphysics clarifies the possible as such because it explicates the changeless character of all possible changes and thus of contingent things or states of affairs. Other than those of greatest possible generality, any possibly true existential statement can be denied without self-contradiction and thus is merely possibly true; that is, every such statement is about the contingent existence of some actual or possible thing or kind of thing.

The scope of this discussion does not permit pursuit of a systematic metaphysics. That system will be most convincing, I can here merely assert, if it is not only transcendental but also neoclassical—and thereby seeks to present the project for which the works of Whitehead, Hartshorne, and Schubert M. Ogden are the most important resources.[23] Neoclassical metaphysics, on my understanding, asserts a plurality of final real things, each of which is an event constituted by a decision to unify its internal relations to actual events in its past and, thereby, to determine a new condition for possible events in its future when they relate to it. Actual events are properly said to occur, but two or more in succession, distinguished by a shared feature or features because the later relate internally to the earlier, constitute an aggregate that may properly be said to exist. An actual or possible existent is, in other words, an actual or possible aggregate, each of whose member events derives from other such members the aggregate's distinguishing characteristic. What does exist may be an individual, that is, an aggregate of this kind whose member events are ordered only sequentially, and some other existents may include several individuals—where "individual" typically designates the most extended series of actualities distinguished by that characteristic (on my usage, "subjective individual" always so designates). Moreover, the metaphysical character of final real things is self-differentiating, implying two metaphysical kinds, namely, those whose unification relates internally to details of the relevant past fragmentarily and those whose unifications relate internally to details of all other events completely—such that events of the first kind define the metaphysical aggregate called the world, and events of the second kind define a necessary or metaphysical individual that may be called divine. God is the individual that completely includes all that has happened and thus will include whatever else happens when it happens.

Within the world, human beings include individuals who, in some of their events or activities, exemplify subjectivity, even if we have no reason to say that all such existence is dependent, as our existence apparently is, on the kind of body we call human. When final real things occur as subjective acts, I propose, a decision by which the future is conditioned becomes a purpose, and a decision for that purpose is a self-understanding of the individual in question as exemplified in that act. On my accounting, the decision is then a moral one, that is, may be moral or immoral, and moral better and worse are distinguished in terms of a metaphysical feature. The implications of "something exists," in other words, define a character exemplified by final real things in greater or lesser measure, and this character defines the good, such that its actualization in greater measure is better. Each final real thing maximizes its own good by so unifying internal relations to its past as to condition the future for maximal good—and it is this metaphysical feature that becomes, when existence occurs with developed understanding, a moral demand. A subjective act is the best it can be when it decides so to condition the future as to maximize the possibilities that subsequent events can maximize the good.

The two preceding paragraphs are offered simply to mention the direction in which, to the best of my reasoning, sound metaphysical thinking seeks to move. Whatever their merit, the principal intent of this discussion is to defend metaphysical necessity against the dictum "all existential statements can be denied without self-contradiction" or, what comes to the same thing, "all existential statements are contingently true or false." To be sure, negative arguments cannot be completely convincing without a corresponding positive argument for whatever is implied by one's negation. Hence, the present defense cannot be complete without presenting a systematic metaphysics. Still, any such system must start somewhere, and one might well assert that one or more statements within a coherent metaphysics are necessarily true in a more transparent way than are others. "Something exists" is, I propose, one such statement. For this reason, I have sought to clarify why the statement "nothing exists" and thus the dictum "all existential statements can be denied without self-contradiction" are impossible.

2

SPEAKING OF GOD AFTER AQUINAS

Whatever their own distinctive formulations and varied points of disagreement, most contemporary Christian theologians continue in some way to affirm that Christian faith and thus Christian theology include speaking of God. In addition, there appears to be a widespread consensus that all positive forms of such speaking must use terms in a manner that differs from their use in speaking of things other than God. On that agreement, religious and theological language can never use positive terms in the same sense to designate both God and nondivine things.

This summary characterization naturally applies to Roman Catholic theologians who seek to maintain essential continuity with the account of theistic predication given by Thomas Aquinas, at least as it has traditionally been understood. But recent Protestant thinkers often evidence a similar continuity with the Protestant project of liberal theology, notwithstanding that, in other respects, they may also depart fundamentally from it. If we trace the beginnings of that project to Friedrich Schleiermacher and include within it the "self-criticism" effected by neo-orthodox thinkers of the earlier twentieth century (see Ogden 1966, 4–5), such major representatives as Schleiermacher himself, Rudolf Bultmann, Reinhold Niebuhr, and Paul Tillich all assert that speaking of God in positive terms is always analogical or mythological or symbolic or metaphorical in character. In this respect, recent Protestant theologians often exhibit continuity with these predecessors.

In both Roman Catholic and Protestant thought, the differing use of terms in designating the divine reality is sometimes said to depend on the divine self-disclosure in or through Jesus Christ and the apostolic witness to it, typically thought to be that of scripture or of scripture and tradition. Speaking of God properly is not possible independently of the Christian community and its discourse. On other proposals, however, the peculiar character of theistic language can be explicated philosophically. When this latter approach is taken, the detailed account of analogical names in Aquinas is often central to the argument. This chapter is focused on this philosophical discussion and, specifically, on the account offered by Aquinas.

To be sure, some interpreters of Aquinas hold that his account of the divine names is solely a Christian theological account—in the sense that his view depends on what can be known about God only in or through sacred scripture. To the best of my reading, however, Aquinas defends analogical predication of the divine by way of natural reason, just as he also seeks to demonstrate God's existence independently of special revelation (cf. Kretzman 1997). I will so present his position, but I will not advocate this interpretation against challenges to it.[1] My purpose here is to argue that Aquinas's account, at least on the traditional reading of it, cannot be sustained as a philosophical defense of our speaking of God. Assuming that this critical argument is correct, I am convinced that similar, if not more apparent, problems characterize all philosophical attempts to show how all positive speaking of God is mythological or symbolic or metaphorical. But I will not analyze any such attempt. Instead, I will conclude with the summary recommendation of another approach to theistic discourse, on which we can use some positive terms in the same sense to designate God and nondivine things. Notwithstanding the criticism of Aquinas I will offer, I will also suggest how this alternative approach maintains its own kind of continuity with him, specifically with his argument for God's existence.

In so taking up Aquinas, this chapter relates to a proposal in philosophical theology that is unsurpassed in systematic complexity and completeness and the discussion of which has been immense. Neither the format of a chapter nor my command of the literature allows me to consider the full range of Aquinas's texts or the full scope of pertinent scholarly treatments. For this reason, I refer to the "traditional reading" of Aquinas's account as the one I will present and criticize. This reading, I believe, can be explicated through attention to the *Summa Contra Gentiles* and the *Summa Theologiae*, and for this reason my presentation is also confined to those sources. Accordingly, there may be other readings of Aquinas I do not engage here. I proceed in spite of this more narrow compass because it marks in relevant respects the reading of Aquinas to which contemporary theologians must appeal if they seek from him philosophical backing for saying that we can apply positive terms to God and creatures only in differing senses. In other words, a metaphysical defense of this assertion constitutes what I mean by Aquinas's account on the traditional reading. In the relevant sense, then, "other readings" means those on which Aquinas does in fact affirm positive terms that designate God and creatures in the same sense. I also proceed with the traditional reading because, as far as my knowledge extends, I am inclined to think that this reading is correct, and I will have some occasion in what follows to give some reasons for rejecting some possible alternatives. Nonetheless, I do not purport adequately to defend my explication of Aquinas.

Aquinas's account on the traditional reading of it has been extensively debated, and it might well be asked what this chapter hopes to add. Given that theologians continue to cite his argument for constructive purposes, even the repetition of effective criticism others have offered may be worthwhile. But a clear explication of the problem in Aquinas, I also think, is inseparable from a coherent approach to theistic discourse, so that the former sets the direction for the latter, and in this respect there is a contribution to be made. As I will try to show, the fundamental problem is metaphysical. Here and throughout this chapter, I use "metaphysical" in the strict sense, that is, to designate an explication of existence as such—in distinction from "metaphysical" in the broad sense, that is, an explication of moral existence as such.

The fundamental problem, then, involves the relation between what Aquinas says about analogical names and the limits he places on theistic arguments. More clearly stated, analogical speaking of God makes sense only given prior success in demonstrating that God exists, notwithstanding that we cannot know God's essence, but success in this demonstration depends on the prior showing that we can name God and creatures analogically. Aquinas's account, in other words, involves a vicious circle. David Burrell has made a similar point, but, as I will discuss below, he does not focus on the metaphysical issue because we should refuse, he believes, a metaphysical justification of our speaking of God. In contrast, I will recommend that Aquinas's problem is more adequately appreciated if, with him, we affirm the metaphysical task and remove the limits he places on metaphysical theism.

A READING OF AQUINAS

On what I am calling the traditional reading, Aquinas holds that all proper and positive speaking of God is analogical because natural reason or, as we may say, philosophical theology can demonstrate the existence of God but cannot establish God's essence. "I say that this proposition, *God exists*, of itself is self-evident.... Now because we do not know the essence of God, the proposition is not self-evident to us, but needs to be demonstrated by things that are more known to us, though less known in their nature—namely, by His effects" (*S.T.* 1.2.1).[2] We cannot know God's essence because "our natural knowledge begins from sense. Hence, our natural knowledge can go as far as it can be led by sensible things. But our intellect cannot be led by sense so far as to see the essence of God; because sensible creatures are effects of God which do not equal the power of God, their cause" (*S.T.* 1.12.12), Through natural reason, as Aquinas also formulates the point, we can know *that* God is but not *what* God is, and therefore this understanding of God is "through negations."

> Many things are set apart from Him, through demonstration, whose removal enable Him to be understood in distinction from other beings. In fact, demonstration shows that God is immutable, eternal, incorporeal, altogether simple, one, and other such things.... Now, we reach a proper knowledge of a thing not only through affirmations but also through negations.... But there is this difference between these two modes of proper knowledge: through affirmations, when we have a proper knowledge of a thing, we know *what* the thing is, and how it is separated from others; but through negations, when we have a proper knowledge of a thing, we know *that* it is distinct from other things, yet what it is remains unknown. Now, such is the proper knowledge that we have of God through demonstrations. (*S.C.G.* 3.39.1)

This means that "names which are said of God negatively or which signify His relation to creatures manifestly do not at all signify His substance, but rather express the distance of the creature from Him, or His relation to something else, or rather, the relation of creatures to Himself" (*S.T.* 1.13.2). Because these names alone express the knowledge of God through demonstrations, it follows, with respect to names said of God positively, that "univocal predication is impossible between God and creatures" (*S.T.* 1.13.5; see also *S.C.G.* 1.32.1). We cannot speak positively of God in terms that signify both God and creatures in the same sense. The very name God itself "is a name of operation so far as relates to the source of its meaning... since all who speak of God intend to name *God* that being which exercises providence over all.... But though taken from this operation, this name *God* is imposed to signify the divine nature." In other words, God "is made known to us from His operations or His effects" (*S.T.* 1.13.8), and the name God cannot express knowledge of God's essence but, rather, expresses our knowledge of God's effects as the effects of "something existing above all things, the principle of all things, and removed from all things" (S.T. 1.13.8.ad2).

Analogical names, then, allow natural reason to understand or speak of God affirmatively or positively. "These names . . . are predicated substantially of God," although they do not predicate between God and creatures univocally because "they fall short of representing Him." They "signify the divine substance, but in an imperfect manner, even as creatures represent it imperfectly." Analogical names are possible because "God prepossesses in Himself all the perfections of creatures, being Himself absolutely and universally perfect. Hence, every creature represents Him, and is like Him, so far as it possesses some perfection" (S.T. 1.13.2). In other words, "our knowledge of God is derived from the perfections which flow from Him to creatures; which perfections are in God in a more eminent way than in creatures" (S.T. 1.13.3). This relation of creatures to God is what permits natural reason to demonstrate that God exists and, thereby, to speak of God negatively. By virtue of the same relation, we may apply to God analogically names with which we speak of certain perfections that flow from Him.

Analogical speaking, Aquinas explains, is distinguished from both univocal and purely equivocal designation of differing things:

> Now this mode of community is a mean between pure equivocation and simple univocation. For in analogies the idea is not, as it is in univocals, one and the same; yet it is not totally diverse as in equivocals; but the name which is thus used in a multiple sense signifies various proportions to some one thing: *e.g., healthy*, applied to urine, signifies the sign of animal health; but applied to medicine, it signifies the cause of the same health. (S.T. 1.13.5)

At the same time, analogical predication of God and creatures must also be distinguished from metaphorical speaking of the divine. "There are some names which signify these perfections flowing from God to creatures in such a way that the imperfect way in which the creatures receive the divine perfection is part of the very signification of the name itself, as *stone* signifies a material being; and names of this kind can be applied to God only in a metaphorical sense" (S.T. 1.13.3.ad1).

In so characterizing metaphorical names, Aquinas refers to terms that "imply or mean a corporeal condition in the thing signified" (S.T. 1.13.3.ad3), as does the term "stone" or "mighty fortress." By implication, then, analogical names for God are terms that also apply to creatures but do not include in their very signification the imperfect way in which corporeal creatures receive the divine perfection; that is, these terms do not or do not necessarily signify materiality. Because the human soul is, for Aquinas, an immaterial substance, terms that signify perfections of the human soul, such as "good" or "wise" or "living," can "be applied to God properly" (S.T. 1.13.3.ad1) and thus are analogical rather than metaphorical names.[3] Moreover, the same is true of metaphysical terms such as "substance," which do not necessarily signify something material.

Since the perfections that flow from God to creatures are in God in a more eminent way than in creatures, the eminent designation of these names is the divine essence. "So when we say, *God is good*, the meaning is . . . *Whatever good we attribute to creatures pre-exists in God*, and in a higher way" (S.T. 1.13.2). But we cannot know God's essence. Thus, we must distinguish between what is designated or signified by analogical predication between God and creatures and our mode of signification.

> Our intellect apprehends them [that is, the perfections] as they are in creatures, and as it apprehends them thus does it signify them by names. Therefore, as to the names applied to God, there are two things to be considered—viz., the perfections themselves which they signify, such as goodness, life, and the like, and their mode of signification. As regards *what is signified* by these names, they belong properly to God, and more properly than they belong to creatures, and are applied primarily to Him. But as regards their *mode of signification*, they do not properly and strictly apply to God; for their mode of signification befits creatures. (S.T. 1.13.3, emphasis added)

This distinction can be clarified through attention to Aquinas's general definition of analogical names.

> In names predicated of many in an analogical sense, all are predicated through a relation to some one thing; and this one thing must be placed in the definition of them all. And since *the essence expressed by the name is the definition*, as the Philosopher says, such a name must be applied primarily to that which is put in the definition of the other things, and secondarily to these others according as they approach more or less to the first. Thus, for instance, *healthy* applied to animals comes into the definition of *healthy* applied to medicine, which is called healthy as being the cause

of health in the animal; and also into the definition of *healthy* which is applied to urine, which is called healthy in so far as it is the sign of the animal's health. (S.T. 1.13.6)[4]

In naming God and creatures analogically, our mode of signification differs from what is signified because the order of signification is reversed. The reality designated by such a term belongs primarily to God and secondarily to creatures. On this order, to name a perfection of creatures is to attribute something to them that flows from the perfection of God, such that God's perfection should be placed in the definition of the creatures' perfection. Since we cannot know the divine essence, however, our mode of signification applies the name primarily to creatures and secondarily to God, and God's perfection is defined as that from which the perfection of creatures flows. "Because we come to a knowledge of God from other things, the reality in the names said of God and other things belongs by priority in God according to His mode of being, but the meaning of the name belongs to God by posteriority. And so He is said to be named from His effects" (S.C.G. 1.34.6).[5]

In sum, Aquinas asserts that we can know by natural reason that God exists but cannot know God's essence, such that univocal names designate God negatively. Still, we can speak of what God is or predicate positively of God by way of analogy, wherein, according to their mode of signification, analogical names apply to God secondarily and by relation to their primary application to creatures.

ANALOGICAL AND PURELY EQUIVOCAL NAMES

On the assumption that the traditional reading of Aquinas and this brief review of it are essentially correct, his account of theistic predication raises the following question: if *all* proper and positive predication of God is analogical, how is it possible for humans to distinguish these divine names from pure equivocals? The analogical sense in which such names apply to God is, for us, by relation to their primary application to creatures. Hence, we cannot understand the former unless we understand the relation between God and creatures, and that understanding requires some understanding of both related things. As Aquinas himself says, "a relation needs two extremes" (S.T. 1.13.7). Moreover, the two related things must be understood independently of the analogical names, because the relation determines the sense in which these names apply to God. But this independent understanding of both extremes is absent in speaking of God and creatures analogically because a proper designation of God that is not analogical is only negative.

Consider Aquinas's favorite example of an analogical term, borrowed from Aristotle: the term "healthy." In application to animals, on the one hand, and to medicine, on the other, "healthy" signifies in primary and secondary ways, respectively. The term is not purely equivocal because medicine is related to animal health as its cause. We can understand the causal relation and thus "healthy" as analogical because we understand independently of "healthy" both animals, on the one hand, and, on the other, something else that is or might be related to animals as the cause of their health. Were it the case that we could not understand anything that is or might be related to animal health as its cause, it would be senseless to say that "healthy" is an analogical name applied secondarily to something else of which animal health is an effect. Hence, to apply "healthy" to animals and to something else would be (in the absence of something related to animal health in a manner other than causally) purely equivocal.

To this it might be objected, "When an effect is better known to us than its cause, from the effect we proceed to the knowledge of the cause.... Since every effect depends on its cause, if the effect exists, the cause must pre-exist" (S.T. 1.2.2). We can proceed, the objection asserts, from our knowledge that animal health exists to the knowledge that it has some cause, which may be called healthy in a secondary sense. But this assertion is an instance of affirming the consequent because it assumes that animal health exists *as an effect*. Just because "every effect depends on its cause," effects presuppose causes, and thus to call something an effect is already to affirm that it is caused. So far from proving that animal health has a cause, proceeding to knowledge of something that may be called healthy presupposes that there is such a cause and thus presupposes that we can understand independently of the analogical term something that is or might be related to animal health in this way. Were it the case that we could not understand independently of the analogical term anything that is or might be so related to animal health, we would have no reason to speak of the latter as an effect.

Mutatis mutandis, it is precisely this last condition that obtains with respect to Aquinas's analogical naming of God and creatures. Proper predication of the divine that is nonanalogical is only negative. Since we cannot have an independent understanding of what is thereby designated, we cannot understand the relation by which the application of a name to God determines its status as an analogical name. To say that "we know God from creatures as their cause [that is, the cause of creatures as such]" (S.T. 1.13.1) is to presuppose that we have an independent understanding of something that is or might be such a cause. Since this understanding is not possible, we have no reason to speak of creatures as God's effects, and speaking of God positively must apply names that cannot be distinguished from pure equivocals.

One might now object that Aquinas has been misrepresented. When he says that "we know God from creatures as their cause, and also by way of excellence and remotion" (S.T. 1.13.1), he means to distinguish speaking of God as cause from both speaking of God *analogically* and speaking only by negation. In the present context, then, the objection asserts that *cause* itself speaks in a different manner than both about creatures as effects. Still, speaking of God as cause, as with speaking of God as *God*, does not express knowledge of God's essence or substance; rather, one thereby names God "from His operations" (S.T. 1.13.8). This is confirmed when Aquinas makes clear that the relation between creatures as effects and God as cause is real only in the creatures.

> Since, therefore, God is outside the whole order of creation, and all creatures are ordered to Him, and not conversely, it is manifest that creatures are really related to God Himself; whereas in God there is no real relation to creatures, but a relation *only in idea*, inasmuch as creatures are really related to Him. . . .
>
> Nor is it incongruous that God should be denominated from relations really existing in things, provided that the opposite relations be at the same time understood by us as existing in God [that is, be relations only in idea], so that God is spoken of relatively to creatures inasmuch as the creature is related to Him; just as the Philosopher says that the object is said to be knowable relatively because knowledge relates to it. (S.T. 1.13.7, and ad4, emphasis added)

Thus, the difference between knowing God as cause and knowing God by way of excellence does not imply differing ways of designating God's substance but, rather, marks the difference between naming the relation of creatures to God and naming God's perfections. It remains, then, that we cannot have an independent understanding of something that is or might be such a cause. To be sure, the term "cause," as the term "God," may be taken from this operation and imposed to signify the divine nature. But "from the divine effects we cannot know the divine nature in itself," so that we have only the ways of "eminence, causality, and negation" (S.T. 1.13.8.ad2). If "cause" is used to designate the divine nature, this term is also applied analogically. "Being a cause" then names a perfection that is "in God in a more eminent way than in creatures" (*S.T.* 1.13.3), and our natural knowledge of causes, which goes as far as it can be led by sensible things, must "fall short of representing Him" (*S.T.* 1.13.2).

Conceding that causality does not provide an independent understanding of God's substance and, thereby, of the relation between God and creatures, this relation, some might say, is given by "eminence." Thus, God is related to creatures as the being that "superexceeds them all" (*S.T.* 1.12.12) and in whom "all the perfections of things pre-exist excellently" (*S.T.* 1.13.5). On this proposal, that comparison determines the status of divine names as analogicals in distinction from pure equivocals. Taken as designating a relation, however, "eminence," as far as I can see, repeats how we understand God by way of causality, since the perfections "that are in God in a more eminent way than creatures" are known by way of God's effects. "God is the highest good absolutely, and . . . . good is attributed to God . . . inasmuch as *all desired perfections flow from Him as from the first cause*" (*S.T.* 1.6.2; emphasis added). This reading is confirmed by the recognition that divine perfection is, for Aquinas, "pure act, without the admixture of any potentiality" and, therefore, "immutable" (*S.T.* 1.9.1), so that anything that exists or is in act is insofar a perfection. Because God is without any potentiality, all other beings depend for their existence and thus their perfection on God, and this is another way of saying that God is the first cause.

But quite apart from explicitly equating the way of eminence with the way of causality, the former cannot provide another understanding of God and thus of the relation between God and creatures, such that one could understand divine names as analogous rather than purely equivocal. In speaking of a being in whom the perfections of creatures preexist excellently, one presupposes that we can understand what such preexisting excellence is. But just this possibility is denied to us because we cannot understand God's essence. Given that we know the application of "good" or "wise" to some creature, for instance, we might well be able to understand that these terms also apply or could apply to others "in a higher way" (*S.T.* 1.13.2), that is, the others are or could be better or wiser. On Aquinas's proposal, however, we can have no positive and nonanalogical understanding of another who is "absolutely and universally perfect" (*S.T.* 1.13.2). Hence, we can have no understanding of the relation between this other and creatures. To the contrary, the relation between eminent and creaturely perfection is what can be signified only by analogical names.

Let us summarize the apparent problem by returning to Aquinas's general account of these names: "In names predicated of many in an analogical sense, all are predicated through a relation to some one thing; and this one thing must be placed in the definition of them all" (S.T. 1.13.6). By relation "to some one thing," a secondary application clarifies a "mode of community... between pure equivocation and simple univocation" (S.T. 1.13.5). If we say, for instance, that God is "wise," we properly define this secondary application in some such manner as follows: "God is wise" means that the wisdom of humans preexists in God's perfection. But this account does not contribute to understanding unless we understand the term "perfection" in application to God. In truth, however, this term (if not solely negative) must itself be analogical and thus in need of a similar definition. Precisely because we cannot properly speak of God positively except by analogy, every account of an analogical term must include an analogical term, and the point becomes apparent when we recognize that God's "perfection" cannot be defined without placing this very application of the term (or some other term that differs only verbally) in the account: "God's perfection" means that the perfections of creatures preexist in God's perfection. Thus, the relation between eminent and creaturely perfection, or of creatures to their first cause, cannot be understood in the manner required to know that "wise" or any other term designating a creaturely perfection is anything other than purely equivocal in application to God.

Given that theistic analogies cannot be distinguished from pure equivocals, one has reason to doubt that we can have any understanding of God. A pure equivocal applies to differing things in "totally diverse" (S.T. 1.13.5) senses. If this is, as far as we can know, the manner in which *all* positive terms name God and creatures, then all of our affirmations of God apply terms in a sense completely unrelated to the sense in which they apply to creatures. This means that we cannot affirm anything in speaking of God or can have no understanding that such speaking might express.

Some might contend that the conclusion reached is only epistemic. The argument, on this construction, shows only that we cannot distinguish between analogical and purely equivocal names in speaking of God and creatures. In itself, as far as I can see, that would be sufficient also to conclude that Aquinas does not by way of natural reason successfully defend analogical predication of the divine. As he himself observes, "if, then, nothing was said of God and creatures except in a purely equivocal way, no reasoning proceeding from creatures to God could take place" (S.C.G. 1.33.5; see also S.T. 1.13.5). Nonetheless, it might be said, there still could be a difference between analogical and purely equivocal predication of God and creatures, notwithstanding that we are unable to distinguish the one from the other.

But the argument here concludes that Aquinas's account of divine predication, at least on the traditional reading of it, prevents an understanding of the relation between God and creatures by virtue of which analogical and purely equivocal names would be differentiated. What we cannot do is *conceive* of this relation. If we assume, as I think we must, that assertions about something inconceivable are not philosophically meaningful, then the statement that there might be a difference between analogical and purely equivocal names of God is itself not meaningful, since this assertion speaks of a relation between God and creatures we cannot conceive. Perhaps the conclusion reached is epistemic; still, it is also ontological: Aquinas's account implies that we cannot speak meaningfully of God.[6]

THEISTIC ARGUMENTS

For all that, however, the previous discussion might now be called tendentious because it abstracts from Aquinas's theistic arguments, which claim to demonstrate the existence of God (see Wippel 1984, 221--22). If one or more of these arguments is or are successful, then surely we can have an understanding of God. Moreover, it might seem that the status of theistic analogies as neither simply univocal nor purely equivocal is established by the prior showing that there is something to which creatures are related as their "first mover, moved by no other," the first principle "of their being, goodness, and every other perfection," which has "of itself its own necessity." Because the existence of that "to which everyone gives the name of God" (*S.T.* 1.2.3) can be demonstrated, we can, contrary to what was said above, "know God from creatures as their cause" (*S.T.* 1.13.1). Indeed, Aquinas's various arguments for God's existence, in the *Summa Contra Gentiles* as well as the *Summa Theologiae*, seem to be so many differing attempts to demonstrate the existence of a first cause of all things. Accordingly, the conclusion reached in the previous section cannot be convincing without attention to Aquinas's conviction that "the existence of God ... can be known by natural reason" (*S.T.* 1.2.2.ad1).

As will become apparent, the purpose of this chapter does not require an extended statement of the theistic arguments Aquinas offers. As far as I can see, the metaphysical principle effective throughout is the priority of actuality to potentiality. "Previous to that which is potential, must be some being already actual, since a potential being can be reduced to act only by some being already actual" (*S.T.* 1.4.1.ad2). Because actuality is prior in this sense, Aquinas argues, there is a being whose essence is to exist, and further, there can be only one such being. There must be a "first being" that is "pure act, without the admixture of any potentiality, for the reason that, absolutely, potentiality is posterior to act" (S.T. 1.9.1). Because pure act must be absolutely infinite and simple, the God whose existence is proved can be univocally designated only by negation. "Our intellect, which first apprehends composite things, cannot attain to knowledge of simple things except by removing the composition" (S.T. 1.10.1.ad1), and thus "demonstration shows that God is immutable, eternal, incorporeal, altogether simple, one, and such other things" (S.C.G. 3.39.1). Having demonstrated God's existence, however, we know that creatures are effects of a being from whom "all desired perfections flow . . . as from their first cause" (S.T. 1.6.2). Accordingly, we have understood the relation of creatures to something that allows us to speak of both analogically.

Whatever else might be discussed in the differing ways that Aquinas reasons to a first cause, the pertinent consideration here is his formulation of their common conclusion. Because God is said to be "pure act," one is led to ask: How can any theistic argument succeed if what is said to be demonstrated thereby can be designated only by negations? Predications that are only negative insofar fail to distinguish their object from sheer nothing. At least to first appearances, then, a God whose essence we cannot know must be simply a God whom we cannot know. To a criticism stated in this way, however, Aquinas has a ready reply, because he does not seek by demonstration to know the essence of God but, rather, solely God's existence. The arguments are said to achieve a conclusion that is distinguished from sheer nothing because they prove that something "immutable, eternal, incorporeal, altogether simple, one, and other such things" *exists*.

Criticism is more circumspect, then, if it attends to this separation between knowing the existence and knowing the essence of God. Can the former be possible if the latter is not? Because God's essence is unknowable, univocal speaking of God and creatures must predicate of God only by negation, but saying of some subject that it exists or is a being necessarily speaks of it positively. To be sure, raising the question in this way may seem to violate the dictum that "existence" is not a predicate. But Aquinas, it would seem, finally cannot accept this dictum, at least with respect to the divine, because the God whose existence he purports to demonstrate is the one being whose essence is to exist. "I say that this proposition, *God exists*, of itself is self-evident, for the predicate is the same as the subject, because God is His own existence" (S.T. 1.2.1).

It seems now to follow that every other being is one whose essence differs from its existence, and for Aquinas, this is another way of saying that its being depends on God as its first cause. On this reasoning, one can predicate of any being its *mode* of existence: either this mode is such that existence differs from essence or, in the case of God alone, the mode is such that existence is essential (cf. Hartshorne 1962a, 49--68). In the former case, the mode of existence is contingent and, in the latter case, necessary. In either case, the predication is positive. Thus, to demonstrate the existence of God is to predicate of God the uniquely divine mode of existence and, thereby, to speak of God affirmatively. There is, I recognize, room for controversy about what Aquinas intends when he concludes through demonstration, "God exists." But we can say this: unless one thereby designates God affirmatively, this statement, too, is indistinguishable from speaking about sheer nothing. But, then, "God exists" appears to be a positive and univocal speaking of God.

Even in this form, however, the critique of Aquinas's theistic arguments is inadequate because he can agree that predicating existence of God is positive, notwithstanding that we cannot know God's essence. On this account, there is no contradiction because "being" is itself an analogical name. "In predications all univocal names are reduced to one first non-univocal analogical name, which is *being*" (*S.T.* 1.13.5.ad1). Indeed, this name is, for Aquinas, analogical quite apart from speaking of God. For instance, he notes, as do many thirteenth-century logicians (see Ashworth 1992), that "being" applies in differing senses to substances and accidents. "In analogicals, a name taken in one signification must be placed in the definition of the same name taken in other significations; as, for instance, *being* which is applied to *substance* is placed in the definition of being as applied to *accident*" (*S.T.* 1.13.10). A more or less complete explication of this "first non-univocal name" would require a more or less complete review of Aristotelian metaphysics as transformed by Aquinas, and that task exceeds the scope of this chapter.[7] But whatever else might be said about it, "being" does apply to God and creatures, and we may focus on its use in theistic predication.

"Since God is simple and subsisting, we attribute to Him simple and abstract names to signify His simplicity, and concrete names to signify His subsistence and perfections; although both kinds of names fail to express His mode of being, because our intellect does not know Him in this life as He is" (*S.T.* 1.13.1.ad2). Or, again:

> Whatever is predicated of many things univocally is either a genus, a species, a difference, an accident, or a property. But, as we have shown, nothing is predicated of God as a genus or a difference; and thus neither is anything predicated as a definition, nor likewise as a species, which is

constituted of genus and difference. Nor . . . can there be any accident in God, and therefore nothing is predicated of Him either as an accident or a property, since property belongs to the genus of accidents. It remains, then, that nothing is predicated univocally of God and other things. (S.C.G. 1.32.4)

Thus, "being," like "good" or "living," is a name that signifies a perfection belonging primarily to God but, as regards our mode of signification, applies primarily to creatures (S.T. 1.13.3.ad1). Indeed, it is just because "being" names God and creatures in differing senses that all other positive names properly applied to God must be analogical. Every other positive predication of God implies that God is, and since the being of God can be known only analogically, we cannot apply any other positive predication univocally to God and creatures. Conversely, were "being" to name God and creatures univocally, we could speak of the essence of God and the essences of creatures in some univocal "mode of community" (S.T. 1.13.5), that is, we could designate what they have in common using some other name or names that apply to both in the same sense.

But if the analogical character of "being" seems to allow the affirmation of God's existence without a positive predication that expresses knowledge of God's essence, the price of this proposed solution is that God's existence cannot be demonstrated. From the being or actuality of creatures, Aquinas argues to the being or actuality of God. But the conclusion of any such argument does not signify with the term "being" what is thereby signified in the premise, and the argument commits the fallacy of equivocation. Avoiding this fallacy requires the additional premise that "being" is in the relevant sense an analogical name. But that premise cannot be established without prior reason to say that absolute perfection in distinction from the perfections of creatures exists. Thus, the theistic arguments must posit their own conclusion and, thereby, commit the fallacy of petitio principii.[8] Finally, this is simply another way of saying that analogical predication requires an independent understanding of the relation between things that allows them to be so named. Since the relation between God and creatures cannot be understood, the "being" or "existence" of God as it appears in the theistic arguments cannot be distinguished from a pure equivocal, and we cannot conceive of what is said when this term is applied to God. In truth, "God exists" says nothing at all.

In sum, the problem in Aquinas's account of theistic predication is this: showing that we can name God and creatures analogically depends on prior success in the demonstration of God's existence, but success in this demonstration depends on the prior showing that we can name God and creatures analogically. This formulation states the problem in terms of a philosophical defense of theistic predication, but the matter may also be stated simply in terms of naming God: the possibility of naming God and creatures analogically depends on the independent possibility of understanding God's existence, but the possibility of understanding God's existence depends on the independent possibility of naming God and creatures analogically. The account is involved in a vicious circle. If it explicates our speaking of God, we are bound to the conclusion that we cannot speak meaningfully of God.

BURRELL'S ALTERNATIVE

In an extended and sophisticated analysis of philosophical language, David Burrell agrees that "any justification for using analogical predicates" in the philosophical theology of Aquinas "will be circular, since the meaning of these predicates is secured only through an analogical use of cause" (Burrell 1973, 133; see also Burrell 1979, part I and especially chapter 4).[9] On Burrell's reading, moreover, Aquinas also shared this understanding. Because "God is proposed as first cause or principle of all," Aquinas means that God "is not, cannot be, *a* being," and thus God is "outside any of the universes of discourse that provide the contextual meanings for the terms we use" (Burrell 1973, 132, 169, 125).[10] This is the point expressed in his affirmation *that* God is, even while we cannot say *what* God is, and thus the point expressed also in Aquinas's insistence that univocal terms name God only by negation. "One can say nothing about him—which is a way of saying what cannot be said: that he is not a thing" (Burrell 1973, 239).

Nonetheless, Burrell continues, Aquinas refuses an easy retreat into "the chaste mysticism of silence" because "to forsake language before it is absolutely necessary would betray the very reason that raises questions"—and specifically, the question about the first cause or principle of all (Burrell 1973, 135). Thus, Aquinas works with medieval accounts of analogy in order to make his point. In our time, his intentions can be honored and analogical names for God understood by refusing, "in the spirit of Wittgenstein," the attempt "to justify such usage." The recognition that "we do evoke notions which resist analysis" is, Burrell asserts, "the first step in a contemporary account consistent with Aquinas's analogical usage" (Burrell 1973, 133). If I understand him correctly, Burrell holds that clarity about our speaking of God requires a refusal to explicate it metaphysically. Because I wish to recommend another course, it is important briefly to consider Burrell's proposal.

Burrell identifies the basic terms used to name what, for Aquinas, are the relevant "perfections" as "transcategorical" terms, those that "appear to be equally at home in every category and mode of discourse" or every "context" or "framework" of inquiry and life (Burrell 1973, 222, 225). The "obvious candidates are the transcendentals [e.g., 'being,' 'true,' 'one'] and that subset of them that fills out the schema 'good.'" Their notable common character is that they function to "point from language to the language user. Or rather they speak of language as emanating from a person with aims and purposes" in discourse or inquiry (Burrell 1973, 240--41, 243). Accordingly, "the meaning of these terms is relative to the inquiry in which they occur." They are "transcategorical" because they have "a proper use within each language framework" but "possess no 'carry-over' meaning of their own" (Burrell 1973, 223--24).

> 'Being' (x is a ...) reflects no answer in particular but simply notes that the *question*, 'What is (the nature of) x?' is a question that will not down. To assert that p is true is simply gratuitous unless the context supplies some clues to the method of verification, to the kinds of statements that would count as evidence. And to say of anything that [it] is *one* (a unity, an individual) suggests little more than the viewpoint from which someone is regarding it and the general character of his intellectual concern about it. (Burrell 1973, 223)

Calling this transcategorical use of language analogical distinguishes it from the ordinary use of terms and from their metaphorical use, and when such analogical terms are employed in speaking of God, their meaning is relative to that context. This is why a given analogical name for God cannot be defined except through the use of other analogical terms as they function in the given context. "Transcendentals and appraisal terms form a set open to use in characterizing a God who must remain uncharacterizable" because God "is not a thing" (Burrell 1973, 231--32). Such speaking has propriety because—or, at least, if—human aspiration includes, as Aquinas says that it does, understanding the universe itself, in the sense that one seeks to make existence as such intelligible.

This brief review abstracts from Burrell's instructive discussion of language use generally and from the development of his proposal through detailed treatment of attempts in Western philosophy to clarify analogical speaking. But if the review as far as it goes is essentially correct, then it allows us to ask: Is Burrell's account of theistic analogies consistent with his thesis about transcategorical terms? "[T]he meaning of these terms," he says, is entirely relative to differing contexts of inquiry "in which they occur"—differing modes of discourse in which it is meaningful to ask about "(the nature of) *x*" and "the kinds of statements that would count as evidence" and thus to pursue some or other "intellectual concern" (Burrell 1973, 223–24). Hence, the propriety of such terms in speaking of God depends on whether it is meaningful to ask a question, the answer to which characterizes what "must remain uncharacterizable."

On Burrell's reading, Aquinas holds that asking about "the grounds for there being anything at all" reflects the "imperious demands" or aspirations of rational life for "order and fulfillment." If this inquiry "is not forced upon us, it nonetheless corresponds to what can only be called the inner structure of the inquirer" (Burrell 1973, 163). But conceding a meaningful question something like the one Aquinas answers in speaking as he does about God does not commit us to the understanding of that question attributed to him by Burrell—namely, that we here enter a context of discourse or inquiry in which we do not ask about *a* being and thus can say nothing positive except in analogical terms. To the contrary, this explication of the relevant discourse is inconsistent with affirming such a question, precisely because "the meaning of these terms is relative to the inquiry in which they occur," and the inquiry is said to ask for the nature of something "one can say nothing about." As far as I can see, then, Burrell's revised account of analogy does not show how we can say anything meaningful about God.

Moreover, his proposal seems to violate his own understanding of transcategorical terms. To say that God is not *a* being and, thereby, to distinguish this context of discourse from all others is to use the transcendental term "being" with a meaning that is *not* relative to a given context of inquiry. By implication, every other context of inquiry involves asking "the *question*: 'What is (the nature of) *x*?'" about something that can be distinguished from other things, and "thing" or "being" so understood must have some "'carry-over' meaning" of its own in order to distinguish all such inquiries from the theistic inquiry that is not about a thing. The transcendental term "being" must have, in other words, some transcendental meaning or set of meanings, and asking about this meaning or set of meanings defines a context of inquiry that is itself transcategorical. On my reading, Aquinas calls this transcategorical inquiry metaphysics. Thus, he intends a metaphysical statement when he calls "being" an analogical name and, thereby, expresses his philosophical conviction that we can speak of something we can signify in univocal terms only by negation.

To the best of my reading, Burrell's analysis of theistic discourse or, as he says elsewhere, of "the grammar appropriate *in divinis*," depends entirely on *his understanding* of our "quest for the sense of it all" and thus our question seeking an explanation for "the fact that there exists anything at all" (Burrell 1979, 17, 74, 67). It is Burrell's understanding of this question that requires us to speak of something one can say nothing about or to use language as a "way of conceiving the inconceivable" (Burrell 1979, 89). As far as I can see, however, this required answer implies that Burrell's proposal repeats the difficulty in Aquinas: asking about God is not a meaningful question if its true answer could only designate "the unknown" (Burrell 1979, 12).[11]

THE PRINCIPLE OF PRIOR ACTUALITY

Whatever the force of this criticism, however, some may still doubt its conclusion because something seems right in Aquinas's arguments for God's existence. To these readers, the metaphysical principle that actuality is prior to potentiality, taken to mean that potentiality cannot be reduced to act without a prior actuality, seems to be sound. If this principle is affirmed, it seems to follow that something about actuality and thus being or existence is necessary, that is, existence as such cannot be the actualization of a mere possibility, as if there might have been nothing. Acceptance of this implication, some may think, implies in turn a being whose essence is to exist, precisely in the sense that Aquinas asserted, so that both his demonstration of God's existence and his analogical naming of God's perfections must, notwithstanding the critical discussion above, be sound.

But nothing said above intends to deny the principle of prior actuality, as I will call it, or its importance for speaking of God. To the contrary, I accept this principle as an expression of the basic metaphysical recognition that existence as such cannot be completely absent, and thus a complete negation of existence is senseless. As far as I can see, a putative thought whose conceptual content is in no way existentially positive cannot be distinguished from a putative thought that has no content at all, for instance, a thought whose conceptual content is self-contradictory. If that is correct, then statements such as "there might have been nothing" or "existence may cease" are, in truth, merely verbal, because they cannot be so much as possibly true. Charles Hartshorne expresses this conclusion in saying that no meaningful statement can be "completely restrictive" of existential possibilities, and thus "we must . . . exclude all statements professing to be free of positive implications"

(Hartshorne 1970, 159–60). The principle of prior actuality may be understood to mean or imply that every meaningful statement is at least in part existentially positive.[12]

Since this chapter cannot attempt to develop an alternative metaphysics,[13] I will not seek further to defend this basic metaphysical recognition, and I assert it only to clarify the respect in which I take Aquinas's principle of prior actuality to be valid. So far from denying the principle, the burden here is that Aquinas himself contradicts it in his account of theistic predication. Because he holds that "being" in the sense of "actuality" is itself an analogical name (whose application to God and creatures cannot, in truth, be distinguished from a pure equivocal), Aquinas asserts that "actuality" signifies in two metaphysical senses, one of which has no positive content. His statements about God violate a basic metaphysical recognition precisely because they seek to designate something inconceivable or to designate only by negation. In truth, Aquinas's putative thought of God cannot be distinguished from a putative thought that is in no respect existentially positive.

To the best of my reasoning, then, the principle of prior actuality means that speaking metaphysically about God requires positive terms that apply univocally to God and creatures. To reach this point is, naturally, only to credit the extensive philosophical discussion of whether there are such terms and, if so, what they are, and a more or less complete argument for some answer to those questions cannot be offered here. As one possibility, William Alston, if I understand him correctly, argues that "Thomas has radically under-supported his claim that... no terms can be predicated univocally of God and creature." Alston also believes that "we [should] jump ship on" Aquinas's "simplicity doctrine," and that doing so will facilitate speaking univocally of God. But "even if we go along with Thomas on divine simplicity, the best position to take on theological predication," Alston concludes, "is that we may be able in some cases to use terms univocally of God and creature" (Alston 1973, 178).

This is because "our conceptual operations" at least may not be "so closely tied to the character of what is conceived that we cannot form concepts that prescind from some of... [its] features" (Alston 1973, 175). Indeed, Aquinas himself allows (see Alston 1973, 175) that "our concepts" need not "reflect precisely the ontological character of their objects" (Alston 1973, 174)—so that the meaning of a concept need not, as Aquinas elsewhere holds (see Alston 1973, 174), be bound to the worldly composite or composites of experience from which it initially occurred. Hence, it may be possible to prescind from the features of worldly things and, thereby, "form a concept of willing, knowing, forgiving or loving that abstracts from the differences in the ways in which these forms are realized in God and creatures" (Alston 1973, 175). Alston does not "know any way of demonstrating this possibility short of exhibiting the actuality by actually constructing such a concept." Further, any such concept will have "a very abstract structure that can plausibly be claimed to be equally found in God and in creatures ... though the mode of realization of this abstract structure is, no doubt, enormously different" (Alston 1973, 176)—and, as a previous citation illustrates, Alston mentions certain abstract psychical concepts.

Assuming that the argument of this chapter is sound, we must, as far as I can see, reject this suggestion—at least if "we go along with Thomas on divine simplicity." To assert that a name applies univocally to God and creatures notwithstanding the difference in mode of being is to imply that a difference in mode of being does not affect the application of the name. But given the divine simplicity (or what comes to the same thing, Aquinas's designation of God as "pure act, without the admixture of any potentiality" and, therefore, "immutable" [S.T. 1.9.1]), the difference in mode of being, in the sense of "actuality," is *metaphysically* dualistic (that is, different in all respects). Metaphysical dualism is the thesis that reality consists of two kinds of things, where each kind is in no way implied by the other and thus the two have nothing in common—or, to say the same thing, each of the two is only the negation of the other and thus differs in all respects. As far as I can see, actuality with some "admixture of ... potentiality," and actuality "without the admixture of any potentiality" (that is, "pure act" or divine simplicity) is the assertion of metaphysical dualism. Hence, Aquinas does not permit some "very abstract structure" (designated by, perhaps, some psychic terms) exemplified by both God and creatures because metaphysically different meanings of "actuality" designate the *most* abstract structure. Metaphysical dualism is the most fundamental divide. For this reason, univocal speaking of God and creatures does indeed require that we "jump ship on the simplicity doctrine" (Alston 1993, 178).

In other words, the principle of prior actuality implies that we cannot speak meaningfully of God unless the metaphysical terms "actuality" and thus "existence" have a single meaning metaphysically and, for this reason, designate univocally of God and creatures. We can also reach this conclusion in the following way: given that completely negative existential statements are not meaningful, the metaphysical task is to clarify what must be the case because existence cannot be completely absent. This means that true metaphysical statements are implied by every meaningful statement because they are, as Hartshorne formulates the point, "completely non-restrictive" of existential possibilities (Hartshorne 1970, 161), and all true metaphysical statements imply each other. On my reading, this is Alfred North Whitehead's meaning in saying that a metaphysical scheme should be "coherent," in the emphatic sense that all the implications of any true metaphysical statement imply it: "the fundamental ideas... presuppose each other so that in isolation they are meaningless" (Whitehead 1978, 3). He calls the metaphysical correlate of this methodological principle the "ontological principle," namely, that "actual entities," in a single sense of the term, are "the final real things" (Whitehead 1978, 18). It follows that philosophy has insofar failed when it pays "metaphysical compliments" to God (Whitehead 1963, 161) because it exempts God "from all the metaphysical categories... applied to the individual things of this temporal world" (Whitehead 1961, 169).

If one accepts this account of metaphysics as necessary for predicating of God philosophically, one is not thereby explicitly bound to accept the specific conception of God that Whitehead or Hartshorne asserts.[14] Still, I take the neoclassical theism that Hartshorne especially has systematically developed to be our most promising resource for the philosophical attempt to clarify our speaking of God, and it may be useful in conclusion to explicate briefly how, on this proposal, we may designate univocally of God and creatures. On Hartshorne's account, the metaphysical designation of "actuality" is creativity or creative synthesis, meaning that an actuality is the unification of real relations to other actualities and to possibilities. The difference between a divine actuality and all others consists in the difference between real relations to strictly all else in all detail, on the one hand, and real relations that are fragmentary, on the other.

Moreover, Hartshorne insists on a metaphysical distinction between God's existence and God's actuality, such that the former is the identity of God as an enduring individual or being that must always be actualized in some way of other, although the divine actualities differ as actualities occur in the world and thus add to the objects of the divine relativity. Thus, Hartshorne can say that God is *a* being or individual, distinguished from all others as the universal or all-inclusive individual, and assert without equivocation that God's essence is to exist. This means that "existence" also names God and creatures univocally, since "existence" in every application signifies that essence is actualized somehow, and the divine individual is distinguished from all others because no other exists necessarily.[15] God is the one being distinguished solely by metaphysical characteristics as the eminently temporal individual.

Some may object that this attempt consistently to affirm the principle of prior actuality suffers from a fundamental flaw of its own and, moreover, one that Aquinas himself identified. On this objection, speaking of God and creatures univocally must itself be impossible because Aquinas, following Aristotle, shows that being cannot be a genus of which God and creatures are species.

> If being were a genus we should have to find a difference through which to contract it to a species. But no difference shares in the genus in such a way that the genus is included in the notion of the difference, for thus the genus would be included twice in the definition of the species. Rather the difference is outside what is understood in the nature of the genus. But there can be nothing that is outside that which is understood by being, if being is included in the concept of the things of which it is predicated. (S.C.G. 1.25.6)

Any pertinence to the present context this argument might have depends on the assumption that "genus" designates an essence or characteristic whose species are defined by the *specific* differences and thus differences not implied by the genus. In contrast, the metaphysical proposal on which "actuality" or "existence" is applied univocally to God and creatures does not understand the difference to be specific in the relevant sense. Rather, the metaphysical terms are understood to be *self-differentiating*, such that they are or imply transcendental disjunctions. By this, I mean that the metaphysical term implies a metaphysical distinction. For instance, "actuality," defined as the unification of real relations to other actualities and to possibilities, itself implies the metaphysical distinction or disjunction between "real relations to strictly all others in all detail" and "real relations to some details of others." This difference between all-inclusive and fragmentary things is the difference between divine and nondivine actualities—and the mutual implication characterizing this transcendental disjunction means that each metaphysical kind of actuality relates all-inclusively or fragmentarily to one or more actualities of the other kind. Again, "existence," defined as essence that is actualized somehow, implies the metaphysical distinction or disjunction between "necessarily actualized somehow" and "contingently actualized somehow," and this is the difference between the divine and all other individuals.

At best, these comments can merely suggest a direction in which philosophical theology might be developed in order to make sense of theistic predication. Moreover, a theologian can always seek to refuse metaphysical speaking and to develop another account of theistic language. But if one intends to avoid exclusive appeal to the specifically Christian community of discourse and, thereby, to use a language authorized only by what Christians take to be the decisive self-disclosure of God, theology is bound to clarify our speaking of God without depending on or essentially restating Aquinas's achievement, at least on the traditional reading of it I have given. In addition, we can say this: if the principle of prior actuality is valid, then one cannot in truth simply refuse metaphysical implications, because the character of existence as such is implied by every meaningful statement. A complete account of theistic language will require philosophical theology in the sense that both Aquinas and Hartshorne pursue it and, moreover, the terms with which we speak of God and creatures in the same sense.

❊ 3 ❊

SCHLEIERMACHER AND TRANSCENDENTAL PHILOSOPHY

What is the relation, if any, between Friedrich Schleiermacher's achievement and transcendental philosophy?[1] Address to this question requires at the outset a relevant definition of "transcendental," because its meaning is contested. In contrast to its principal use in scholastic thought, the term now readily invokes reference to Kant's critical philosophy, where transcendental conditions are those necessary to human reason as such, theoretical and practical, and thus equivalent to what Kant calls metaphysical principles. Mindful of this reference, I will use "transcendental" in a broad sense to mean the following: transcendental conditions constitute subjectivity as such; they are, in other words, conditions of the possibility of subjectivity as such, so that every possible subject presupposes them. Transcendental philosophy seeks to explicate these conditions.

It follows that true transcendental statements are pragmatically necessary, in the sense that every subject who denies what any such statement asserts engages in a pragmatic self-refutation, implying in the act of denial what is denied. For instance, if subjects as such are, with Kant, bound by the moral law, then "something that is bound by the moral law exists" is pragmatically necessary, and every subject who denies this statement implies in doing so the existence of something bound by the moral law. This is because the subject making the denial must exist and, moreover, is bound by the moral law. I have formulated the statement as one about existence, but it might also be presented as a statement about subjectivity, for instance, "a subjective act is bound by the moral law." Again assuming, with Kant, that subjects as such are so bound, we can see that this statement, too, is pragmatically necessary; every subject who denies it implies in the act of denial the statement "a subjective act is bound by the moral law." On the assumption, moreover, the denial is also semantically self-contradictory: being bound by the moral law is a property entailed by a subjective act because being so bound is a condition of the possibility of all possible subjects.

Still, the formulation of transcendental statements as existential statements—that is, statements of the form "something that is x exists"—has the following advantage: it allows a clear distinction between two kinds of transcendental statements, namely, those whose necessity is only pragmatic and those whose necessity is also semantic. Thus, "something that is bound by the moral law exists" is, while perhaps pragmatically necessary, not semantically necessary—at least if we allow that subjects do not necessarily exist. But "something that is temporal exists" is, on some understandings of existence, both pragmatically and semantically necessary. The condition this statement asserts is presupposed not only by every act of subjectivity but also by strictly every possibility. In other words, "something that is temporal exists" is, on those understandings, unconditionally necessary because its denial is said to be semantically self-contradictory; hence, the sheer absence of existence and thus the statement "nothing exists" must be impossible.

Confining oneself to statements about what exists, then, clarifies how transcendental conditions might be present in a strict as well as a broad sense. In the broad sense, statements about such conditions include all pragmatically necessary existential statements, and in the strict sense, statements about such conditions are existential statements that are also semantically necessary.

SCHLEIERMACHER'S INTRODUCTION TO DOGMATICS

To stipulate these designations of "transcendental" is not explicitly to assert that subjectivity as such or existence as such does have necessary conditions, and thus there are transcendental statements. Here at the outset, I mean only to provide some precision for the question: What is the relation, if any, between Schleiermacher's achievement and transcendental philosophy? The pertinence of this question might be seen when his introduction to *The*

Christian Faith proceeds through propositions borrowed from philosophical reflection on human life. But whether that perception has merit depends on how the character of Schleiermacher's introduction should be understood.

This understanding can be approached through the arresting statement found in the introduction's last part: "Our dogmatic theology will not... stand on its proper ground and soil with the same assurance with which philosophy has so long stood on its own, until the separation of the two types of proposition is so complete that, *e.g.*, so extraordinary a question as to whether the same proposition can be true in philosophy and false in Christian theology, and *vice versa*, will no longer be asked" (§ 16, postscript).[2] I will not seek to sort out all this statement might mean but, rather, will focus on why, for Schleiermacher, dogmatic and philosophical truth are so separated that asking whether true dogmatic statements are true in philosophy is an improper or pointless question. This focus, I will argue, will suffice to clarify the relevant function of Schleiermacher's introduction and, further, the respect in which his achievement is related to transcendental philosophy. Also, I will not seek to detail the definition or definitions Schleiermacher gives to "philosophy." It will suffice if this term, in its relevant meaning, designates the science of self-conscious life in general, including therein any specific forms of experience and activity whose definition can be derived from self-conscious life in general. For present purposes, then, I take philosophy to be, at least roughly speaking, what Schleiermacher calls ethics, and I take what he calls philosophy of religion to be, at least in part, itself an aspect of ethics.

That Schleiermacher begins with propositions from ethics and philosophy of religion confirms what he says at the outset, namely, that his introduction is not itself a part of dogmatics: "since the preliminary part of defining a science cannot belong to the science itself, it follows that none of the propositions which will appear in this part can themselves have a dogmatic character" (§ 1). This means that his statement separating truth in dogmatics and truth in philosophy, appearing in the final part of the introduction, is not itself a dogmatic but is, rather, a philosophical statement. Defining a "science" of dogmatics is a philosophical task. Logic commends the same conclusion. Were the separation itself dogmatic, Schleiermacher would wrongly state that the "extraordinary question" is improper because philosophers might still have good reason to ask whether supposedly true dogmatic statements are true in philosophy.[3]

Were the separation itself dogmatic, moreover, its assertion would, on my accounting, be problematic in a way characteristic of any attempt to circumscribe the meaning and truth of Christian faith entirely within the Christian experience of Jesus and thus completely independent of philosophy. So to assert is to imply that self-conscious existence includes no general or common human experience on the basis of which the difference between dogmatics and philosophy can be explicated. To be sure, this implication is negative in form: philosophy can neither ask nor answer the question about self-conscious existence in general that Christian dogmatics asks and answers. Still, that negation is a statement about self-conscious existence in general and thus is philosophical in character—and thus the complete independence of Christian faith from all philosophical implications becomes self-refuting.[4]

Indeed, a similar problem invades every assertion that meaning and truth are in all respects circumscribed by tradition or lifeworld or epoch in the history of Being and, therefore, by some specific location in the human adventure—however generously that location might be marked. The supposed meaning and truth of *this* assertion are about all locations of understanding, and thus any subject who so asserts engages in a pragmatic self-refutation. Karl-Otto Apel, I believe, has it right: "Whoever seriously speaks of the conceptual meaning of 'meaning' and 'truth' as being in the last instance dependent on events or fate—that is [asserts] that the *logos* of our discursive claim to meaning and truth is in principle subordinate to time—thereby cancels the claim to the meaning and truth of their discourse" (Apel 1994, 178). Or, more tersely: reason cannot function "as object and no longer as subject of critique" (Apel 1998, 164). In any event, Schleiermacher's account is not vulnerable to this problem because he is quite clear that the separation of dogmatic from philosophical truth obtains for reasons philosophy itself can provide. Hence, this difference is not a dogmatic truth or, to say the same, the introduction is not itself a part of dogmatics.

Whether the introduction's philosophical discussion is intentionally transcendental is, however, another question. Against that reading, one might argue, Schleiermacher's apparently persistent appeal to introspection (see, e.g., § 4.1) at least suggests that he presents a kind of empirical inquiry, summarizing the general facts of self-consciousness as they appear. Still, the generic description seems to explicate features of self-conscious existence as such and invites a reading of them as transcendental conditions, especially when Schleiermacher uses such phrases as "essential element of human nature" (§ 6.1) and "absolutely general nature of man" (§ 33.1).[5] For instance, his assertion that every moment of self-consciousness includes both a feeling of partial dependence and a feeling of partial freedom and, thereby, "our coexistence with the world" (§ 4.2) of others seems to preclude the possibility that self-conscious existence could ever be otherwise. If this is so, then every denial that these feelings exist would be pragmatically self-refuting, the act of denial implying what it denies.

Indeed, I am persuaded that transcendental arguments for these two feelings can, with suitable changes in their characterization,[6] be successfully formulated—because a moment of self-consciousness can never be conscious only of self (and, therefore, is partially dependent on some other or others) and can never be entirely determined by others (and, therefore, is partially free). But I will not further pursue these arguments. Clarity about the logic of Schleiermacher's philosophical introduction to Christian dogmatics is served, I will argue, by taking his general conclusions, whether so intended or not, to explicate transcendental conditions.

The relation to Christian dogmatics is approached when general self-consciousness is said to include a feeling of God, a relation unlike any relation to the world because the co-determinant is not given and, in that sense, is not an object. "As regards the feeling of absolute dependence. . . . this feeling cannot in any wise arise from the influence of an object which has in some way to be *given* to us" (§ 4.3). If one takes Schleiermacher's account to allow transcendental arguments for feelings of partial dependence and partial freedom, one can see in his discussion of absolute dependence the potential for similar reasoning. Because we are always partially dependent, there can be no feeling of absolute freedom—or, to say the same, self-conscious existence is finite or within the world. But our very existence as finite, "the whole of our spontaneous activity" (§ 4.3), cannot be its own source. Moreover, no finite thing in relation to which we are partially dependent and partially free and thus exist in reciprocity—nor, for that matter, all finite things together (see § 32.2)—can be the source of finite existence as such. Hence, immediate consciousness of our existence as finite includes a feeling of the infinite source of all and, in that sense, of a nonobjective or nongiven "Whence" (§ 4.4): "the self-consciousness which accompanies our whole existence, and negatives absolute freedom, is itself precisely a consciousness of absolute dependence" (§ 4.3).

For the moment, at least, I am not concerned to assess this argument. Whether or not it is sound, the importance of a transcendental formulation here becomes apparent. To be a self *is* to be finite, and thus one cannot be *self*-conscious without an awareness of one's finitude. If we thereby feel our absolute dependence, then self-conscious existence without this feeling cannot be so much as possible. Anticipating discussion to be pursued shortly, we may also state the point as follows: if human existence without this feeling were so much as possible, then the feeling when it is present must depend on some condition or conditions particular or specific to certain self-conscious individuals. The feeling then becomes indistinguishable from what Schleiermacher calls a particular or specific religious affection, for instance, specifically Christian faith, and dogmatics cannot have a philosophical introduction. Whether a transcendental account is read out of or into Schleiermacher's discussion, the general human relation to God could not be what he asserts it to be except as so understood, and my assumption that his analysis has this transcendental character is, in truth, essential to his conclusion. Certain subjective necessities are explicated philosophically, including, in the self-consciousness of absolute dependence, the feeling of an existential necessity—even if, as discussed below, the existential necessity itself (that on which humans are absolutely dependent) cannot be explicated philosophically.

As is well known, Schleiermacher's description of this feeling has been widely criticized as nonsensical because it asserts a consciousness independent of any intentional object, that is, independent of an object the experience of which depends on thought and thus on conceptual content. For instance, Wayne Proudfoot writes: "The religious consciousness is said to have the ... independence of thought ... characteristic of sensations, and yet to include an intuitive component whose object is the infinite.... This combination, required for Schleiermacher's program, is impossible" (Proudfoot 1985, 11).[7] On this reading, if I understand correctly, Schleiermacher describes the feeling in a manner analogous to Kant's description of "intuitions without concepts," even while the feeling is, Schleiermacher says, a conscious relation to God. For Kant, there is no human experience without concepts; "intuitions without concepts are blind" (Kant 1956, A51/B75). Similarly, Proudfoot argues, there can be no human experience of God independently of thought. But whether or not Schleiermacher's account is finally convincing, this criticism is, I am persuaded, misplaced or, at least, misleading. Schleiermacher never denies that one's immediate relation to God is intentional and, to the contrary, persistently speaks of its object as its "co-determinant" (for instance, § 4.2 and § 5.1). What we require, on my reading, is attention to his differing meanings of "object" as something to which a subject does or might relate.

In one sense, all feeling, whether of God or of something in the world, is nonobjective. Having said that every self-consciousness involves "another factor besides the Ego," Schleiermacher continues: "But this Other is not objectively presented in the immediate self-consciousness" (§ 4.1). If, for the moment, we limit attention to things in the world, the "Other" is, on my reading, objectively presented only when consciousness reflects on and thereby represents (re-presents) what is immediately present—or, as we may say, when consciousness is explicitly focused on something that is or has been immediately given. In the sense that having objects involves such reflection, immediate consciousness has no object. For this reason feeling is to be distinguished from knowing and doing, both of the latter two being, on Schleiermacher's use of terms, aspects of activities of objective consciousness. But this accounting implies that feeling also relates the subject to objects in another sense, that is, to objects as immediately given—or, as we may also say, as objects of implicit consciousness. Although nothing is reflectively represented in these feelings, they nonetheless have intentional objects. Were this not the case, one could not be immediately conscious of being partially dependent and partially free, since consciousness of oneself as related in those ways necessarily distinguishes the self from what is given (that on which the self is dependent) and thus distinguishes the given as an object.

With respect to being absolutely dependent, immediate consciousness occurs in distinction from God—and, thereby, a "co-determinant" or intentional object is also present. But this object is unique because it is not *given*—or, as Schleiermacher also says, "we do not set ourselves over against any other individual being, but, to the contrary, all antithesis between one individual and another is in this case done away" (§ 5.1). What, then, is this difference between an object that is given and one that is not? On my understanding, Schleiermacher here differentiates objects that reflection or objective consciousness can designate literally in positive terms, on the one hand, from, on the other, the object that reflection can designate literally only by negation. Speaking of our immediate relation to God can designate the object literally only with such terms as "*not* another individual being" or "*not* an object of reciprocity" or "the absolute *un*divided unity" (§ 32.2, emphasis added) or "*in*finite"—and only in this sense is the co-determinant, unlike those in our feelings of the world, "nonobjective." Thus, Schleiermacher speaks of God in the manner relevantly similar to Kant's conception of noumena, which Kant designates only as "not-phenomena." For Kant, to be sure, we have no intuition of noumena, even if we can think them with this solely negative designation—and, accordingly, we have no intuition of God, even while we can think of God as the completely unconditioned and can affirm God's existence in a postulate of practical reason. For Schleiermacher, unlike Kant, the God whom we literally represent only by negation is also the object of an immediate or implicit consciousness, an intuition or feeling or absolute dependence that is prior to either theoretical or practical reason.[8]

It then follows that our feeling of absolute dependence has no content reflection might call metaphysical or moral—at least if metaphysics represents beings as such in literal and positive terms, and moral thinking represents purposes or ends of action in literal and positive terms. Perhaps metaphysical content so understood is present in a subject's feeling of partial dependence, and moral content so understood is present in a subject's feeling of partial freedom. But both require immediate objects that are given, and the intentional object in our immediate relation to God is not given, that is, can be literally designated only by negation. In this sense, the feeling of absolute dependence is the "indispensable third" (Schleiermacher 1958, 38) to metaphysical and moral content in our immediate self-consciousness.

Precisely because its co-determinant is not given or cannot be designated literally in positive terms, this feeling in itself "is not the consciousness of ourselves as individuals of a particular description, but simply of ourselves as individual finite existence in general" (§ 5.1). But human existence actually occurs only in the moments of a particular individual, and for this reason, the constitutive human consciousness of God is never present except as "conjoined with" or in "reciprocal relation" with (§ 5.3) the sensible self-consciousness, the feelings of given or worldly objects that partially determine us as particular individuals and with respect to which we are partially free:

> Since the feeling of absolute dependence is in itself perfectly simple, and the conception of it provides no basis of differentiation [because, we may add, its object can be designated literally only by negation], such a basis can be derived only from the fact that that feeling, in order to realize itself in an actual moment, must first unite with a sensible stimulation of self-consciousness, and that these sensible stimuli must be regarded as infinitely various. (§ 9.1)

In this reciprocal relation, the feeling of absolute dependence becomes "a particular religious emotion" (§ 5.4) or a particular religious piety, that is, a feeling that varies depending on the sensible consciousness with which it is conjoined. Still, actual moments in human life integrate two things, which may be called the higher consciousness and the lower consciousness, whose "co-existence" may also vary depending on whether the one or the other is more or less dominant in "the unity of the moment" (§ 5.3). "The more the subject, in each moment of sensible self-consciousness, with his partial freedom and partial dependence, takes at the same time the attitude of absolute dependence, the more religious is he" (§5.3).

We can also make the point this way: against theologians for whom the meaning and truth of Christian faith are entirely circumscribed by Christian experience of Jesus, Schleiermacher asserts a common human experience of

God. But God as thereby presented can be designated only by negation, and thus there is no common human experience of *God in relation to the world*.[9] How the higher consciousness integrates with the lower consciousness cannot, therefore, be given philosophical or transcendental formulation. *That* such integration occurs is transcendental, but *what* integration occurs is entirely a particular religious piety. In this respect, as far as I can see, Schleiermacher repeats with reference to immediate self-consciousness what Aquinas says of theistic demonstration: "through affirmations . . . we know *what* a thing is, and how it is separated from others; but through negations . . . we know *that* it is distinct from other things, yet what it is remains unknown. Now such is the proper knowledge we have of God through demonstrations" (S.C.G. 3. 39. 1).[10]

In this sense, Schleiermacher's conclusion denies anything that might be called "religion in general." If that expression is used, "nothing can fitly be understood by it but the tendency of the human mind in general to give rise to religious emotions, always considered, however, along with their expression, and thus with the striving for fellowship, *i.e.*, the possibility of particular religions" (§ 6, postscript). That conclusion, then, warrants Schleiermacher's arresting statement about dogmatic and philosophical truth, at least insofar as asking whether true dogmatic statements are true in philosophy is a pointless question. Because positive awareness of God is not transcendental but always specific to some or other religious emotions, the science of dogmatics can only be the precise and systematic description of the "common distinctive quality of the religious emotions" (§ 10, postscript)—or, we may also say, the faith—specific to the Christian community (or a particular Christian community). Statements that are true within that description can never be philosophically true or false precisely because there is no common human experience of God in relation to the world.[11]

To be sure, certain dogmatic statements about God and the world may indeed sound like general statements of a philosophical kind, in part because the dogmatic theologian not only may but also must borrow language from philosophy to formulate her or his systematic description. But this dependence on philosophy is "only in form" (§ 19, postscript); that is, the language is used to describe feelings of God in relation to the world (that is, religious emotions) to which philosophy has no access. Even then, there are certain philosophical views "unfit for use in dogmatic language," namely, "those which make no separation between the conceptions of God and the World, admit no contrast between good and evil, and thus make no definite distinction in man between the spiritual and the sensible" (§ 28.1). Language used to articulate such views will misrepresent the Christian experience.

When needed, if I understand correctly, "it is... the business of Apologetics" (§ 28.3) then to confirm by philosophical argument, perhaps through the general analysis of self-consciousness, that these views are unconvincing. One is again reminded of Aquinas, for whom natural reason cannot know the essence of God but can show that proofs for the nonexistence of God do not succeed (see S.T. 1.1.8).

Because it describes the specific religious affections of the Christian church (or a Christian church), dogmatics systematically redescribes feelings of God in relation to the world. The initial expression or communication of these feelings is symbolic because their positive content is inseparable from a specific or particular determination of the sensible self-consciousness. Dogmatics is, we can say, an interpretation of Christian symbolic expressions that makes no philosophical claim to truth, and for this reason, dogmatic statement is, in its own way, inescapably symbolic, precisely because it articulates systematically God in relation to the world. Insofar, at least, there is common ground between Schleiermacher and Paul Tillich, for whom theology can speak positively of God only in symbolic terms. In the end, this common ground is also marked by their conviction that God as a co-determinant of our constitutive awareness—or, in my terms, an object of transcendental consciousness—can be literally designated only by negation.[12]

AN ASSESSMENT OF SCHLEIERMACHER'S ACHIEVEMENT

The foregoing is, at best, a terse reading of how transcendental philosophy might be read out of or into Schleiermacher's achievement and thus be seen to warrant his separation of dogmatic and philosophical truth. Summarily stated, meaning and truth in dogmatics imply transcendental philosophy because the former systematically interprets a particular religious faith or piety and thus depends on a logically prior explication of religion as a common human possibility. At the same time, dogmatic truth is separated from philosophy because the "corresponding co-determinant" (§ 5.1) humans commonly experience and on which religion is based has no positive character a particular religious faith might in its specific way actualize.

If that summary will suffice, we may turn to the question: Is Schleieracher's account convincing? We can approach this assessment by returning to the final note in my reading, namely that all positive language about God is symbolic. At least to first appearances, that view seems to be self-defeating. If positive designation of God can never be literal, then the possibility of speaking symbolically about God seems to be destroyed, since we could only explicate a symbol's meaning in terms of other symbols and thus could not clarify of what any given symbol is symbolic. Thus, we could not distinguish speaking *about God* from merely misusing language whose literal use designates something within the world. In this respect, Schleiermacher's conclusion seems problematic in a manner similar to Aquinas's account of theistic analogies. Seeking to distinguish such analogical speaking from both univocal and purely equivocal use of terms, Aquinas nonetheless holds (or, at least, implies) that no theistic analogy can be explicated except by way of other analogies. Arguably, therefore, all such speaking of God becomes purely equivocal, and such speaking cannot be distinguished from designating nothing at all.

For Aquinas, the God of whom we speak analogically can be distinguished because we can through demonstration know *that* God is distinct from other things, even if we cannot thereby know *what* God is. In other words, we can demonstrate the existence of that which can be univocally named only by negation. For Schleiermacher, this reminds us, dogmatic explication of specific religious affections designates positively or in relation to the world the God to whom subjects as such relate in the feeling of absolute dependence, even if the co-determinant of that common human experience can be reflectively and literally represented only by negation. Schleiermacher's solution, then, turns on whether an object of immediate consciousness can be designated by complete negation, just as Aquinas's arguments for God's existence turn on whether a being can be distinguished in the same way.

With this recognition, we reach, to the best of my reasoning, a thoroughly fundamental issue in philosophy and theology, and I wish to argue that designation by complete negation is meaningless, not a genuine thought. In sum, the reason is this: a supposed thought whose content is completely negative cannot be distinguished from another that is merely putative because it has no content at all. Consider any supposed thought whose content is, in fact, self-contradictory, for instance, the supposed thought of a colorless yellow thing. Although one may utter the words, one cannot in fact have the thought because its supposed object has no content. One may think of something colorless and one may think of something yellow, but one cannot think of something simultaneously colorless and yellow. Moreover, this supposed thought is completely negative. Purporting to think of something colorless, one designates something as not yellow; purporting to think of something yellow, one designates the same thing as nothing other than yellow—and "something not yellow and nothing other than something yellow" is a complete negation. Hence, if some other complete negation—for instance, the "co-determinant" in our feeling of absolute dependence, as Schleiermacher intends this term, or "God," as Aquinas intends that term—is to make sense, it must somehow be different from merely putative thoughts that have no content at all. In truth, however, there can be no such difference because the supposed content of each is completely negative, and a difference must be positive. A supposed difference in content that is in no way positive is no different than no difference at all. Hence, a supposed thought whose supposed content is completely negative is no different from a merely putative thought that is, in truth, no thought at all.

We might repeat the point as follows: Every supposed designation only by negation is or implies an existential statement, "something that is x exists" (or, if one prefers, "something that is x is real") that is said to be semantically possible, where the grammatical subject, "something that is x," has no positive content. At least insofar, then, every such statement is equivalent to statements of the form "something that is x exists" (or "something that is x is real") that are semantically impossible because the grammatical subject is self-contradictory and thus meaningless—for instance, "something that is colorless and yellow exists (or is real)." If statements such as "something that is a noumenon exists" or "something that is an absolutely undivided unity exists" or "something that is a completely nontemporal God exists" are to be so much as semantically possible, their grammatical subjects must somehow be distinguished from those that are nonsense. But no such distinction is possible if the former, as the latter, are completely negative.[13]

This argument, I recognize, begs for sustained development in relation to objections.[14] But if, as I am persuaded, it can be sustained, we should conclude that every assertion purporting to designate something by complete negation is meaningless. It then follows that Schleiermacher's project is profoundly problematic. Because the co-determinant in our feeling of absolute dependence is not given and thus cannot be literally designated or represented in positive terms, the assertion that this feeling is real, or coexists with every sensible consciousness as a religious emotion, cannot possibly be true. As far as I can see, Proudfoot is wrong if he reads Schleiermacher to mean that a feeling of God has no intentional object. Still, Proudfoot is right in this respect: an impossible combination in Schleiermacher's philosophy of self-consciousness is indeed present, namely, his affirmation of an intentional object and its completely negative designation. The immediate consciousness of absolute dependence, as Schleiermacher understands it, is a feeling no subject could have on land or sea. Because his account of that feeling is what warrants his separation of dogmatic and philosophical truth, we should also conclude that something is fundamentally problematic in Schleiermacher's conception of the dogmatic theological task.

Nothing in this critique says that we are not immediately aware of God. But if we are, the meaning of "God" cannot be what Schleiermacher takes it to be. If a philosophical analysis of self-consciousness shows that subjectivity as such relates to a unity beyond the world, the intentional object of this feeling must be one that reflection can designate literally in positive terms. An implicit consciousness of God does indeed, I am inclined to think, constitute existence with understanding. But I will not here seek to argue for that conclusion. Instead, I will assume it in order, first, to pursue what must be the case if Schleiermacher's philosophical introduction to dogmatics is so transformed as to be convincing, and then, second, to comment on what is implied for the Christian theological task.

As a reality reflection can designate literally in positive terms, God as an intentional object in common human experience must be, in its own way, *given* and experienced in distinction from ourselves and all others in the world. What is thereby present, therefore, must be God in relation to the world. Immediate consciousness of this relation, then, is something to which philosophical analysis does indeed have access, and Schleiermacher's denial of such access (because, for him, the feeling of absolute dependence is found only in the symbolic statements of religious emotions) must be mistaken. Because this consciousness constitutes subjectivity as such, moreover, it must be a transcendental condition, a necessary condition of being a subject, so that every subject who denies an implicit awareness of God in relation to the world engages in a pragmatic self-refutation.

Indeed, this awareness, we may conclude, involves transcendental conditions in both the broad and strict senses defined at the outset. They are transcendental in the broad sense precisely because the awareness constitutes subjectivity as such. But if aware of God in relation to the world, self-consciousness also has transcendental conditions in the strict sense, that is, conditions of existence as such. This is because God is a reality other than anything within the world and, therefore, can be literally and positively distinguished from all worldly individuals only in terms that designate conditions of existence as such—worldly existence as such, on the one hand, and divine existence, on the other. To be sure, many have held that no existential affirmation can be *semantically* necessary because, to cite Hume's dismissal of all a priori reasoning to God's existence: "Whatever we conceive as existent, we can also conceive as non-existent, there is no being, therefore, whose non-existence implies a contradiction" (Hume 1975, 58). But this objection has already been turned aside if, as previously argued, designation only by negation is impossible. The conclusion there reached implies that "nothing exists," the sheer absence of all existents, is meaningless, so that "something exists"—that is, "something in its most general sense or otherwise unspecified exists"—is a semantically necessary statement, its denial being semantically impossible. Moreover, anything implied by "something exists," any statement in which a condition of existence as such is designated, is also semantically necessary and thus transcendental in the strict sense.

Contrary to Schleiermacher, then, constitutive awareness of God includes metaphysical content, that is, content whose literal and positive representation by reflective consciousness has as its object existence as such. If we assume, with Schleiermacher, that every moment of human life is marked by a feeling of partial freedom, our immediate consciousness also includes moral content. Awareness of self in relation to conditions of existence as such implies awareness of one's own subjectivity as a specification of those conditions—and the conscious freedom of subjects that is transcendental in the broad sense cannot specify transcendental conditions in the strict sense unless the latter define the good one should decide to pursue. More than some others, I recognize, this last implication may elicit a call for further argument in relation to objections. But perhaps it is sufficient here that such objections are not likely to come from theists, for whom an understanding of God's character typically implies and is implied by a comprehensive good to which all human purposes ought to be directed.

In sum, the transformation of Schleiermacher I propose understands our common human experience to be an implicit understanding of self in relation to God and the world that defines the self in terms of a divine telos. As a condition of subjectivity as such, this self-understanding is a transcendental condition in the broad sense, and it includes the transcendental character, in the strict sense, of God and the world. At the same time, however, subjects consciously decide in some measure what to become, and thus we humans live by way of an implicit decision for a self-understanding, that is, an understanding of ourselves in relation to God and the world as such. Because this decision may be, in its deepest sense, immoral as well as moral, we thereby either embrace the immediate consciousness constitutive of every subjective moment or become what we are with some false understanding of existence as such. But the latter can never be merely a mistake, because we are always also aware of the true alternative we ought to elect. The decision is always between authenticity and inauthenticity, as we may call the alternatives, and a self-understanding at fault is always duplicitous because one is inescapably aware of the alternative that defines integrity.

I will simply assert that this transcendental understanding of human life finds its most adequate resource in the neoclassical metaphysics first comprehensively presented by Alfred North Whitehead and subsequently refined for philosophical theology by Charles Hartshorne. Naturally, that assertion will not approach critical acceptance without a thoroughly extended discussion. Still, their basic contribution is, I believe, a systematic formulation that does not, in Whitehead's terms, pay "metaphysical compliments" to God (Whitehead 1925, 179) by making the divine reality an exception to the most general categories applicable to all other things. Literal designation of God only by negation pays such a compliment. In this respect, Schleiermacher speaks of God, the "Whence" that determines our feeling of absolute dependence, in the manner found throughout classical theism. I have especially in mind the putative conception of God as eternal or unchangeable in all respects and thus the reality to which none of the general categories applicable to things in the world literally applies.

Literally speaking of God only by negation is what led Kant to deny possible knowledge of God and to call such supposed knowledge "transcendental illusion," and Schleiermacher's inheritance of classical theism is, or so I have argued, the basic reason why he does not successfully discover in our immediate self-consciousness the God who relates to the world. In contrast, neoclassical theism allows literal and positive designation of the divine character because God is conceived as the eminently temporal one. For this reason, God is not a co-determinant with whom we have no reciprocity or an object not given. To the contrary, the eminently temporal reality is the universal individual, the only one who affects and is affected by strictly all others in all detail and thus the one on whom the exercise of our freedom has everlasting influence.

Still, we need not pursue an argument for neoclassical metaphysics in order to see what the previous discussion implies for Christian theology. If the transcendental transformation of Schleiermacher I have outlined is convincing, the dogmatic task cannot be adequately defined in the way he does. It is, on my accounting, perfectly proper to understand dogmatics as the precise and systematic description of Christian faith—or, we might say, disciplined or critical reflection on the meaning of Christian faith. Moreover, we may quite agree that "religion in general" is an expression fitly understood to designate only the possibility of particular religions, whereby systematic description of the faith symbolized by a particular religion is not itself philosophy. Given the transformation, however, the designation of "religion" and "religious" is also altered. Schleiermacher takes any feeling of God in relation to the world, of the higher consciousness as combined with sensible consciousness, to be a religious emotion and thus particular to some individual or, through communication, specific to some community of faith. But if subjectivity is necessarily conscious of God in relation to the world, we may speak of all self-conscious life as an implicit decision of faith, whose authenticity or inauthenticity can be defined philosophically. Thereby, our common human experience has a positive character that a particular religious piety may in its specific way actualize. Hence, a particular religion can only consist of expressions that claim to represent decisively our constitutive awareness of God and the world, and the function of religion is to mediate or cultivate implicit decisions that are authentic.

The implication for Christian theology is this: asking whether a true dogmatic statement is true in philosophy is no longer improper—at least insofar as dogmatic statements are about ourselves in relation to God and the world. For Schleiermacher, the question is pointless precisely because feelings of God in relation to the world are all particular religious affections to which philosophy has no access. But if subjectivity as such is a decision of faith, then a true dogmatic statement, one that correctly describes the meaning of Christian faith, may be false in philosophy because Christian faith does not, at least in the respect explicated by the statement, include a true representation of subjectivity as such. Similarly, a true dogmatic statement may be true in philosophy precisely because Christianity is a true religion. This does not imply that dogmatics, which explicates the meaning of Christian faith, itself pursues whether its understanding of God in relation to the world is philosophically true. But neither can truth in dogmatics be separated from truth in philosophy. Instead the dogmatic task implies not only a prior transcendental analysis of religion as a common human possibility but also a subsequent transcendental assessment of its conclusions. In both respects, then, Christian systematic theology includes philosophy even while remaining a distinctive form of reflection because constituted by its distinctive question about the meaning and truth of Christian faith. Whether true dogmatic statements are true in philosophy is, moreover, finally the all-important theological question, because finally the task of theology is to assess whether Christian faith is a true representation of our common human experience and, thereby, a servant of our authentic humanity.

4

THE SOURCE OF TEMPTATION

Reinhold Niebuhr's Gifford Lectures begin: "Man has always been his own most vexing problem" (Niebuhr 1941--43, I, 1). In the directly succeeding paragraphs, the problem discussed is theological; that is, he replies to the question of how human existence in general or as such is properly explicated. But the work as a whole leaves no doubt that Niebuhr also has in mind an existential problem. Humans are their own deepest predicament because they live at fault, as sinners. "The Christian view of human nature is involved in the paradox of claiming a higher stature for man and of taking a more serious view of his evil than any other anthropology" (Niebuhr 1941--43, I, 18). Moreover, the work as a whole gives every reason to combine the theological and existential meanings: explicating the problem of sin in human life is the most vexing theological problem, even if the divine response to sin is our most important existential condition and thus the point of theology. In his own way, Augustine, to whom Niebuhr avows a great debt, might well have agreed.

AUGUSTINE: THROUGH ADAM TO THE DEVIL

My discussion here is concerned with what Augustine, in *On Free Choice of the Will*, called the source or sources of sin—and, further, of sin in what he there calls the strict sense: "We use the word 'sin' not only for what is really sin in the strict sense, which involves actions performed knowingly and by free will, but also for the necessary result of the punishment of sin in the strict sense" (Augustine 1993, 108).[1] Here, "free will" means the capacity to decide among alternatives such that actualizing one alternative rather than another has no cause other than the decision. Sin performed by free will is distinguished, then, from sin as the penalty all humans subsequent to Adam suffer for his sin in the strict sense. Toward the end of *On Free Choice of the Will*, written after his move to Hippo, Augustine is already working on the solidarity of all human beings in Adam. "All sinful souls have been afflicted with these two punishments: ignorance and difficulty.... When someone acts wrongly out of ignorance, or cannot do what he rightly wills to do, his actions are called sins because they have their origin in that first sin, which was committed with free will. The later sins are the just results of that first sin" (107).

Still, Augustine continues, this would give cause for complaint only "if there were no Victor over error and inordinate desire. But in fact there is one who is present everywhere" (107), and "in the midst of their ignorance and difficulty he leaves them the free will" to "turn back to God so that he might overcome the penalty that had been imposed for turning from God" (108). In the course of the Pelagian controversy, Augustine's most radical statements on the matter denied even free will in this sense. Since all good things come from God, even the decision of faith that sets one on the way is God's gift, and absent grace, we are free to choose only *how*, not *whether*, to sin. At the same time, Augustine is sensible of the paradox in this radical formulation and, we may note, allows in *The Spirit and the Letter* that faith as consent to grace, in distinction from righteousness, "must be in our power," even if dependent on God's calling "through the inducement of impressions which we experience" (Augustine 1955, 238, 244).

In any event, I seek here to discuss sin in whatever respect it occurs by free will of the sinner. On my accounting, Augustine was right to say in *On Free Choice of the Will*, "defect would not be worthy of condemnation unless it were voluntary" (100), and thus "the will is the cause of sin" (104). Absent that assertion, as far as I can see, one cannot protect what Augustine himself, in *On Free Choice of the Will*, always sought to assert as fully as he insisted on God's goodness, namely, the sinner's responsibility for sin. I will also abstract from any complications introduced by Augustine's christology, specifically, any idea that faith in God is possible only in or through Christ in a sense that requires conscious relation to Jesus. To the best of my reasoning, it is senseless to call all humans sinners in the strict sense unless it is also true that "one is present everywhere" who makes faith in God an open alternative. But I will not argue that point further and, in discussing Augustine, will simply attend to free choice of the will whenever faith in God is possible—or, to use Augustine's terms, whenever embracing what is eternal and unchangeable or embracing what is temporal and changeable as if it could secure true happiness are both alternatives for decision. Given this focus for discussion, *On Free Choice of the Will* is an appropriate conversation partner.

Clarity within this focus will be served by marking the distinctive freedom involved in this decision. Many have noted the difference Augustine articulates between free choice, on the one hand, and true or genuine freedom, on the other, where the latter is present, for Augustine, only when or insofar as free choice embraces what is eternal and unchangeable—a distinction found also in Paul and, in a different way, in Kant. But there is another distinction present or clearly implied in *On Free Choice of the Will* between what I will call primal freedom, on the one hand, and specific freedom, on the other. The freedom to turn toward or away from God, the primal movement of the will, is simultaneously expressed or embodied in whatever choice one makes among the specific actions or purposes possible for a given individual in a given time and place—specific alternatives that will vary depending on the individual and circumstances in question. Moreover, the exercise of primal freedom is all-important because it sets the terms in which the specific alternatives are evaluated and specific freedom thus exercised. In other words, the primal movement of the will is expressed in and thus implied by the specific choice. Together, then, these two aspects of the one decision constitute a distinctively human activity, and I will call this self-creation the exercise of original freedom or decision for a self-understanding. A single exercise of original freedom is complex because it includes the primal movement of the will and its embodiment in some or other specific decision.

Even were it not anachronistic, calling Augustine an existentialist would be false because, if for no other reason, it ignores his cosmology and his sweeping chronicle of human events. Still, his view of original freedom is similar to the existential condition Paul Tillich calls the freedom "we ourselves" are (Tillich 1951, 62), at least in the following respect: the primal fact of human action, expressed in and implied by whatever occurs specifically, is a movement of the will for which there are two fundamental alternatives, toward or away from God, and in which one elects an understanding of one's ultimate good or significance. In this respect, on my reading, Augustine asserts in his own context that humans live by way of decision between these fundamental alternatives, whereby, to use more contemporary terms, we decide to be authentic or inauthentic. Not spelled out but still present in the apostle Paul's writings, says Alasdair MacIntyre, freedom in this primal sense was first articulated by Augustine (see MacIntyre 1988, 155–58). Be that as it may, I intend sin in the strict sense—as does Augustine, at least in his earlier work—to mean an exercise of original freedom, inclusive of a primal decision at fault. Confusion might be avoided by noting that a primal decision need not be taken explicitly, in the sense that consciousness is centered on it. Indeed, I am inclined to think that a turn toward or away from God always occurs implicitly in human life, in the background or in the dim recesses of our awareness. The difference between what is explicit or centered and what is implied in consciousness will be important to Niebuhr, but it will not be necessary to defend that view here.

With these preliminary comments as the setting, I can state in Augustine's words the question about sin I wish to discuss: "What is the source of this movement by which the will turns away from the unchangeable good toward a changeable good" (69)? In *On Free Choice of the Will*, he returns repeatedly, in one way or another, to this question—and it becomes apparent that "source" has another meaning besides "cause." Augustine is decisive in showing that movement of the will "belongs to the will alone, and that it is voluntary and therefore [if evil] blameworthy" (72). Still, the question about "source" recurs, and the closing pages of this work make apparent that it asks not only about the cause of sin but also about temptation. What prompts or tempts the will to turn away from God? That Augustine has this question in mind becomes clear when, in those later pages, he identifies "two *sources* of sin: one's own spontaneous thought, and someone else's persuasion." In either case, he continues, sin is voluntary; "just as no one sins unwillingly by his own thought, so no one yields to the evil prompting of another unless his own will consents" (91). In order to keep the question clear, I will henceforth speak of the source of temptation.

This question recurs, I believe, because Augustine is so thoroughly a theist. An exercise of primal (and hence original) freedom includes an awareness of God, the embrace of whom alone is happiness rather than misery, true good rather than emptiness. Absent something that makes the changeable good tempting, the turn to God would be a ready movement of the will because the alternative has no credence. A drowning person to whom a rope is thrown may have the choice to refuse it, but that alternative is, as it were, not a live option, is a mere theoretical possibility, an absurdity summarily dismissed as she or he decides to be saved. Unless the sinful alternative is for some reason attractive or alluring, it could not compete for election, and the free will marking human nature would not be sufficient to account for sin. Making this point might be aided by underscoring that original freedom as the cause of sin is *moral* freedom, which means the capacity to decide for the immoral even while one knows which alternative is right. This is, on my accounting, one meaning of "ought implies can." Commonly taken to assert that a prescribed act must be among the alternatives for choice, the dictum also means that a prescription is senseless if the person in question cannot decide accordingly because she or he ought to do so, that is, with awareness of the obligation. As immoral, original freedom decides for a false commitment or self-understanding knowing it to be false and, in that sense, is duplicitous. One tells a lie to oneself, and an intellectual being has no reason to do so unless the wrong alternative is provocative, appears with some appeal, or is tempting.

On my reading, one reason why Kant denies that some object or telos to be pursued can define moral worth is his intent to protect the significance of temptation in human decisions. Were there such an object, he writes, "it would destroy every concept of duty and fill its place with a merely mechanical play of refined inclinations" (Kant 1956, 40–41). As defining moral worth, the telos or object to be pursued would have to be both desired and constitutive of practical reason as such; but a desire by which all rational creatures are constituted would be controlling. All other desires would be impotent as competitors, and the choice, while still perhaps a choice, would be nonetheless a mere "mechanical play of refined inclinations" (and for Kant, rational beings are not necessarily marked by desire, which may be peculiarly human). It follows, Kant holds, that duty and thus moral freedom are not properly conceived unless the moral law is independent of desire, defined solely by the formal universality of reason, and this law becomes a categorical imperative because we are not only rational but also sensuous. Characterized also by desires, the human will "stands between its *a priori* principle, which is formal, and its *a posteriori* spring, which is material" (Kant 1949, 18). In other words, we are tempted.

Whether Kant's proposal solves the problem might itself be doubted. That a rational being, aware of the moral law, is tempted by her or his desires appears to be stipulated rather than explained—and we might ask why human obedience to the categorical imperative is not a mere "mechanical play of reason." As far as I can see, moreover, the price Kant pays for separating moral worth from desire is a formal law in the sense that it has no material implications and is thus an empty law, providing no distinction between moral and immoral alternatives. For Augustine, in any event, there is no such separation. Free choice of the will decides between our authentic desire for unchangeable good and inauthentic desire for changeable good as if it could provide true happiness, so that Kant's reference to a "mechanical play" serves to restate the question: Given our true desire, what makes the desire for temporal things competitive? What is the source of temptation in the sinful will? Absent another answer and given his concept of God, Augustine could only attribute temptation to the Creator, so that God, although not the cause of sin, is the cause of temptation. Naturally, this is unacceptable because temptation to sin is not a good, and only good can come from God.

But Augustine does have another answer, at least for all of Adam's descendants: temptation belongs to the penalty for Adam's sin. On this account, we are born with inordinate desire and thus find changeable goods alluring—not because cupidity belongs to our created nature but, rather, as Augustine puts it in one formulation, because "it was not right for his [Adam's] offspring to be better than he was himself" (108). Let us here repeat that temptation is one thing, and sin is another. To desire inordinately is not sin unless one acts on the desire, and yielding to a desire for changeable goods remains, at least in Augustine's earlier work, the free choice of the will. Hence, the penalty we suffer in this respect does not contradict or remove our responsibility. Still, this proposal, while it explains the allure of evil in all those descended from the first man, leaves the question with respect to Adam himself: why was he tempted to turn away from God?

Augustine has another ready reply: the serpent suggested that Adam's freedom "succumb to the allure of those inferior things" (121). To be sure, this response appears only to displace the question, since one may then ask, as Augustine does, about the devil: "But from what source did the devil himself receive the suggestion to desire the impiety by which he fell from heaven" (121–22)? But Augustine is again ready with this answer: there are, recall, "two *sources* of sin: one's own spontaneous thought, and someone else's persuasion" (91). The first "originates in the things that are present to the attention of the mind or the senses of the body." As it contemplates, "the highest wisdom," Augustine continues, "the changeable soul also looks upon itself and somehow enters its own mind." Thereby, "the soul realizes that it is not the same as God, and yet that it is something that, next to God, can be pleasing" (122), and this spontaneous awareness of self prompted the devil to pride.

As far as I can see, this answer begs the question. We may and should grant that human freedom requires awareness of self and, thereby, the possibility of willing "to enjoy . . . [oneself] in a perverse imitation of God" (122). But the devil, Augustine adds, saw itself as "something that, next to God, can be pleasing"—and why, aware that "contemplation of the highest wisdom" (122) alone is blessed, the self would ever find itself instead of God *pleasing* is precisely the question in view when one asks for the source of temptation for the devil. Indeed, I suspect that Augustine himself is sensible of his non sequitur. He may be more candid earlier in the work when he writes: "Perhaps you are going to ask what is the source of this movement by which the will turns away" from God. "If I told you that I don't know, you might be disappointed; but that would be the truth. For one cannot know that which is nothing" (69). Thereby, Augustine anticipates his formulation in *The City of God*: "'evil' is merely a name for the privation of good" (Augustine 1985, 454), because whatever has being or is substance is, just insofar, God's creation and, therefore, good. Hence, sin has no efficient cause but, rather, a "deficient" cause (Augustine 1984, 480)—and, we might add, temptation has a "deficient" source. Since it is evil, that source is finally something that cannot be known. With that resolution, however, the question of temptation remains begged.

Still, one might think, a prompting for the devil's sin is not needed. Having traced temptation back through Adam to the devil, one might simply insist that free will is, after all, free to choose. All one needs is a single demonic decision, and among the many angels, that one choice can be asserted simply as a fact—after which the temptation of Adam and, through him, the presence of temptation throughout the human adventure is explained. But even allowing the devil as mere fact, we cannot also allow the entire account without a return to Adam and to the second source of temptation, namely, "someone else's persuasion." Attention to the devil's suggestion is not only pertinent to an assessment of Augustine but also will be, as I hope to show, important in our subsequent discussion of Niebuhr.

"In the Garden of Eden," Augustine writes, "the commandment of God was seen among superior things; the suggestion of the serpent was seen among inferior things. Man had no control over what the Lord commanded or over what the serpent suggested. But ... he was indeed free not to succumb to the allure of those inferior things" (121). Notice how, again, the question of temptation is answered by stipulation. Why did Adam, whose created nature as yet suffered no penalty, find the serpent's suggestion *alluring*?[2] Aware that God's commandment presents the only good and thus true happiness, would not Adam have seen this suggestion as transparently absurd and thus not a live option? The point here is this: that another seeks to persuade one's original decision does not itself constitute temptation unless the suggestion is received with *persuasive power*. A second someone on the shore proposing that the drowning person refuse the rope might be heard but would, as it were, be dismissed without a hearing, and the allure of inferior things cannot itself be explained by the fact of a suggestion. As Augustine himself writes in another context: "If a flawed nature approaches a nature that has no flaw and attempts to corrupt it, it does not approach it as an equal; the flawed nature is weaker precisely because it is flawed" (98). How, then, can attempted persuasion be tempting unless the one to be persuaded is already flawed, that is, unless she or he is somehow complicit in the effect, whereby she or he entertains the suggestion with persuasive power or finds it attractive?

To be sure, Augustine speaks of the flawed nature as weaker when speaking of those who are created equal. "Nothing can be corrupted *by its equal*" unless it, too, is flawed (98; emphasis added). "But if a stronger nature corrupts a weaker," it may happen "through a flaw in the more powerful nature, if that nature is so much superior that it remains more powerful even when it has become flawed" (98). Perhaps, then, the serpent's success with Adam was consequent on the devil's superiority, notwithstanding its fall, as an angel. Nonetheless, it follows that no *human* suggestion could have persuasive power unless its recipient is complicit. If that complicity is explained for all subsequent humans through their inheritance from Adam, Augustine also requires his cosmology inclusive of the devil (as mere fact) in order to explain how the first man could be tempted. Both conditions are rejected by the now classic account formulated by Niebuhr. Indeed, Niebuhr's insistence that Adam is not a historical person and that Augustine's cosmology is no longer credible imply convictions that are modern and likely irreversible—such that Niebuhr might well be included in the liberal theological tradition that is often said to be initiated by Schleiermacher. In any event, Niebuhr's explication of sin, however dependent on Augustine, also becomes something significantly different.

REINHOLD NIEBUHR: SIN POSITS ITSELF

Although calling Augustine an existentialist is false, this is not the case with Niebuhr, at least with respect to his explication of original sin in the *Nature and Destiny of Man*. That discussion, unsurpassed in modern theology, seeks to describe how every decision of human life is an exercise of original freedom in which a "rebellion against God" (Niebuhr 1941–43, I, 279)[3] occurs. Self-conscious freedom, he writes, "forces us to relate our action in the last resort to totality conceived as a realm of meaning" (Niebuhr 1942, 44). Rebellion against God is the decision for a misconception of our total context or the ground of our ultimate worth, because "totality conceived as a realm of meaning" is one way in which Niebuhr formulates the divine ground of all things. Thereby, Niebuhr also asserts, with Augustine, that whatever has being somehow belongs to God or is God's creation and thus is insofar good. As with Augustine's christology, I will here abstract from complications introduced by Niebuhr's account of revelation, on which the reality of God is generally revealed in common human experience and the character of God is specially revealed through particular historical events, decisively in Jesus as the Christ (see Gamwell 2015, especially chapter 6). As far as I can see, the occurrence of sin as Niebuhr describes it depends on a general revelation of God's character as the center of ultimate meaning—because Niebuhr asserts the strict universality of sin in a sense that requires trust in God as an alternative for decision. For present purposes, however, I will simply assume the universal presence of this alternative.

The complication from which we should not abstract is Niebuhr's clarity about the difference between existential and explicit consciousness. If he sometimes calls the former unconscious, the discussion as a whole makes apparent that he means "not explicitly conscious." For Niebuhr, as for Augustine, our specific purposes, chosen among alternatives that the given situation presents, express a primal decision, and for Niebuhr, the latter is not, at least not typically, taken explicitly. "The experience of God," Niebuhr writes, "is . . . an overtone implied in all experience. The soul which reaches the outermost rim of its own consciousness, must also come in contact with God, for He impinges upon that consciousness" (127). The rebellion against God occurs in the same dim background of consciousness. "Sin is . . . both unconscious and conscious. The degree of conscious choice may vary in specific instances of course. Yet even the more conscious choices do not come completely into the category of conscious perversity" (250). The exercise of freedom he describes is the more plausible by virtue of its existential or implicit character, and, among other things, this allows Niebuhr to explicate how self-deception is typically an aspect of our sinful self-understanding: an implicit lie to oneself includes an exclusion from explicit consciousness, so that we explicitly understand ourselves to serve more righteous ends (see 204, note 2).

The occasion for sin, Niebuhr explains, is existential anxiety. Acknowledging his debt to Martin Heidegger, Niebuhr sometimes speaks of anxiety as nothing other than the internality of finite self-awareness. As the occasion for duplicity, however, anxiety has a more precise character. It "is the internal description of the state of temptation" (182) and is present because a false interpretation of one's ultimate meaning "is suggested to man by a force of evil which precedes his own sin" (181). Thus, when Niebuhr says "anxiety is the inevitable concomitant of the paradox of freedom and finiteness" (182), he means, on my understanding, that temptation to sin is universal. Absent the suggestion, finite self-consciousness would be only what Niebuhr, citing Søren Kierkegaard, calls "the dizziness of freedom" (252), the awareness that decision concerns nothing less than how totality as a realm of meaning and thus one's ultimate worth are defined. But this dizziness would not be troubling because one is simultaneously aware of the God who assures ultimate meaning and in whom one may trust.

"Suggested by a [prior] force of evil" reminds us of the devil in Augustine's Garden of Eden. For Niebuhr, however, the Genesis story is a "myth" (179) describing the situation of every human in every decision. Adam is "representative man" (261). Niebuhr is, as mentioned earlier, a modern theologian, for whom history cannot have the character it had for Augustine, and Genesis cannot be the literal description Augustine could take it to be, and this is to repeat that Niebuhr's account is, in the relevant sense, existentialist. On my reading, moreover, the term "*force* of evil" (181, emphasis added) expresses Niebuhr's recognition that the false interpretation is tempting. The force is the lure of persuasive power. Indeed, this is why the suggestion makes one anxious. One is attracted to a self-understanding that is, one is simultaneously aware, false, and it is, therefore, experienced as a threat to one's ultimate meaning.

Having rejected Augustine's literal appeal to Adam, in which the penalty paid by all others for Adam's fall is inordinate desire, Niebuhr must turn elsewhere to explain why humans are tempted. The alternative he proposes can be explicated if we pursue the sense in which a force of evil *precedes* the sin. To first appearances, the priority here might seem temporal. Each human in each moment of decision is tempted because she or he inherits from the larger human setting the sinful self-understandings or false interpretations actualized in her or his own past deeds, proposed by other people, carried in the culture, or embodied in institutions and associations—which then become lures for duplicity in the present. Let us call this the social character of temptation. Whatever its importance, it is not, for Niebuhr, a sufficient accounting because it does not explain why duplicitous suggestions from the past bear persuasive power. This is, we may recall, the point previously made in discussing how, for Augustine, Adam was tempted. That another human seeks to persuade one's original decision does not itself explain why the false interpretation is received with persuasive power, since the new decision is simultaneously aware that only trust in God offers ultimate meaning. Absent something further, that decision would see the suggestion as transparently absurd.

For Niebuhr, then, the priority marking this "force of evil" as tempting is not temporal but, rather, itself existential—by which I mean prior in constituting the moment of decision. This becomes apparent when he calls the temptation a "mystery" and offers as its best description Kierkegaard's "statement that sin posits itself" (181). Niebuhr does not mean a socially prior sin, the wrongdoing of others, or a prior fault in the course of one's own life. Nothing about priority in that sense would be relevantly mysterious.[4] To the contrary, present sin posits, as he also says, a "defect" or a "bias toward sin" (242, 249) in the present exercise of original freedom itself. Insofar, he agrees with Augustine: the flawed suggestion of another human (or one's own past) could not be a force of evil absent a flaw in the present self. But this defect, Niebuhr holds, must be in the will (see 242); that is, it cannot be a fate suffered or a necessity of our created nature. Because temptation is an evil, God cannot be responsible for it, and it follows, Niebuhr holds, that each moment of decision must be complicit in the force of evil. The will as it decides is already at fault and thus entertains its alternatives in a defective way. "Man," he writes, "could not be tempted if he had not already sinned" (251).[5] "Sin posits itself" (181).

As far as I can see, Niebuhr's existentialist account is, given his theistic understanding, driven to this assertion. Clarity about it, in any event, reveals at least one reason why he famously insists that sin is inevitable, notwithstanding his equally firm insistence on the sinner's responsibility. Because temptation itself requires a defective or sinful will, it is inevitable that one will yield to the temptation, even while one is responsible for that duplicity because both temptation and inevitable sin are consequent on an existentially prior sin. "Sin is natural for man in the sense that it is universal," he writes, "but not in the sense that it is necessary" (242). To be sure, Niebuhr is also known for endorsing the aphorism that original sin is the one empirically verifiable doctrine of the Christian faith, and this may suggest that he intends with the term "universal" a statistical universality. To the contrary, however, he means strict universality, precisely because temptation, as he says, "lies . . . in the human situation itself" (251) and already implicates the self's fault. In a sense, perhaps, one might still speak of empirical evidence verifying the inevitability of sin, since only a defective will can be tempted, and thus sin would not be empirically pervasive unless it were inevitable, inescapable precisely because the will is defective.

But if Niebuhr's explication effects an existentialist transformation of Augustine, it is also incredible. "Sin posits itself," in Niebuhr's sense, says that every moment of human decision decides prior to its decision, and since the prior decision was sinful, it posits another decision prior to itself, and the exercise of original freedom becomes an infinite regress of duplicitous decisions.

One original decision cannot itself be many such decisions, much less an endless series thereof, and Niebuhr's distinction between what is inevitable and what is necessary is empty because his account of original sin is incoherent. If the will is inevitably defective, this can only be a fate, which Niebuhr, in order to protect the goodness of God, attributes to our use of the very freedom so fated. In his own way, then, he asserts the radical view formulated by the later Augustine: we are free to choose only *how*, not *whether*, to sin. Calling the will's defect a mystery does nothing to change the matter, and Niebuhr's reference to faith in God as an "ideal possibility" (182, see 251) within the human situation is simply an attempt to have it both ways.

Indeed, nothing more fully confirms that Niebuhr intends what I have read him to say than his candid recognition that his account is self-contradictory: "It expresses a relation between fate and freedom which cannot be fully rationalized, unless the paradox be accepted as a rational understanding of the limits of rationality and as an expression of faith that a rationally irresolvable contradiction may point to a truth which logic cannot contain" (262). He himself is immediately troubled by this conclusion: "Formally there can be of course no conflict between logic and truth. The laws of logic are reason's guard against chaos in the realm of truth. They eliminate contradictory assertions" (262–63). When he then attempts to reconcile the conclusion with this affirmation of rational consistency, Niebuhr in effect throws up his hands. "There is no resource in logical rules to help us understand complex phenomena, exhibiting characteristics which *seem* to require that they be placed in contradictory categories of reason. Loyalty to all the facts may require a *provisional* defiance of logic, lest complexity in the facts of experience be denied for the sake of a *premature* logical consistency" (263, emphasis added). But phenomena cannot exhibit characteristics that merely *seem* to require contradictory categories of reason unless one can show why what appears to be provisional and premature is not finally the case. In other words, Niebuhr's assertion that his understanding of sin is not a final defiance of logic cannot be true unless he can clarify how the account finally is not the "rationally irresolvable contradiction" that, as he concedes, it is.

ANOTHER ACCOUNT: HUMAN FRAGMENTARINESS

The validity of Christian belief in God is challenged if the explication of human fault is finally inconsistent. Self-contradiction in theological anthropology calls into question the credibility of theism. But there is, I am persuaded, another accounting that avoids incoherence. Here, I will assume that Niebuhr rightly rejects Augustine's cosmology, at least insofar as it includes explanatory appeal to a devil, and Augustine's chronology of human events, at least insofar as it appeals to the solidarity of all humans in the penalty for Adam's sin. I will assume, in other words, that Niebuhr is right to pursue an existentialist explication of sin. For present purposes, I will also stipulate that totality is a realm of meaning, to which original freedom relates authentically or duplicitously in deciding for a self-understanding, so that everything, insofar as it is, is good, and evil is privative. It then follows that all human understanding, whether its object is something actual or something possible, occurs with a feeling or sense of worth. To be conscious of something is to sense it having some value, better or worse. Everything understood is somehow within the divine totality and insofar good, although one may also sense privation or negative worth through comparing what is with what might have been or comparing one possibility with others.

Given that context, an alternative to both Augustine and Niebuhr may be approached through two citations from Niebuhr's discussion. Consider this first citation: "Man knows more than the immediate natural situation in which he stands and he constantly seeks to understand his immediate situation in terms of a total situation. Yet he is unable to define the total human situation without colouring his definition with finite perspectives drawn from his immediate situation" (182). I will not pause to pursue what, for Niebuhr, this description means or entails. Taken solely on its own, the citation is puzzling for the following reason: in one sense, we humans must be truly aware of totality, because a sinner's responsibility would be erased were she or he unable to understand the total situation in the sense required for original freedom to decide against God. But we finite creatures, Niebuhr here says, are unable to define the total situation. In what sense, then, is this latter the case? Clarity is aided, I believe, by the second citation, drawn from a discussion in which Niebuhr seeks to show how self-centeredness prevents obedience to the "law of love." "There is no simple possibility . . . of a perfect coherence of love so that the man in China or America would affirm the interests of the man in America or China as much as he affirms his own. The human imagination is too limited to see and understand the interests of the other as vividly as those of the self" (296).

This second citation explicates by way of illustration the fragmentary character of our consciousness, noting that a person's capacity to understand or appreciate the specific possibilities of other individuals is far more limited than her or his capacity to imagine possibilities of her or his own future. These facts are, I will assume, noncontroversial. A person typically remembers her or his own past activities and anticipates her or his own future in a measure that dramatically exceeds the capacity of one person to appreciate the actual or potential activities of another. More generally, a human's awareness is inescapably fragmentary, understanding details of the past and more specific possibilities of the future in a manner that is highly partial and largely circumscribed within a proximate temporal and spatial environment.

With this comment on fragmentariness, we may revisit the first citation: a human is "unable to define the total human situation without colouring his definition with finite perspectives drawn from his immediate situation." Because we must understand God truly in the sense required for original decision, the definition we are unable to give must transcend the fragmentariness of human consciousness and thus be a fully concrete appreciation of totality. In the latter, everything actual would be fully appreciated as actual, and all possibilities would be appreciated with whatever specificity and probability obtain. All things would enter consciousness with full vividness, the kind of definition possible only to God. What we require, in other words, is a distinction between (1) the divine character or the character of totality, human relation to which defines authenticity in any possible situation and in terms of which we ought to understand our immediate situation, and (2) totality in all of its concrete detail.[6] With respect to the former, we humans can define "the total human situation" because we decide for or against God. With respect to totality in all of its concrete detail, however, any human's approach to understanding can only "colour" the definition "with finite perspectives drawn from his immediate situation."

Let us focus, then, on alternatives for human decision, possible ends or states of affairs one might pursue, some of which are more specific and others more general, and among which choice is to occur. Because totality is a realm of meaning, consciousness of these possibilities, as all understanding, occurs with a feeling or sense of worth, positive or negative. Allowing that humans can be mistaken about what is truly good and truly evil, we can reestablish contact with Augustine by saying that possible futures we take to be good are insofar objects of desire, and those we take to be evil are insofar objects of aversion. Whether worth is sensed as positive or negative, in any event, the feeling of it is stronger or more intense, other things equal, the more vividly a possibility is entertained, that is, the more our fragmentary consciousness understands or imagines in detail the realization of a given alternative for purpose. Were this not the case, seeking to realize some possibilities and to prevent the realization of others would be worthless, since realization is full actualization or making fully concrete. In other words, totality as a realm of meaning is fully concrete.

For instance, the mere thought of a yellow rose one might retrieve from the garden, in the sense that one conceives of "yellow" and "rose" as universals that might be exemplified, is one thing; imagining the color and fragrance one would experience as being similar to past experiences is something else—and, other things equal, makes the prospect more attractive. The mere thought that one could have a serious automobile accident is quite different from a vivid understanding of the trauma to oneself and others it would inflict, and, other things equal, the latter is more likely to prevent reckless driving. An eloquent and detailed portrayal of the debasement imposed by racism is typically more effective than more abstract descriptions in keeping those of us who practice it sensible of our complicity. As the last of these examples suggests, the difference they all illustrate is similar in principle to a distinction generally between artistic expressions and philosophical or scientific formulations; the former have, other things equal, a greater capacity to represent possibilities in a manner that attracts or repels.

To restate the principal point, our sense of worth is stronger or more intense, other things equal, the more concretely a possibility is appreciated. Thus, alternatives for purpose to which desire is attached may differ with respect to the intensity with which one entertains them because one appreciates them concretely in differing measure. I may, for instance, affirm abstractly that my own satisfaction and that of my neighbor are equally good, but I may feel the worth of my own more intensely because "the human imagination is too limited to see and understand the interests of the other as vividly as those of the self" (296).

Moreover, the sense of positive worth with which an alternative is entertained may be called its persuasive power, so that pursuit of my own satisfaction has, other things equal, greater persuasive power than pursuit of my neighbor's—and, thereby, I am tempted to believe that my own future is inherently more important as I interact with her or him. Recall, now, the distinction between primal freedom and specific freedom in which a decision for or against God is simultaneously expressed or embodied in a specific choice among the alternatives for purpose possible in one's given situation. Because the two are one complex decision, every choice among specific possible ends implicates a decision about totality as a realm of meaning. Thus, when the greater concreteness with which I appreciate my own future tempts me to give it undue regard, it must also tempt me to duplicity. In other words, the intensity with which specific alternatives are desired will be included in the persuasive power of alternatives for primal freedom.

This returns us to the question Augustine solves by appeal to Adam and Niebuhr solves by the mystery of a defective will: If original freedom is aware of God, how could a false interpretation of one's primal situation be tempting? The answer, I believe, is this: the sense of worth attached to trust in God may not be significantly strong or, to say the same, the divine calling present "as an overtone" may not be experienced with significant persuasive power. In fact, God's character constituting totality as a realm of meaning defines terms for assessing worth that are indifferent to how concretely we do or do not see the interests of self and others or, more generally, how concretely we appreciate specific possible ends. As the principle or purpose of authenticity as such, in other words, the divine calling is maximally general or abstract. Thus, a duplicitous alternative for self-understanding may be tempting because, at some level of specificity, its evaluation of alternative ends is sensed more intensely than is the chance for integrity.

The point is illustrated most clearly, perhaps, when a sinful alternative tempts someone to a specific purpose at odds with her or his moral responsibility. For instance, I am tempted to a self-understanding expressed in selfish deception and manipulation of other people or through complicity in larger structures of injustice because I sense more strongly the worth to be gained in my own future than the worth that will be sacrificed in the lives of those whom this choice mistreats. But duplicity does not require a specific end different from the one in which authenticity is expressed. I may be morally obligated to assist my neighbor in some specific way and still be tempted to do so. The greater sense of worth with which I appreciate certain future possibilities may still invade my original freedom, so that I act for this specific purpose because, for instance, the recipient will be indebted to me, and I likely will benefit in the longer run.

This is the reason for saying that a sinful self-understanding is tempting because we sense its evaluation more intensely "at some level of specificity." Having previously distinguished between decision for or against God and its expression in a specific purpose, we should add that specific purposes can include various levels of specificity. For instance, one chooses a specific phrase in order to complete a given speech in order to help elect a given candidate in order to maximize what one sees as the common good for one's country, and one's conception of the common good for one's country implicates an understanding of totality as a realm of meaning. At some level of specificity, the purpose in which duplicity is expressed may coincide with the expression of trust in God, but the former diverges from the latter in some wider context. There, the evaluation is "coloured" by the differences with which possibilities are concretely appreciated. I may have made the right choice among the candidates for Congress but did so in terms of an understanding of the common good biased toward the greater advantage of some part of the country to which I belong. Accordingly, the inference from some morally good specific purpose to an authentic exercise of primal freedom is always uncertain. At least in this respect, a person cannot know her or his own deepest motivations.

In giving this account, we must recognize that one's original awareness of God carries a sense of truth, and thus the chance for authenticity is always more persuasive in the following respect: it is free from the sense of internal dissonance or self-contradiction—or, with Niebuhr, overcomes the anxiety—with which every false alternative is entertained. Still, this singular advantage may have to compete with the greater intensity marking false interpretations by virtue of the greater concreteness with which their specific alternatives for purpose are, at some level of specificity, appreciated. We can be tempted when our fragmentary capacity to feel the worth of future possibilities gives persuasive power to possible self-understandings in which the future we appreciate more concretely is given inordinate worth. In contrast, such differences in our concrete awareness are irrelevant to trust in the divine good, and this alternative may not be present with significant persuasive power. Hence, there is nothing absurd in saying that duplicitous alternatives are rivals to our primal awareness of God.

Resolving the problem of temptation by way of human fragmentariness also explains why sin so widely appears as the turn toward self or self-centeredness. Just because a person typically anticipates her or his own future far more concretely than the future of any other individual, duplicitous alternatives in which special worth is attributed to one's own life as an individual are, other things equal, likely to have the greatest persuasive power. Another merit of this resolution is that we may now fully credit the social character of temptation. What gives the evil suggestions of another or others persuasive power is, again, the fragmentariness of our awareness. It is this fragmentariness that makes us complicit. If possible futures are, other things equal, sensed more intensely insofar as they are more concretely understood, so proposals for our evaluations have, other things equal, greater persuasive power when we evaluate their authors positively and relate to them more concretely—and, thereby, receive those invitations with a more vivid sense of worth.

Given a person's especially detailed relation to her or his own past, suggestions from her or his previous duplicity may be especially persuasive. But other individuals who are prominent in our experience may also have, other things equal, the capacity to suggest, intentionally or not, tempting evaluations. The proposals of certain people or simply the kind of purposes they elect may be entertained with greater persuasive power for one's own choice—because these are people who are concretely important or whom we know, or think that we know, well. Moreover, the same may be true of institutional and cultural patterns with which we are more concretely familiar by virtue of their regular exemplification in our experience, in distinction from alternatives that are experienced only as objects of thought. Human fault is socially reinforcing.

The social character of temptation will be more effective, other things equal, when the suggestions one receives commend alternatives that already have the advantage derived from the person's more concrete understanding of future possibilities—as, for instance, when people or communal orders commend inordinate importance for one's own nation or race or parochial way of life or family. Persuasion will be especially effective, then, when it commends giving special worth to the self. If, for instance, the other people or institutionalized patterns more concretely significant to me exemplify certain general forms of undue self-assertion, the temptation to my own similar self-assertion will be the more forceful. This suggests that social reinforcement also shapes the content of self-assertion—what it is about one's future to which one is tempted to give excessive importance. Whether one is most attracted to maximizing one's own sexual pleasure, financial status, prestige, participation in a privileged class, or domination over others may be consequent on the suggestive power of social and cultural context.

Both Augustine and Niebuhr, each in his own way, say or appear to say that self-assertion or undue love of self is *the* form of sin and thus *the* form of temptation, at least in the sense that any temptations seeming to be otherwise are still in some distorted way the lure of pride. To pursue briefly one application of the point, Niebuhr is well known for his discussion of "immoral society" and, specifically, for his analysis of why groups and especially nations become the false gods of "group pride" (208). One might wonder whether duplicitous self-understandings in which the importance of some group centers totality as a realm of meaning could require or, at least, allow differing forms of sin among members of the group. Assuming that the society is unjust, perhaps oppressors, on the one hand, and oppressed, on the other, exemplify the "collective egoism" (212) in differing ways—such that pride is a more appropriate characterization of the former than of the latter. But Niebuhr generalizes over all members of the community by calling the group's pretension "a pretension" each "individual makes for [her or his own] ... self-aggrandizement" (212) and, thereby, harmonizes his insight into group pride with his Augustinian assertion that pride is the form of all sin, even if sometimes expressed in a distorted way.

A longer discussion is needed to assess this assertion. But it cannot be redeemed, I judge, unless its meaning somehow includes the following fact: because the singular capacity to envision one's own future can be given a distinct content by social persuasion, it follows that negative evaluations of the self can also be learned. Self-abasement is a duplicitous self-understanding to which individuals are tempted because they have learned to attach a negative sense of worth to the future they most concretely appreciate and, thereby, desire a future in which they will be oppressed or exploited. This evaluation acquires persuasive power because it is taught through potent experiences of condemnation or threat by the culture or institutional setting or by prominent individuals in one's own life, that is, by a social context evaluated positively and more concretely inherited. At the same time, as far as I can see, self-abasement differs from self-assertion in this respect: temptation to the former has to be taught. Humans do not attach a negative sense of worth to the vivid sense of their own possibilities without the false interpretations suggested by important others, including the larger communal context. In contrast, the temptation to undue self-importance is, as it were, natural. Unless specifically prevented by learning, this temptation will be intense because given with the fragmentariness of human understanding itself and the dramatically heightened appreciation of one's own past and future—and that is why self-assertion is the most apparent form of sin.

In sum, we can explicate the consistency between our original awareness of God and the source of temptation and, at the same time, the pervasiveness of human fault without recourse to a penalty for Adam's sin or a mysterious defect of the will. The fragmentariness and social character of human consciousness are sufficient to offer a rational account of, in Niebuhr's term, the "facts of human wrong-doing" (248). Still, nothing that has been said *explains* those facts, if "explains" means giving an account of sin independent of the exercise of freedom. What has been explained is temptation. But however powerful the persuasion attached to false interpretations, no human activity is sinful unless it chooses a duplicitous self-understanding and, therefore, is responsible for its fault. Temptation is one thing, and sin is another. In the sense that decision has no explanation, there is, perhaps, "mystery" in the fact of sin. But it is not temptation that is mysterious, and there is no need to say, with Niebuhr, that a human "could not be tempted if he had not already sinned" (251). To the contrary, temptation can be explained without contradicting the freedom of distinctively human existence to decide for or against the divine good.

CONCLUSION

Given this understanding of the facts of human wrong-doing, it follows that socially and culturally persuasive power may also be used to weaken temptations. On my accounting, this possibility includes the proper function of religion in human life. Because our original decisions are, on my view, taken implicitly, we may seek to influence ourselves through specific activities designed to increase the vividness of our authentic alternative. In these activities, we focus on concepts and symbols that re-present explicitly our true understanding of totality as a realm of meaning, thereby seeking to cultivate or persuade our own implicit decisions accordingly. Thus, religious expressions tend to assume a highly figurative form, including symbolic practices, because they have a function analogous to artistic expression, namely, to represent possibilities in a way that heightens sensibility.

But an adequate account of religion requires another discussion. If the one pursued here is convincing, the important question remaining is why neither Augustine nor Niebuhr explains the source of temptation in terms of human fragmentariness. As far as I can see, both hold that theism, as they understand it, prevents this accounting: the fragmentary character of human consciousness is a mark of our worldly character; as a consequence, temptation and thus an evil would be caused by God as creator, and this conclusion contradicts the divine perfection. But this reasoning is compelling to Augustine and Niebuhr, on my reading, only because both also hold that theism means divine omnipotence, in the sense that creation as such is caused by a completely eternal God; that is, divine agency is the cause of there being a world at all. The complete goodness of God then implies that creation would be without evil absent the fault of lesser agencies, angelic or human.

If both accounts are incredible, this is one good reason for theology to reassess the classical view of God and entertain the neoclassical alternative, of which Charles Hartshorne provides the most developed statement (see Hartshorne 1948): omnipotence can only mean the greatest conceivable power one being can have, given that there must be other beings with some power. Accordingly, the world as such, in distinction from any individual within it, has necessary existence along with God, and God as the necessary and thus perfect individual is the eminently temporal one who constitutes again and again the totality of all nondivine individuals, those whose nondivine character entails their fragmentariness. Indeed, only this neoclassical understanding of God, as far as I can see, permits a consistent distinction between the character of God as constituting totality, of which all humans are truly aware, and the concrete totality God constitutes again and again, which humans can only fragmentarily understand or appreciate. Insofar as it derives from this necessary fragmentariness, temptation is no one's fault, that is, not caused by anything other than the necessity of God and of the world, when both become the content of self-consciousness. In this respect, life with temptation to duplicity is the only life we could possibly be given when we are also given life for which the goodness of God gives rest to the restless heart and assures everlasting worth.

PART TWO

MORALITY AND DEMOCRACY: METAPHYSICS IN THE BROAD SENSE

❧ 5 ❧

MORAL CREATURES
AND THEIR DECISIONS

The Western philosophical and theological tradition has given substantial attention to the difference between moral and immoral decision. Relatively less attention has been directed to the difference between moral and nonmoral creatures. These two distinctions are related because an individual cannot decide between the moral and the immoral unless it is moral in distinction from nonmoral. The difference between moral and nonmoral creatures may be called the meta-ethical distinction, in contrast to the difference between moral and immoral decision, which may be called the normative distinction. This discussion seeks to clarify both distinctions—and in the process, also seeks to show how the meta-ethical difference implies a principle in terms of which the normative difference is explicated. That principle, the discussion will argue, is both transcendental to subjective existence as such and is teleological, because the good is defined metaphysically in the strict sense. I will also argue, at least briefly, why neither nontranscendental nor nonteleological theories can be true.

As mentioned in the introduction, transcendental metaphysics is systematically ambiguous because it has two meanings: in its strict sense, it means critical reflection designating literally features of the possible as such or existence as such, so that every denial of any such statement is semantically self-contradictory; in its broad sense, transcendental metaphysics means critical reflection designating literally features of subjectivity as such, so that every denial of any such statement is pragmatically self-refuting (that is, the denial contradicts what is implied by every subjective act of denying). In what follows, I will use the term "strictly metaphysical" to mean features or statements thereof designated by metaphysics in the strict sense and "broadly metaphysical" to mean features or statements thereof designated by metaphysics in the broad sense. Also, I will reserve the terms "necessarily true" and "self-contradictory" for the semantic character of statements. In its strict sense, then, transcendental metaphysics is a systematic set of necessarily true existential statements, that is, statements of the form "something that is x exists." Many contemporary philosophers clearly allow that certain statements about existence are necessarily true, but, typically, all such statements are said to be conditional—for instance: "if a subject exists, then something that is self-conscious exists." All such necessity is said to be conditional because all existential statements can be, it is said, denied without (semantic) self-contradiction or are contingently true or false. In contrast, a necessarily true existential statement (that is, a statement of the form "something that is x exists") is *unconditionally* necessary, and transcendental metaphysics in the strict sense has this character.

Chapter 1 sought to defend such metaphysics (see chapter 1), but a brief argument for it can be presented here: if all existential statements can be denied without self-contradiction, the statement "nothing exists" is possibly true; to the contrary, that statement is impossible because, as far as I can see, it cannot be distinguished from a self-contradictory existential statement. In each case, "exists" is said to be the predicate of a grammatical subject designated only by negation. For instance, the statement "something that is colorless and yellow exists" designates something said to be not yellow, because it is colorless, but also nothing other than yellow, because yellow—and "not yellow and nothing other than yellow" designates the something only by negation. But complete negation cannot be distinguished from complete negation—and given the identity of what cannot be distinguished, the statement "nothing exists" is identical to a self-contradictory existential statement. Hence, designation only by negation is not to designate, is impossible. It then follows that "something exists" (where this means "something" in its most general sense or "something that is otherwise unspecified exists") is necessarily true, as are all implications of "something exists," that is, all features of "something" by which it is distinguished from complete negation.

In addition, transcendental metaphysics in the strict sense is possible, on my accounting, only if also neoclassical—which, in a word, means that becoming rather than being is the basic character of reality. In what follows,

I will first state and briefly defend certain metaphysical conclusions in the strict sense that are both transcendental and neoclassical and, thereby, necessarily true existential statements, such that every denial of any one is semantically self-contradictory. In doing so, my debt to Charles Hartshorne, and through him, to Alfred North Whitehead will be apparent. Less apparent, perhaps, is my debt to Schubert M. Ogden: in his vocation as a Christian systematic theologian, he has advanced a metaphysics in the strict sense that is, as he says, both "austerely transcendental" and "neoclassical." In any event, this attention to strictly metaphysical features is required, I hope to show, in order to clarify the two distinctions—moral creature/nonmoral creature and moral decision/immoral decision—and why a principle for the latter is implied by the former.

NEOCLASSICAL METAPHYSICS IN THE STRICT SENSE

Given that transcendental metaphysics in the strict sense consists in a set of necessarily true existential statements, each implies all of the others and is implied by all of its implications. Necessarily true existential statements constitute a necessarily true set; thus, all things in the metaphysically final sense exemplify each metaphysical feature; that is, each thing in the metaphysically final sense exemplifies all such features. Thus, in Whitehead's words, a metaphysical scheme in the strict sense "should be 'necessary,' in the sense of bearing in itself its own warrant of universality throughout all experience," where "experience" includes "everything of which we are conscious, as enjoyed, perceived, willed, or thought" (Whitehead 1978, 4, 3). This follows because these statements describe the possible as such; that is, "something exists" (in the sense given above) is necessarily true—and both implies and is implied by statements of the metaphysical features. Hence, all such features together must designate a single kind of thing, which Whitehead calls a "final real thing" or fully determinate thing—and I will call an actuality.

Although strictly metaphysical features must together designate a single kind of thing, reality cannot be exhausted by determinate actualities; that is, all reality cannot be fully actual or fully determinate in distinction from partially possible or indeterminate. Were that the case, reality would be in all respects changeless and eternal ("Without motion and change," Augustine rightly said, "there is no time, while in eternity there is no change" [Augustine 1985, 435]), and what is in all respects changeless or eternal can be designated only by negation. Still, if reality must include what is possible, whatever is actual must be prior to what is possible, in the sense that what is determinate must condition or limit what is indeterminate. Absent that limitation, indetermination would be infinite in all respects, and infinite indetermination in all respects can be, again, designated only by negation.

For this reason, so-called hylomorphic metaphysicians in the Western tradition (for instance, Aristotle and Aquinas) spoke of "prime matter" (*hylo* designates matter), meaning thereby infinite indetermination, which could not be at all unless combined with "form" (*morphic*), that is, unless something is actual. Because possibility requires some prior actuality or actualities, without which what is possible would be designated only by negation, what is possible must be a feature or aspect of what is actual. In other words, relation to what is possible or the limitation on possibility is itself a constitutive feature of actuality, and what is possible or indeterminate can only be what must or may (or may not, or did not) become actual or determinate—which confirms that all necessarily true existential statements designate one kind of final real thing, namely, actualities.[1] Transcendental metaphysics in the strict sense is nothing other than the most general explication of a final real thing or actuality—those that are actual and the possibilities for those that must or may (or may not, or did not) become so (see Whitehead 1978, 19).

Also, reality must include more than one actuality; were there only one, it, too, would be completely changeless and eternal. Given more than one, each must imply and thus be internally related, in some measure, to others, else that actuality could be the only one. Further, each actuality must be unique because no two can be identical.[2] Thus, the internal relations of any given actuality must be to more than one other actuality because uniqueness requires a unification of those relations. Each actuality is distinct by virtue of its internality, that is, *how* each relation becomes unified with the others. Indeed, a given actuality can be constituted *only* by its unification of internal relations; were there something else (for instance, a substance) that "has" the relations, it, too, could be designated only by negation, namely, as what remains when one removes all of the relations. Moreover, as previously said, what is actual includes its limitation on what is possible; thus, some of the internal relations unified must have as objects what is indeterminate or merely possible.

This unification of relations to other actualities, on the one hand, and to possibilities, on the other, is self-determined by the actuality in question—and decision is, in that sense, strictly metaphysical. "Causal explanation," writes Hartshorne, "is incurably pluralistic: on the basis of many past events, it has to explain a single present event or experience. It is, then, simple logic that something is missed by the causal account" (Hartshorne 1970, 2). What the decision creates, in the measure available, is the determinate internality with which each relation—to what is already actual or to what is possible—becomes the single actuality. Moreover, the decisions actualities take are the reason why actualities and some possibilities are contingent; wherever it occurs, contingency is the consequence of one or more decisions.

On my accounting, the strictly metaphysical concept of an actuality constituted by its internal relations is self-differentiating because it implies and is implied by both ordinary and extraordinary exemplifications, where the latter actualize a necessarily existing or transcendental individual rightly called divine. This strictly metaphysical distinction expresses the difference between relation to some and relation to all—such that ordinary actualities are fragmentarily related to details of what is actual and possible, and extraordinary actualities are entirely inclusive of those details. Here, however, I will leave aside for later discussion whether and, if so, how to speak of the divine or strictly metaphysical individual and pursue the features of fragmentary actualities.

If we attend to any ordinary actuality, its internal relations to other actualities, on the one hand, and to possibilities its decision conditions or limits, on the other, are relations respectively to past and future. Hence, the actualities that condition or limit the given one are already determinate or in its past, and the possibilities a given actuality conditions or limits are those of its future. Possibilities or indeterminates, then, are contingent insofar as they are conditioned by decisions of the actual or determinate past—and the contingent range of what is possible is (other things equal) less as the future is more proximate, being more extensive insofar as the future is more distant. That there is a future is, however, itself necessary, because "nothing exists" is impossible.

Contemporary actualizations define space, and location within space makes an actuality ordinary. There is no ordinary relation to contemporaries. Were such relations possible (perhaps only to contemporaries whose completion occurs prior to completion of the actuality in question), the relations to be unified would be increased, such that another decision would be required. But more than one decision implies more than one actuality because each decision unifies a differing set of internal relations and thus creates a differing particular or determinate internality. Given its relations to past actualities and future possibilities, in other words, a given actuality *is* its decision; that is, the one decision must be present throughout as a determination of how relations are unified; or, again, the decision is what becomes actual. For this reason, contemporary "space," writes Whitehead, "expresses the halt for attainment" (Whitehead 1938, 139). To be sure, we humans consciously perceive things as contemporaries. But these appearances are, in fact, perceptions of particular objects rather than mere sense data because we relate internally and through our bodies to actualities of the immediate past. There is, then, the usually valid assumption that certain more general features of the past, experienced presently as mere sense data appropriately projected into space, endure into the contemporary world (see Whitehead 1927).

The present, on this account, is an actualization, which occurs all at once in some finite spatial and temporal extension and in which the most immediate and conditioned possibility becomes something actual and determinate. Indeed, actualization can be only in the present—because the past is what has been effective on it, and the future is what will be affected by it. Also, an actualization must have extension because each "moment" of an infinitely divisible present could be designated only by negation. Actualities or final real things (still leaving extraordinary ones aside) are, as far as we know, microscopic events—in each of which a decision about unification of relations to the past occurs as a condition of the future. On Whitehead's now classic formulation: "the many become one, and are increased by one" (Whitehead 1978, 21).

Moreover, past actualities must be infinite in number and future possibilities must extend without ending because each actualization implicates others in its past to which it relates, and the future possibilities to which it relates are indeterminate that, when actualized, will relate to future possibilities—or, again, "something exists" is necessarily true.

Because these final real things are, as far as we know, microscopic occurrences or actualizations, everything else is an abstraction from one or more or an aggregate of them. The macroscopic objects of our experience—for instance, human beings, buildings, chairs, stars—are all alike aggregates or aggregates of aggregates. The most significant aggregates are genetic in character: some identifying characteristic by which the given aggregate is distinguished from all others is exemplified by all actualities that are members of or actualize it, and this identity is thereby shared because later members internally relate to past others. Given that its identity is fragmentary, as are its earlier and later actualities, an aggregate in the world endures through a contingent period of time.[3]

Individuals, then, are genetic aggregates in which the member actualities are ordered sequentially (that is, no two are contemporaries), and other aggregates may include individuals. If the many become one and thereby increase the many by one, that is, thereby condition or limit the future, a given individual is a series of unifications, such that no two are contemporaries, and its identifying character or its identity is present throughout this individual's actualities because the later or succeeding are conditioned by the earlier or preceding. Also, an individual (at least for present purposes) means the most extended sequence of actualities distinguished by its identity. It seems apparent that we humans are such individuals who relate to a larger world (that is, the larger past and future) through relations to the actualities and their aggregates in our own bodies, the distinctively human individual likely existing somewhere in the brain. Perhaps because we participate in a developed language, moreover, we humans are individuals who have or quickly acquire the capacity both to remember our own past and anticipate our own future actualities in a measure dramatically greater than we remember or anticipate those of other individuals in the larger world.

Removing the restriction previously placed on the discussion, namely, its attention to ordinary actualities, we can call the concept of a final real thing or actuality, as mentioned previously, self-differentiating: two kinds of actualities, ordinary and extraordinary, are implied by the very concept and each implies it—and thus they can be distinguished by metaphysics in the strict sense. The self-differentiation turns on the difference between some and all. Ordinary actualities relate only in some measure to other actualities and possibilities (in fact, as far as we know, only a small measure); extraordinary actualities relate completely to whatever has occurred and might occur. In other words, ordinary actualities are fragmentary; extraordinary actualities are all-inclusive, and thereby each of the latter constitutes the whole of reality. Because all-inclusiveness is a self-differentiation of "actuality" and thus is strictly metaphysical, the aggregate of all-inclusive actualities cannot have a beginning or ending, and no two such actualities can be contemporaries because they cannot be spatially related.[4] Hence, extraordinary actualities must define a necessary or divine individual whose character (complete internal relation to all the world) can be formulated in a necessary existential statement. The identity of this individual is, in other words, itself strictly metaphysical, namely, to be, again and again, the whole implied by actuality as such, so that unification of all that has been and all that might be occurs again and again throughout all time.

Absent some or other world, there would be nothing for a divine individual to include. Thus, "something that is the world exists" and "something that is divine exists" are both necessarily true, even if the latter is necessarily a class of one. In contrast, the world's necessity can mean only that a nondivine class of individuals and other aggregates, none of which necessarily exist because no one is distinguished metaphysically in the strict sense, cannot be empty. Also, there must be an "infinite qualitative difference" between any worldly actuality or contingent individual and the divine actualities or their strictly metaphysical individual, just as the difference between "fragmentary relation to others" and "complete relation to others" is infinite. We may call the difference between ordinary and the extraordinary individuals the difference between the world and God, such that God always includes all of the world and, thereby, preserves forever every worldly decision in its entirety. For humans, that everlasting inclusion is arguably presupposed in taking any decision at all: practical reason is always "all things considered," and what has no ultimate worth ultimately has no worth (see Ogden 1966, 36).

This summary of a neoclassical metaphysics in the strict sense is likely terse, may well leave or elicit questions, and is subject to objection or controversy. Here, it is principally intended as a context in which to pursue the difference between moral and nonmoral creatures and, given moral creatures, the difference between moral and immoral decisions. On my accounting, metaphysics in the strict sense is essential to both distinctions. Because the summary of such metaphysics is terse, however, I can only ask readers to review the following discussion and, if they find its proposal with respect to the two distinctions promising, then to assess whether it implies at least something like the metaphysical background I have offered.

MORAL UNDERSTANDING

The difference between moral and nonmoral creatures depends on whether an actuality occurs with understanding; that is, understanding is a necessary condition (although not a sufficient condition; an additional condition will be mentioned later) of taking either a moral or immoral decision. This is because that decision is impossible absent relation to one's obligation that is distinct from the decision, and there is no such relation unless one understands what ought to be chosen. Without the distinction, the decision would be a good one; that is, the range of possibility present would include only what is best in the given situation. Because the understanding is different than the decision, one can decide with understanding *between* the moral and the immoral. Kant's dictum "ought implies can" has two meanings. On its more familiar intent, a prescribed action must be something the individual to whom the prescription is applicable can choose to do. On the less familiar intent, an individual is not subject to a prescription unless she or he *can* act accordingly because (for the reason that) she or he *ought* to do so; that is, unless she or he understands the obligation. Kant thereby states the reason why moral theory in the Western tradition has typically said that action contrary to some specification of the moral law is not culpable if taken in ignorance of that specification—at least if the ignorance itself is not itself culpable (see Aristotle 1109b35–1110a2).

It is, we may assume, noncontroversial that understanding implies consciousness, but whether consciousness implies understanding may be questioned. Perhaps consciousness without understanding is possible—and if so, I will suggest in a moment how that might occur. In any event, consciousness here designates a certain internality of an actuality, *how* it relates to something. Specifically, consciousness means the internality of an actuality that discriminates—and *x* is discriminated when contrasted with everything other than *x*: "*x* and nothing other than *x*" is, in other words, the object or content of a conscious relation—or that to which an actuality relates consciously. Consciousness of a yellow rose, for instance, marks an actuality's internality when it relates to a yellow rose in contrast with strictly everything else. Phenomenologically, at least, human awareness seems to discriminate in this way: to be conscious of the yellow rose is to see or smell it there and then, in contrast to strictly any other time and place; to be conscious that Democrats may control the next US Congress is to be aware of a possibility within the specific future of the United States in contrast to strictly any other past or future location.

It does not follow that one must be conscious of all things in detail in order to be conscious of any given thing, any more than one must be conscious of all humans in detail in order to be conscious of this given thing as a human being. To the contrary, relation to this given thing and to thing as such, the common character of all possible things, is sufficient if they form a contrast in which "nothing other than *x*" simply means "no other exemplification or specification of the possible as such"—just as relation to this being as human and human being as such is sufficient if they form a contrast in which "no other human being" means "no other possible human." It then follows that consciousness of any given thing includes an awareness of the character common to all possible things, that is, the metaphysical character of the possible as such—even if this metaphysical content is, in most conscious actualities, only inchoate. Discrimination is not possible without that awareness.

In this context, "inchoate" means that awareness can be implicit—and implicit consciousness or understanding means "contained in the nature of something although not readily apparent" (American College Dictionary). Because ordinary actualities and, therefore, actualities with understanding are fragmentary, what is readily apparent in consciousness is itself a fragment of the more pervasive awareness that includes a dim consciousness surrounding the focus or center of attention—and thus both consciousness and understanding can be implicit as well as explicit. At least with respect to human life, I take this distinction to be noncontroversial. Whitehead is, I think, phenomenologically correct when he says of consciousness: "Even at its brightest, there is a small focal region of clear illumination, and a large penumbral region of experience which tells of intense experience in dim apprehension" (Whitehead 1978, 267; see also 1958, 78). Moreover, every denial of the difference between implicit and explicit awareness is, I think, self-refuting, so that consciousness as such implies it. Explicit consciousness is always present; something occupies the focus or center of attention (perhaps absent in dreamless sleep, but present when a denial thereof is possible). Also, implicit consciousness is always present because its denial entails that all content of consciousness depends on learning. Given that discrimination of x is a contrast between x and strictly everything else, learning itself presupposes an awareness of the possible as such that is not learned and thus must be implicitly or inchoately present.

If consciousness *without* understanding is possible, I suggest, "everything other than this yellow rose" could then mean a contrast with the possible as such but not with any specific future possibility, so that a given yellow rose is discriminated only from other actual things but not from any contingent future the actuality might condition—and the awareness of the possible as such remains always implicit. Because that metaphysical character is common to past and future, consciousness without understanding would not discriminate the difference between past and future, even implicitly. It then follows that consciousness without understanding is not self-conscious—because, as I will suggest in a moment, self-consciousness requires understanding the difference between past and future and, thereby, the present. This does not deny that creatures without understanding act for their own futures and thus relate to specific future possibilities; the point is, rather, that relations to the future are not conscious. Thus, a creature of this kind does or would not discriminate itself from the objects of consciousness.

Whether or not consciousness without understanding can occur, in any event, understanding, on my accounting, marks an actuality when it is also conscious in some measure of the specific future to be conditioned. Thereby, consciousness of the contingent past occurs in terms of possibilities or indeterminates or universals. For instance, a yellow rose (which is a genetic aggregate) is understood when an actuality is conscious of a particular flower as exemplifying the abstract possibilities (or indeterminates or universals) "yellow" and "rose." Given the account of past and future previously asserted, an actuality's understanding of something past involves both relation to the given past, relation to the specific future, and relation to the possible as such. For instance, to understand a given yellow rose as exemplifying the abstract possibilities "yellow" and "rose" means to be conscious of the immediate past (the determinate yellow rose), the specific future (the indeterminates or universals "yellow" and "rose"), and the common character of all things (nothing other than this particular exemplification of "yellow" and "rose").

It now follows that an actuality with understanding includes an understanding of itself, a self-understanding. To be conscious of the difference between some given determinates (and, thereby, the past) and some specific possibilities or indeterminates (and, thereby, the future to be conditioned) is to understand the present—and the present is the actuality itself. Consciousness of the difference between the past by which one is conditioned and the specific future one's decision will condition is a self-understanding because the present self *is* that difference. To be sure, self-understanding is a seemingly paradoxical concept. The self is said to be both the one that understands and the one understood, the subject and the object of understanding—and yet the two are the same self. Still, any creature who says or thinks "I do not understand myself" implies the very self-understanding thereby denied. Some thinkers resolve this seeming paradox by explaining that a present actuality understands the past (perhaps immediate past) actuality or actualities of the individual in question. This explication is, however, problematic because it implies that a present actuality does not understand itself and thus cannot decide with understanding. In other words, a present actuality cannot be moral or immoral—because being either requires an understanding of one's obligation that is distinct from the actuality's decision. But, then, making sense of moral creatures depends on resolving the seeming paradox involved in a self-understanding.

Actualities that understand themselves can be clarified, I propose, if and only if self-understanding is explicated as a self-expression. "Self-expression" designates, on the one hand, something that is expressed and, on the other, the expression of that thing—and yet the two are one in the sense that expressing adds nothing to the something expressed except an effect on the future. What an actuality understands when it understands itself, then, is its expression—and thereby the self as subject and the self as expressed object are the same self. Accordingly, self-understanding is not retrospective, attending to an object preceding it (as memory, for instance, is retrospective) but, rather, prospective, attending to the self's effect on the future. What a self understands when it understands itself is the difference it makes. "The many become one, *and are increased by one*" (Whitehead 1978, 21, emphasis added).

If we now underscore that an actuality unifies its internal relations to the past by way of a decision, such that existence with understanding decides for a self-understanding, we can speak of the past presenting a range of possible alternatives for how the self-expression might condition the future, alternatives that are themselves understood and thus presented as differing possible ends or telé the actuality might pursue. Given that an understanding includes future possibility as its object, each alternative must be related to and defined by some indeterminate or universal, such that pursuit of t_1 rather than t_2 or t_3 or ... t_n is abstract because more than one actuality might pursue that telos. Moreover, a decision for this pursuit is the actuality's self-understanding because the actuality—given the past to which it relates and, thereby, its alternatives for purpose—*is* that choice. Its internality, then, is one of conscious choice or choice with understanding, and what is chosen is pursuit of the telos, such that decision within the range of possibility presented by the past is understood solely as pursuit of that telos. The self as subject is also the self as object because the chosen purpose with which the given past is unified then becomes the self when expressed and, therefore, when so presenting itself to the future as to pursue the chosen telos.

An actuality with understanding, we can now say, takes pursuit of the chosen telos to be the good decision. This is because decision for a self-understanding is an understanding of the alternatives for purpose *with respect to choosing*, and an understanding with respect to choosing *is* an evaluation of the alternatives. It does not follow that all evaluations distinguish better and worse, or moral and immoral alternatives—because a given evaluation may compare two or more alternatives as equally best. Still, it remains that a self-understanding understands the difference one makes to be the good decision. Aristotle was right, at least in this respect: "The good . . . has been well defined as that at which all things [he meant, I think, all human things] aim" (1094a1–3). Actualities *without* understanding also make decisions directed by the good because the good, as I will argue in the next section, is rightly defined metaphysically in the strict sense, so that every actuality is constituted by a final cause. Hence, the telos of each actuality without understanding cannot be distinct from its decision, and the range of possibility received from the past includes only the best it can be.

It may be useful here to recall that understandings, because they are conscious, may be implicit or inchoate as well as explicit—in the background of consciousness rather than its focus or center of attention. In most human life, at least, specific universals not now readily apparent but still understood within the actuality were likely entertained explicitly—and, thereby, learned—at some previous time within the individual in question and are now implicitly remembered. A present reading of, say, the Supreme Court ruling in *Shelby v. Holder*, which declared a central provision of the 1965 Voting Rights Bill no longer constitutional, may focus on what the Court said about this provision. But the ruling could not possibly be understood absent background understandings about US politics, the US Constitution, the civil rights movement, and so forth that are *brought to* the reading because they were learned by the individual in question at some prior time and are now implicitly remembered. At least as a general rule, moreover, the greater the complexity of relevant understandings implicitly present, the more profound the understanding of whatever occupies the center of attention. Still, *all* implicit understandings cannot depend on previous explicit understanding because this cannot be the case with an understanding of the possible as such. As mentioned earlier, it must be present whenever there is any understanding at all (and a fortiori any learning), because understanding requires the contrast of consciousness, namely, "*x* and nothing other than *x*," where *x* designates either some past actuality or some future possibility. In addition, a self-understanding and thus the choice thereof are present whenever there is understanding at all, so that these, too, cannot depend on prior learning.

THE STRICTLY METAPHYSICAL DEFINITION OF GOOD

If a self-understanding is a necessary condition, it is not, on my accounting, a sufficient condition of taking a moral or immoral decision, so that some further condition is required in order to be a moral creature. Still, the need for a further condition depends on whether and, if so, how the good is defined. On the view that good has no definition because no moral prescriptions can be valid or invalid, for instance, it is difficult to see how any condition at all for the distinction is needed. Or, again: if the good is, with Kant, said to be defined solely by a good will, so that what is pursued is said to be irrelevant to moral and immoral, it is difficult to see how a further condition beyond the self-understanding of an actuality is required. I now wish to argue for a strictly metaphysical definition of the good, and this argument should not avoid a summary engagement with how prominent Western theories have understood subjective decisions. This section, therefore, will seek to define the good in contrast to alternatives offered by prominent thinkers in the Western tradition, after which I will return to the difference between moral and immoral creatures.

Some thinkers have indeed asserted that human action is amoralist, that is, has no moral principle or principles and thus cannot be the object of reasoning or cannot be understood because decisions are solely subjective or arbitrary. Thomas Hobbes famously writes: "good, evil, and contemptible are ever used in relation to the person who useth them; there being nothing simply or absolutely so; nor any common rule of good and evil, to be taken from the nature of the objects themselves" (Hobbes 1962, 48--49). David Hume also asserts this position: "In moral deliberations," he writes, "we must be acquainted beforehand with all the objects, and all their relations to each other; and from a comparison of the whole, fix our choice or approbation. No new fact to be ascertained; no new relation to be discovered. All the circumstances of the case are to be laid before us, ere we can fix any sentence" (Hume 1975, 290). Hume argues, in other words, that alternatives must be understood in their entirety because one or another can be chosen only as a whole thing. But, he continues, "after every circumstance, every relation is known, the understanding has no further room to operate, nor any object on which it could employ itself. The approbation ... which then ensues, cannot be the work of judgment, but of the heart, and is not a speculative proposition or affirmation, but an active feeling or sentiment" (Hume 1975, 290)—even if Hume also finds empirically in human nature an overriding "sentiment of humanity" (Hume 1975, 235). In the early twentieth century, so-called emotivism in moral theory, on which utterances about what is good or evil are never valid or invalid but, rather, mere expressions of emotion, was widely endorsed. Unlike Hume, moreover, emotivists typically found no sentiment of humanity among human emotions.

On my accounting, Kant shows why the denial of all moral reasoning is self-refuting. Every theory or statement of practical reason as such is, he argues, a moral theory. In other words, every statement about how practical decision as such properly relates to alternatives as such purports to be an a priori practical law and thus to include a definition of the good; any such statement formulates an understanding of alternatives as such not in terms of what Hume calls their "circumstances" (Hume 1975, 290) but, rather, *with respect to choosing*. Given that any such theory or statement claims to be true, moreover, it claims to be a practical law of which all moral creatures are aware—because it defines moral obligation as such, and "ought implies can": a prescription implies that one *can* act accordingly because (for the reason that) one *ought* to do so. Hume himself, even while he asserts, with respect to choosing, that "understanding has no . . . room to operate," allows that a subject might misconstrue how alternatives as such are properly compared in choosing among them. For instance, a subject might take practical decision to be morally bound—and this is, for Hume, a misunderstanding because decision among alternatives is said to be always a matter "of the heart" and thus solely arbitrary. In conceding that subjects might misconstrue their decisions, Hume thereby acknowledges, at least by implication, that his focus on sentiment, which he considered true, is an understanding of approbation and disapprobation. But, then, his theory itself illustrates Kant's point: Hume's very statement can only be a comparative understanding of how practical decision as such relates to possible alternatives as such, not with respect to their circumstances but, rather, with respect to choosing.

In other words, the amoralist denial cannot be a solely descriptive understanding of similarities and differences among those alternatives because it denies all supposed misunderstandings *of the decision*. Hence, the assertion that practical thought as such is solely arbitrary is, in fact, how the alternatives *ought to be* compared—is, in other words, a moral law—and evaluates them all as equally good, whereby the decision is said to be always an exercise of preference. More generally, Kant rightly concluded, the statement of Hobbes or Hume is self-refuting: every assertion about subjective freedom as such purports to be true with respect to choosing (even a statement that denies any such understanding) and thus, for moral creatures, purports to be the moral law.

To be sure, one might deny, as many have, all universal theories of practical reason as such. In other words, one might deny any universal moral law or definition of the good and assert that good is always entirely relative to some historically specific situation. But if "good" is in any context defined entirely in terms of some historically specific situation, "good" must be so defined in all such situations; if absent anywhere, a universal law is absent everywhere. Hence, moral relativism is also self-refuting because it asserts the character of *all* practical reason—and thereby implies a comparison with respect to choosing of subjective decisions as such. Relativism is, against itself, a universal moral law, which prescribes for moral creatures a decision that considers nothing beyond one's own historically specific situation. Moreover, one cannot escape Kant's conclusion by asserting that moral and immoral are defined relative to certain universal kinds of decision (for instance, those with respect to keeping a promise or telling the truth). Any such limitation on the universal definition of "good" implies a moral comparison of subjective decisions as such because that limitation itself implies another moral principle: one should, with any decision, consider it a moral decision if and only if it belongs to one or more of those universal kinds. But this prescription purports to be a moral principle for *all* subjective decisions. To prescribe evaluations that consider nothing beyond context, whether the context is historically specific or universal to kinds of decision, is always to prescribe something beyond context.

In the more recent history of Western moral thought, Kant himself and those in the Kantian tradition (I have in mind recent thinkers such as Jürgen Habermas and Alan Gewirth [see Habermas 1990, 1993; Gewirth 1978]) hold that evaluative understanding is bound by a universal principle in terms of which alternatives for purpose are compared in some partial respect. Let us call this the nonteleological tradition. Kant's own nonteleology, for instance, asserts that alternatives for purpose, defined for humans by their "subjective ends," are properly compared with respect to choosing insofar as each does or does not treat other persons as persons, that is, individuals of practical reason—and for him, the freedom of a person is "the supreme limiting condition of all our subjective ends," something "which we must never act against" (Kant 1949, 48, 54). Kant seems to allow, at least for humans, what I take to be transparent, namely, that alternatives for decision can be distinguished only in terms of their possible purposes (their matter or subjective ends, rather than their form) and, with Hume, agrees that a possible purpose can be chosen only as a whole thing or in its entirety. "Now it is certainly undeniable that every volition must have an object [of desire or inclination] and therefore a material" (Kant 1956, 34). On Kant's account, however, purposes cannot be morally evaluated in their entirety (see, for instance, Kant 1956, 26).

Thus, the categorical imperative must be defined solely as the formal universality of reason—"an action done from duty derives its moral worth, *not from the purpose* which is to be attained by it" (Kant 1949, 17). The prescription never to act against a free will, which evaluates purposes in part, is sufficient to define the difference between moral and immoral decision.[5] In any event, subsequent nonteleologists have indeed distinguished morally among alternatives for purpose by way of evaluating each in some part. Gewirth, for instance, asserts that alternative ends are properly compared, not in their entirety but, rather, insofar as each does or does not treat recipients as individuals who necessarily should have, whatever else they have, equal generic freedom and well-being (see Gewirth 1978, 1996). Habermas, as one more example, holds that his discourse ethics "acts like a knife that makes razor-sharp cuts ... between the good and the just" because normative statements intend solely to adjudicate conflicts of human interests "brought to them from outside" (Habermas 1990, 104, 103). Thus, alternatives for purpose are not evaluated in their entirety but solely insofar as they do or do not conform to such norms.

To be the best of my reasoning, however, such nonteleological theories always presuppose what is also denied, namely, the moral comparison of alternatives for purpose in their entirety. The respects in which they are said to be not evaluated are, by implication, said to be indifferent to the moral comparison. But moral indifference is itself a moral conclusion, requiring a moral comparison. In other words, only comparison of the alternatives in their entirety could warrant the conclusion that they differ morally only in some partial respect. Indeed, one may even appeal to Kant's reasoning against the Kantian tradition: if every theory of practical reasoning as such is a moral theory, the Kantian tradition has its own theory of practical reasoning as such—namely, that human alternatives are always chosen in their entirety, even while they are moral or immoral only in part. But that very theory is a moral theory and thus requires a moral evaluation of human alternatives as such in their entirety. As mentioned above, decision among alternatives for purpose considers each as a whole thing; it cannot be evaluated, because it cannot be chosen, in part.[6] Hence, a comparison with respect to choosing cannot be, as the Kantian tradition asserts, nonteleological.

At least for moral creatures, then, the affirmation of some alternative telos as the good decision is inescapably teleological; that is, the telos chosen is said to be maximally good in its entirety. To be sure, it may be objected that no worldly actuality, given that all are fragmentary, can understand its alternative telé in their entirety. But the above argument against nonteleology also implies the following conclusion: insofar as alternatives for purpose, distinguished by their telé, are not understood, they are, by implication, understood to be equally best. If, for instance, the alternatives in a given situation are understood solely in the respect that each conduces to income for the poor, then, by implication, the respects in which each conduces to environmental integrity are understood to be equally good. Hence, the supreme principle of morality prescribes for every moral creature a comparison with respect to choosing of alternatives for purpose insofar as they are understood and thus, by implication, in their entirety.

We may now recall that specific alternatives for purpose, each defined by relation to its telos, cannot be understood except in contrast with all other things and thus as specifications of "something" in its most general sense. To discriminate x, where x is a specific possible telos, is to be conscious of "x and nothing other than *x*" and thus to be conscious of *x* as just this specification of the common character of all things. An aspect of every specific alternative telos is its specification of the possible as such. Hence, no decision for an understanding with respect to choosing can compare its specific alternative telé in their entirety without understanding them in terms of this common character—that is, in terms of a comprehensive or strictly metaphysical purpose. Any proper comparison of them as a greater or lesser good will be, in one or another way, a specification of the possible as such. If, for instance, a comparison of alternatives in a given situation insofar as each conduces to income for the poor is proper, this can only be the case because being so conducive specifies in that situation the strictly metaphysical good. Hence, no contingent variable, that is, a variable that is not strictly metaphysical, can *define* the good—because that variable does not compare the alternative telé in their entirety.

Some have said, for instance, that distinctively human flourishing, rightly understood, *defines* the good, such that human flourishing ought to be maximized. On one reading, at least, this is the proposal John Dewey advances: "the supreme test of all human actions ... shall be the contribution they make to the all-around growth of every member of society" (Dewey 1957, 186). But comparison of its possible purposes in terms of an actuality's contribution to maximal human flourishing does not compare those alternatives in their entirety because some among them may contribute to the flourishing of nonhuman creatures. Only as specifications of the strictly metaphysical character are alternative telé compared with respect to choosing as whole things or in their entirety—a conclusion confirmed by recognition that an alternative for purpose may, for someone, include any given thing, actual or possible, at least in the respect that a given person might think about it.

We may also state the point this way: Let us suppose that a given moral creature defines the good in terms of some character other than the possible as such; for instance, one might compare alternative purposes solely in terms of their contribution to the power and well-being of one's own political community. In the event of any such definition, some possible things would be, by implication, morally valueless; for instance, the power and well-being of other political communities. But *that* conclusion, namely, that some things are morally without value, is itself a moral conclusion requiring a moral comparison with things whose realization is said to morally good. Hence, only the character of all possible things can define the good—and moral teleology is defined by a comprehensive purpose whose telos is strictly metaphysical.

Perhaps this assertion will provoke the question: if good is defined by the possible as such, all things are good—and if all things are good, the good cannot distinguish moral and immoral decisions. From this strictly metaphysical definition, I think, it does follow that all things are good, so that "not good" is always a privation, meaning that something is good but worse than it could have been—allowing that being "worse than it could have been" is not necessarily a moral fault or a consequence of immorality. But "all things are good" does not entail that all things are equally good. To the contrary, the strictly metaphysical definition of good must be a variable, exemplified in greater or lesser measure. Indeed, given that strictly metaphysical statements are mutually implicative and thus define a single kind of final real thing, this definition must itself be a variable; two or more final real things can be different only if the strictly metaphysical scheme defines the necessary character of diverse exemplifications. Hence, the strictly metaphysical definition of good defines a comprehensive purpose; as a moral obligation, it prescribes that actualities so condition the future as to maximize the good.[7]

Moreover, that metaphysical definition can, I judge, claim the implied agreement of Kant. Against most of the Western philosophical tradition, Kant seeks a nonteleological moral law because, for him, metaphysics in the strict sense is impossible: theoretical reason is confined to things-as-they-appear because knowledge of things-in-themselves is denied to humans. For Kant, in other words, all statements of the form "something that is x exists" are, if true, contingently true—and practical reason, whose supreme principle must be a priori, cannot be defined by a telos. Still, Kant was lucid that a moral law on which alternatives for purpose are evaluated in their entirety requires an a priori telos, a state or character of existence as such that cannot be denied without self-contradiction, and thus a strictly metaphysical state or character. Because metaphysics in that sense is, for Kant, impossible, the categorical imperative can only constrain subjective ends among which humans decide by prescribing that which "we must never act against" (Kant 1949, 54). But if, as argued above, a nonteleological moral law implies a teleological one (that is, comparison of alternatives with respect to choosing only in part implies comparison of alternatives with respect to choosing in their entirety), the telos by which practical reason as such is defined can be, Kant holds by implication, only strictly metaphysical.

Both the comprehensive purpose as a moral obligation and the definition of good to be maximized are then transcendental—but in differing senses. On the one hand, that purpose is transcendental specifically to moral creatures as such, so that any statement of it is pragmatically necessary to subjects, and any denial of that statement is pragmatically self-refuting. Because the good is defined metaphysically in the strict sense, the statement "something that is good exists" is, on the other hand, a necessarily true existential statement, and its denial is semantically self-contradictory. Hence, the comprehensive purpose is transcendental to moral creatures as such, and the telos they are required to pursue is transcendental to existence as such.

MORAL CREATURES AS SUBJECTS

We can summarize this notion of the comprehensive purpose by noting that a meta-ethical account implies a normative theory; that is, any theory about the difference between moral and nonmoral creatures implies the most general difference between moral and immoral decision. This follows because explicating the former requires understanding as a necessary condition for being a moral creature—and the understanding in question includes awareness of the moral law, because "ought implies can." Moral creatures always understand, explicitly or implicitly, how subjects as such relate to their alternatives with respect to choosing. In Kant's terms, the metaphysics of morals is "nothing other than the investigation and establishment of *the supreme principle of morality*" (Kant 1949, 8). Against Kant, however, the understanding in question includes a strictly metaphysical good, and the supreme principle of morality is a comprehensive purpose.

Still, if an understanding of the strictly metaphysical good is necessary to a decision between moral and immoral, I am not satisfied that such understanding is sufficient to being a moral creature. As far as I can see, an actuality cannot be moral in distinction from nonmoral unless its understanding is *developed*, such that a subject actuality—which I will henceforth call an activity—understands itself to actualize a contingent individual, a genetic series of activities with a beginning and an ending and the most extended sequence distinguished by its identity. A subject actuality, in other words, is aware that its individual is contingent, that it lives and will die. This is because the moral question concerns *what* future is good and, therefore, should be maximized. Absent a response to that question, an actuality cannot be immoral, that is, cannot choose to disobey the moral law by defining the good in terms of something other than the comprehensive purpose.

Hence, the basic moral question to be asked and answered is whether the activity should so understand itself that good is defined by (1) the future as such (that is, the future without concern for any aspect thereof) in its strictly metaphysical respect, or (2) the future, in some other respect or in some undue measure, of the particular individual or of some specific group or community to which that individual is attached.[8] "Morality of outlook is inseparably conjoined with generality of outlook. The antithesis between the general good and the individual interest can be abolished only when the individual is such that its interest is the general good" (Whitehead 1978, 15). If an actuality occurs with understanding but without subjectivity, the strictly metaphysical future as such has no competitor; the telé among which choice for a self-understanding is taken all maximize the good.[9]

On the whole, I expect, we typically do not speak of actualities that decide for a self-understanding but do not actualize subjects—that is, actualities characterized by a self-understanding exclusive of the individual to which they belong. This fact, I suspect, likely results from a long tradition, beginning with Aristotle, in which each human individual has been conceived as a substance, itself actual, such that its states or relations are accidents thereof, and a self-understanding *is* an understanding of the individual in question. On the neoclassical metaphysics outlined above, however, the individual's identity is not substantial, in the sense of being itself actual, but is, rather, abstract and is actualized by its momentary states. Hence, an actuality may be self-conscious notwithstanding its failure to understand the individual to which it belongs. This may be the case with very small human children, even if a human's understanding of itself as an individual apparently begins at an early age.

Although speculation here is probably unavoidable, certain animals on earth other than humans (for instance, dogs) appear also to include actualities that are conscious of specific possibilities they will condition, but these actualities do not discriminate the contingently existing individual they exemplify. For this reason, the actuality is not conscious that its individual will die. If so, a given actuality of this kind, because it discriminates in some measure both its past and the specific future, understands itself, and decision for a self-understanding among possible telé occurs, perhaps implicitly or inchoately. With respect to the future, however, the telé understood are likely within the near future alone. Thereby, the animal's self-understanding cannot consider its own future as an individual or the future of some specific group or community to which that individual is attached as competing definitions of the good, and the telé of which the animal is aware are all consistent with maximizing good in the future as such.

In saying this, I do not deny that such animals may decide for their own well-being or that of a group to which they belong; I mean only that alternatives for purpose of which the creature is aware are equally best and so evaluated, whereby decision among them is a matter of preference. Often good in the future as such is maximized when an actuality gives principal attention to the future that will likely be most fully related to it or on which it will likely have the greatest effect. In addition, nonhuman animals that do choose a self-understanding may inherit or anticipate far more extensively than their consciousness of past and future extends, so that special attention to themselves or to some specific group to which the individual is attached is nonconscious, and insofar as these are nonconscious, the telos to be pursued is not distinct from the decision.

If actualities become activities when they understand the contingent individual so actualized, becoming a subject requires learning—and some may object that a feature (for instance, being a moral creature) cannot be transcendental to human life if it requires learning. If awareness of oneself as an individual is, indeed, something humans acquire, then, to be sure, being a moral creature is not strictly transcendental to *human life*. Still, each human *is* a contingent individual, and this fact remains transcendental to the actualities of all humans, even if very small children do not understand that fact. Because the good is defined by existence as such, moreover, the telos defined metaphysically in the strict sense characterizes all actualities, even if some such actualities are not subjective and thus decide only within a range of possibility that maximizes the good. Hence, this telos is the final cause for which all human existence with understanding does or, alternatively, should decide, and the comprehensive purpose becomes a moral law as soon as the contingent individual learns to understand itself. In other words, a decision between moral and immoral alternatives is transcendental to *subjects*, that is, to moral creatures.

A moral creature is present, then, when an actuality is a subjective activity, that is, when the choice of a self-understanding must decide what future is good and thus may choose against the future as such in its strictly metaphysical respect. The good, one may decide, is defined by some contingent possibility (or universal or indeterminate) also understood, so that something other than the maximal good in the future as such is taken to be the supreme telos to which all more specific telé in their entirety should contribute. For instance, a subject may take its own power or success to be the supreme telos of one's action, or may be a chauvinistic US citizen, for whom the well-being of the United States identifies the good. More generally, a subject may so decide that, in some respect or in some undue measure or both, one's own individual future or the future of some specific group or community to which that individual is attached is taken to be good. This general decision defines immorality because a strictly metaphysical good is indifferent to where and when it is realized; a strictly metaphysical good requires pursuit of the future as such.

Understanding what decision it ought to take, an immoral activity decides for the false even while knowing what is true and, thereby, tells a lie to itself. This lie, I suspect, is not explicitly conscious, at least not typically. Immorality, at least typically, includes self-deception; the lie is excluded from explicit understanding, and the activity understands itself explicitly to be for the best—however much, in retrospect, the individual may be self-critical. Indeed, it is precisely because one understands what ought to be decided that one can claim an immoral activity to be the best; without that self-contradiction, the decision would not be aware of what "the best" means. When focus on decision for or against the comprehensive purpose is pertinent, I will call it the choice of authenticity or inauthenticity.

On my accounting, then, this primal choice, as we may call it, defines the terms in which the specific alternatives for purpose, that is, the range of possibility presented by the given situation in which an activity is set, are evaluated as better and worse. In other words, the one decision constituting a subjective activity is complex: specific alternatives for purpose are evaluated in accord with a primal choice that determines the evaluation of them, and the specific alternative chosen expresses, even as it implicates, the authenticity or inauthenticity of the activity. For instance, a subject evaluates her or his specific alternatives inauthentically in terms of what conduces to her or his popularity—and, accordingly, calls good the keeping of a given promise because she or he believes that doing so will be thus conducive. Or: a subject evaluates her or his specific alternatives authentically in terms of the strictly metaphysical good—and, accordingly, calls good the keeping of a given promise, notwithstanding that she or he risks popularity in doing so.

In fact, the subjective activities of humans typically pursue some more immediate telos in order to pursue some more distant telé: for instance, one may choose a specific phrase in order to complete a given speech in order to help elect a given candidate in order to aid control of the US Congress by a given political party in order to maximize what is taken to be the common good of the United States. Together with the specific purpose, in any event, the decision for or against authenticity constitutes an activity, and this is, I propose, the original (and originating) decision of a moral, in distinction from a nonmoral, actuality. It also follows, then, that every original decision is moral (in distinction from nonmoral) in a systematically ambiguous way because the term "moral" designates, within the given situation, the complex decision inclusive of both the choice to be authentic or inauthentic and the choice of a specific purpose. Moreover, even a decision for the comprehensive purpose and thus what is best in one's situation is typically implicit in a subject's consciousness because one cannot be explicitly aware of whether a decision that accords with authenticity at some lesser level of specificity may be inauthentic in terms of some more inclusive telos. For instance, one may keep a specific promise in order to advance one's popularity.

For all that, however, the comprehensive purpose does not imply that principal attention to the individual actualized or to groups or communities to which that individual is attached is immoral. An activity that pursues maximal good in the future as such expresses this commitment in some or other specific purpose available given the inherited past, and the commitment often requires expression focused on special relationships—for instance, on the subjective individual in question, her or his family, or her or his work institution or political community. Indeed, as mentioned previously in passing, good in the future as such is often maximized when each individual gives principal attention to the future that will likely be most fully related to her or his present or on which she or he will likely have the greatest effect. For this reason, the mere fact that some specific purpose is so focused does not itself imply whether the activity's original decision includes a choice for authenticity or inauthenticity. But that choice makes all the difference—as can become apparent when an individual continually so defines the good that inordinate or undue worth is given, in some respect, to some specific future and, thereby, a kind of egoism or chauvinism betrays duplicity in her or his original decisions.

THE TRANSCENDENTAL MORAL PRINCIPLES

If a creature is moral only when its actualities are activities, that is, understand themselves and the individual to which they belong, and if the good for which they ought to decide is defined by the possible as such, we have not yet clarified the character of that good and thus the distinction between moral and immoral decision. That good is defined metaphysically in the strict sense does not, as noted earlier, entail that all things are equally good. To the contrary, the good defined by the possible as such is a variable, such that all actualities exemplify it, and all future possibilities if and when realized will or may exemplify it in greater or lesser measure—and the decision activities ought to take is for the maximal good in the future as such. On the neoclassical metaphysics summarily argued above, the final real things exemplify "the many become one, and are increased by one" (Whitehead 1978, 21), that is, exemplify creative unification for the future of given internal relations to actualities and aggregates. Because the diversity of what is given may be more or less extensive and, therefore, the creative unification achieved may be greater or lesser, the character of these unities-in-diversity as such varies.

Transparently, this metaphysical character is variably exemplified by ordinary actualities in our world. To all appearances, the past received by all actualities constituting an inorganic aggregate (for instance, a stone or a star) is relatively trivial compared to the past received by actualities within distinctively human individuals whose participation in language yields a developed understanding of past and future. Other things equal, moreover, a comparison of the experiences constituting differing humans—one of whom is, say, sufficiently poor that attention to survival dominates her or his life, while the other is, say, sufficiently secure, educated, and politically powerful that opportunity for profound experience is often present—itself reveals that unification achieved, notwithstanding its definition of all actualities, is widely diverse. Given this variable character of the good, we may now formulate the following moral law: so act as to maximize unity-in-diversity in the future as such. That principle expresses the comprehensive purpose. Whitehead calls "the many become one, and are increased by one" the category of creativity (Whitehead 1978, 21), and in that sense, greater and lesser unity-in-diversity is greater and lesser creativity. Hence, the comprehensive purpose may also be formulated: so act as to maximize creativity in the future as such.

Pursuit of maximal creativity as such may appear to postpone realization of creativity forever; when future possibilities become present, nonsubjective actualities do and subjective activities should themselves pursue realization in the future as such. But this appearance overlooks the following: the complex moral decision is how a present activity unifies its relations to the past and thus realizes its own unity-in-diversity. Maximal creativity is not postponed, then, if the decision to pursue it *is* the decision by which a subjective activity makes the most of its chance for creativity. To the best of my reasoning, neoclassical metaphysics is incoherent unless this is the case, precisely because maximal good is otherwise forever postponed: maximal creativity cannot define what should be pursued unless it is, in that pursuit, realized.

Some thinkers committed to neoclassical metaphysics have asserted that a moral creature not only decides what a given activity becomes in the present and its intended effect on the future but also the two are not coincident—even if the latter contributes to the former. Each activity, then, ought somehow to balance the creativity realized in the present and pursued in the future. Indeed, Whitehead himself may suggest this interpretation (see Whitehead 1978, 27). To the best of my reasoning, however, that interpretation makes no sense. For one thing, I doubt that decision with understanding can include in its purpose what the present actuality becomes, although I will not seek here to argue the point.[10] Be that as it may, the interpretation in question implies that a relevant activity should not pursue the future realization of creativity; rather, the present should seek so to condition its future that activities therein, when they occur, maximize their own balance between their present and future creativity, and maximal good is then indeed forever postponed.

But realization of the balance makes no sense unless what should be pursued is the realization of maximal creativity. If we are now told that both realizations are equally good (such that we ought to decide either to maximize present or to maximize future creativity), one or the other is insofar sacrificed, and maximal creativity is still forever postponed. Hence, another moral principle is needed to warrant the supposed equality. But maximizing creativity is *the* moral principle or comprehensive purpose. What subjects ought to decide, I conclude, is a purpose defined by maximal creativity in the future as such—and the particular final real things they then become realizes maximal creativity in the present, the best each can be. Our moral obligation is to pursue maximal creativity in the future as such—and in the decision for that comprehensive purpose an actuality maximizes its present creativity. The two are, in other words, coincident.

Perhaps the most persistent critique of teleological ethics asserts that decisions prescribed by deontological norms become solely "guiding rules" subject to cancellation by pursuit of the maximal good.[11] Accordingly, no such norm is truly deontological, where this means a prescription with which action ought to accord regardless of overall consequences. Among other norms of this kind, then, there can be no principles of human rights, that is, rights characterizing any human simply by virtue of her or his humanity—because human rights are meant to be morally controlling regardless of overall consequences, even when action in accord with them conflicts with pursuit of the maximal good.

But this general indictment of teleological ethics cannot be sustained if pursuit of the maximal good is rightly applied indirectly through social practices defined by deontological norms—for instance, the norm by which the practice of promising is defined, namely, that promises should (barring an overriding practice) be kept, as should the democratic norms constituting government through full and free political discourse. I mean here to distinguish deontological from nonteleological norms: the former can be the indirect application of a teleological purpose, while nonteleological norms assert that alternatives for purpose are morally evaluated solely in some partial respect. Moreover, the pursuit of maximal creativity in the future as such seems to call for application through this kind of social practice because creativity will be greater if there is social coordination among humans. Each person will be the more creative if she or he acts with awareness of the roles and responsibilities others will enact in a common practice or practices.

Given that human activities, compared with other creatures in the known world, have the chance for especially increased unity-in-diversity, the past delivered to any given human individual and thus her or his chance for creativity will be greater insofar as it includes human achievements favorably ordered—that is, insofar as she or he receives the achievements of a favorably ordered community or community of communities. Favorably ordered communities require social practices—among them, institutions—to which each participant is committed (barring an overriding social practice) regardless of overall consequences. Indeed, absent social practices, favorably ordered communities or social coordination becomes impossible because the unpredictability for each member thereof is cumulative. Once all actors must decide without settled expectations regarding the actions of others, what any given actor can expect of others becomes radically indeterminate. Without commitment to democratic practices, for instance, a democratic community is impossible. At least to first appearances, then, maximal creativity in the future as such requires the deontological norms through which its pursuit can be a common enterprise.

Still, critics might turn the previous paragraph against moral teleology. Notwithstanding that creativity cannot be maximized without deontological application, this criticism insists, the internal inconsistency of that moral theory is thereby revealed: it does not permit what it nonetheless requires because pursuit of maximal creativity prescribes that action should always sacrifice social coordination to the maximal good. But that critique is unconvincing if subjectivity as such implies a deontological principle. Given this implication, the comprehensive purpose and the implied deontological practice are both transcendental to subjective activity, and the two are mutually implicative, such that denial of either is pragmatically self-refuting. Hence, the deontological principle can only be an indirect application of the comprehensive purpose—whereby that purpose is so applied because maximal creativity in the future as such requires social coordination. On my accounting, then, the comprehensive purpose and a universal social practice of subjective rights are both transcendental to subjectivity as such.

The argument here for that social practice is indebted to Karl-Otto Apel, a Kantian theorist for whom a principle of communicative rights is presupposed by every activity (see Apel 1979). To the best of my knowledge, Apel speaks of rights held by all humans and, therefore, begs questions of whether very small children are subjects and whether all subjects are human—and because I wish to leave these questions open, I will speak of subjects rather than humans.[12] In addition, I have appropriated Apel's Kantian discussion in order to place it within a strictly metaphysical definition of the good, which he does not affirm.

Here, then, is the argument: In taking what one understands to be a good decision and thus a decision consistent with what is claimed to be the comprehensive purpose, any subject whose activity affects any other subjective activity, whether of the same individual or another, thereby affects an activity and its subject also bound by that purpose. The actor then addresses to any affected subjective activity a prescription, namely, the recipient activity ought to receive those effects as consistent with the comprehensive purpose. But "ought implies can," which here means that recipients must be able to obey the prescription because it is valid. In other words, the initial activity is bound to respect the moral freedom of all recipient activities, that is, their right to accept or contest what the initial activity claims to be the comprehensive purpose. In other words, respect for the right to moral freedom of any affected subjective activity is self-prescribed by every subjective activity and, in that sense, is transcendental.[13]

Respect for this right of all subjects, including other individuals, is, then, a principle to which subjects ought to conform regardless of overall consequences. It cannot be overridden by pursuit of the maximal good because moral principles transcendental to subjects as such imply each other; that is, the comprehensive purpose implies and is implied by this deontological principle—so that failure to obey the latter would be failure to obey the former. Hence, the principle of subjects' rights can only be an indirect application of the comprehensive purpose itself, that application being required because maximizing creativity is a common enterprise among individuals who are subjects. Having asserted this deontological principle, we can, I think, derive from it other practices prescribed for the sake of social coordination. These include a form of politics that is, wherever possible, democratic—as well as the legal ordering a democratic polity prescribes and whatever voluntary associations it permits. But I will not seek here to defend these derivations or qualifications of them. Perhaps it will suffice to have shown that pursuit of maximal creativity in the future as such cannot be indicted by the general criticism typically directed against moral teleology.[14]

That moral creatures are required to decide for the comprehensive purpose and its indirect application is one reason why neoclassical metaphysics implies a difference between worldly and divine actualities. The comprehensive purpose prescribes subjective activity through which the future is so conditioned that its multiplicity of actualities, when they become present, will each have opportunity for the greatest possible unity-in-diversity. But this prescription is senseless unless realization in this actual multiplicity is somehow unified. There can be no maximal creativity in the future as such absent a summation thereof—and because creativity in each of the multiplicity is, when it becomes present, actual, the summation itself must be actual. This is possible only if some actuality will completely include each of the multiplicity in its entirety. In short, the strictly metaphysical definition of good to be pursued implies a strictly metaphysical individual. Creativity in the future as such is the future of God.

… 6 …

ON THE INTERPRETATION OF RELIGIOUS FREEDOM

A Conversation with Ronald Dworkin

The death of Ronald Dworkin in 2013 was an immense loss. His moral, political, and legal theories constitute an exceptional academic legacy, and through his reflections on issues in contemporary politics and jurisprudence, he leaves a similar gift to our public life. He persistently—and, I believe, rightly—advocated conceptions and analyses in which politics is responsible to universal moral principles, and I join many who were often persuaded by his address to specific public problems. In recent books, Dworkin discussed more fully how democratic politics properly relates to religion and thus how a constitutional principle of religious freedom should be interpreted. The debt we all owe to him counsels those whose thought about democracy includes express interest in that constitutional provision to consider critically his account of it. Another understanding is, I believe, more coherent.

This chapter will not pursue how the alternative it commends provides a better context in which to affirm many of the political sensibilities Dworkin advocated, but that wider purpose is the background for the engagement here with him. Further, I will in this conversation dramatically abstract from his detailed arguments, although I intend sufficiently to capture his proposal that I do not neglect something relevant to the critique. Also, I will not seek to relate his more recent discussions to earlier work in his massive legacy but, rather, will focus on three publications: *Is Democracy Possible Here? Principles for a New Political Debate*; *Justice for Hedgehogs*; and his final book, *Religion without God*.[1] In what follows, then, I will first summarize Dworkin's position as best I can, turn next to a critical discussion of it, and then seek to outline an alternative account of religious freedom.

The religion clauses initiating the US Constitution's First Amendment, Dworkin holds, should not be construed in terms of "common understandings or dictionary definitions" of religion. To the contrary, those clauses and other "basic constitutional concepts" articulate "political ideals" and should be so interpreted "as to make sense of that crucial role" (2013, 108). What the clauses protect should be so defined as "to justify the assumption that freedom of religion is an important basic right" (2013, 109)[2]—although the definition, Dworkin clearly implies, should at least include what are commonly understood to be religions. With this formulation of the task, he surveys and finds wanting interpretations of religion, both functional and substantive, designed to clarify religious freedom as a special right. In *United States v. Seeger* (1965)—whose decision found Daniel Andres Seeger entitled to conscientious objector status, his atheism notwithstanding—the Supreme Court promulgated a functional view, accepting as grounds for religious exemption "a sincere and meaningful belief which occupies in the life of its possessor a place parallel to that filled by . . . God" (cited in 2013, 120). At least by implication, Dworkin objects, that account identifies religious conviction by "the fervor with which" a belief is held and, thereby, the class of protected beliefs is potentially too extensive (2013, 120; see 118–20). In contrast, substantive views designate a certain kind of conviction as religious—for instance, any "comprehensive account of why it is important for people to live well and what it is to live well" (2013, 122).[3] But these definitions rely "on the assumption that it lies within the power of government to choose" which convictions do and which do not accord with the substantive criterion—and this affirmation "seems itself to contradict the basic principle that questions of fundamental value are a matter of individual, not collective, choice" (2013, 123).[4]

Dworkin proposes "a more radical approach" (2013, 129), namely, that religious freedom is a special case of a more general right to ethical freedom: "We deny a special right to free exercise of religious practice, and rely only on the general right to ethical independence" (2013, 135–36). Clarity about the latter requires attention to how and why he uses "ethical" in distinction from "moral"—and his argument for that distinction is, in turn, part of his larger project in moral and political theory. That larger project, I will argue, is troubled by two basic problems: (*a*) At least by implication, Dworkin rightly affirms, with Kant, the necessary character of moral truth but also wrongly denies, against Kant, a necessary moral law. Given the denial, moral proposals become, against Dworkin's intention, nothing more than mere assertions of the proposers, confirming Kant's insistence on a necessary principle defining moral and immoral. (*b*) Dworkin's moral and political theory is nonetheless broadly Kantian or nonteleological, a character that requires and is required by his distinction between ethics and morality, and his interpretation of religious freedom is incoherent because it applies this nonteleological distinction to a democratic constitution.

In conclusion, I will give summary reason why democracy cannot be coherently explicated unless both troubles are overcome: having rightly affirmed, against Dworkin and with Kant, a necessary moral law, one will not provide a convincing interpretation of religious freedom unless one also affirms, against Kant, moral teleology—and I will make this point in the context of outlining the alternative account. But that proposal, I should here note, is not offered as an interpretation of the US Constitution's religion clauses. Whatever Dworkin's intent in his "more radical approach," I seek only a summary statement of how democracy with religious freedom should be understood in order to be coherent, thereby leaving for other inquiries the relation of this conclusion to US constitutional law.

DWORKIN'S INTERPRETATION

In *Justice for Hedgehogs*, Dworkin "defends a large and old philosophical thesis: the unity of value" (2011, 1)—and defends, as that thesis implies, the presence of "objective truths about value" and, specifically, moral truth (2011, 7). This defense occurs through a distinctive integration of Hume and Kant—or, at least, of what Dworkin calls "Hume's principle" and "Kant's principle." The former "describes the independence of morality from science and metaphysics," and the latter "chart[s] the interdependence of morality and ethics" (2011, 19). My summary discussion will turn in due course to Kant's principle and will focus now on the principle attributed to Hume, which Dworkin formulates as follows: "No amount of empirical discovery about the state of the world—no revelations about the course of history or the ultimate nature of matter or the truth about human nature—can establish any conclusions about what ought to be without a further premise or assumption about what ought to be" (2011, 17). Or, again: "No series of propositions about how the world is, as a matter of scientific or metaphysical fact, can provide a successful case on its own—without some value judgment hidden in the interstices—for any conclusion about what ought to be the case." In moral theory, we can say, naturalism is always a fallacy. Hume's principle, Dworkin writes, "seems to me obviously true" (2011, 44).

The separation of science and metaphysics from evaluative or moral truth means, for Dworkin, that religions "commonly have two parts: cosmological and evaluative" (2011, 340) or "a science part and a value part" (2013, 23). The cosmological or science part answers "the question of what there is and why" (2011, 340), that is, answers "important factual questions" about the universe and human life, often doing so with "godly commitments" or in terms of activity by a god or gods (2013, 23, 24).[5] The evaluative part answers "the question of what there should be and why. What is right and what is wrong? What is important and not important? What must I do with my life?" (2011, 341). This part "offers a variety of convictions about how people should live and what they should value" (2013, 23). But "Hume's principle holds that . . . we cannot derive an ought from an is" (2011, 341); that is, "the science part . . . cannot ground the value part because . . . these are conceptually independent" (2013, 24). More generally, then, scientific and evaluative thinking are "two great domains of intellectual activity," each "standing as a full partner . . . in an embracing dualism of understanding" (2011, 123).

As for Hume, so for Dworkin, all possibly true statements about the world are logically contingent; that is, their denials are also possibly true. "Judgments about the physical and mental world can be *barely* true"; that is, "physical facts . . . can stand alone." They are "just stubbornly there," and "at some point it would be correct to say, 'That's just the way things are'" (2011, 114). For Hume, statements about what is the case cannot imply statements about what ought to be the case because none of the former can be necessarily true, necessity being confined to mathematics and formal logic—and Dworkin also denies that what is has a necessary character. Hence, when he speaks of "metaphysical fact" (2011, 44), he means, to all appearances, the most abstract contingent character of contingent facts—and he regularly denies what he calls the metaphysical view on which objective value requires a kind of moral facts or "moral particles," which he calls "morons" (2011, 43). For Dworkin, in any event, "metaphysics" in what I will call its strict sense, namely, pursuit of knowledge about the necessary conditions of all things or about reality as such, is impossible—and, in this, he is at one with both Hume and Kant.[6]

The second great domain of intellectual activity within our embracing dualism of understanding is interpretation. Unlike science and its concern with how the world is, interpretation is concerned with values—and thus moral and political theories are interpretive. These theories do not exhaust the genres of interpretation—which include historical, sociological, anthropological, legal, and literary thinking, to name a few others—but all such intellectual activities have this is common: "We find it natural to report our conclusions, in each and every genre of interpretation, in the language of intention or purpose" (2011, 125)—and thus in terms of "the best account of the value served by interpreting in the genre in question" (2011, 149). On Dworkin's proposal, "interpretation is a social phenomenon" (2011, 130); any given instance of it participates in some or other social practice or tradition, each of which is "truth-seeking" because "we assume that something of value is and ought to be served" by those who join the practice (2011, 131). Interpretation is, then, an independent intellectual activity—thereby exemplifying Hume's principle—even while presupposing the pursuit of truth.

Although empirical or scientific judgments "can be *barely* true," this "is not the case with ... value judgments"; if "a value judgment is true, there must be a *reason* why it is true." Values "are not just stubbornly there" (2011, 114)—and the reasons for true interpretive judgments can only be other interpretive judgments. "Interpretation is therefore interpretive ... all the way down" (2011, 131)—or, to repeat the point: "Interpretation is holistic ... so an interpreter seeks, though usually unawares, an integration of background values and concrete interpretative insights" (2011, 134–35). Every interpretation of some or other particular object or event is "also interpreting the practice of interpretation in the genre that we take ourselves to have joined: we interpret that genre by attributing to it what we take to be its proper purpose." Accordingly, Dworkin formulates interpretive success in the following way: "A particular interpretation succeeds—it achieves the truth about some object's meaning—when it best realizes, for that object, the purposes properly assigned to the interpretive practice properly identified as pertinent" (2011, 131).

As interpretive, moral theory and its application to politics properly pursue truth through such holistic reasoning. "Our moral epistemology—our account of good reasoning about moral matters—must be an integrated ... epistemology," such that "we are always guilty of a kind of circularity" (2011, 100)—but not, Dworkin thinks, a vicious one: "it is not viciously circular to say that morality provides its own only justification" (2011, 193). In truth, "interpretation knits values together. We are morally responsible to the degree that our various concrete interpretations achieve an overall integrity so that each supports the others in a network of value that we embrace authentically" (2011, 101).

To all appearances, Dworkin means a "circularity" of contingently held beliefs; that is, no one of them is necessary to moral interpretation as such.

Thus, a defense of any one appeals to others whose defense depends on the first—the kind of circularity captured in John Rawls's notion of reflective equilibrium, a concept Dworkin seeks to extend or make "more ambitious" (2011, 263; see also 263–64). "Faced with someone who holds moral opinions radically different from my own, I cannot count on finding anything in my set of reasons and arguments that he would be irrational not to accept. I cannot *demonstrate* to him that my opinions are true and his false." Still, "I can hope to convince him . . . that I have acted responsibly"; that is, the moral opinions evidence overall integrity (2011, 100; see also 101). As one consequence of prescribing mutual support among value affirmations, an integrated moral epistemology denies any supposed separation of so-called meta-ethics (that is, answers to "questions *about* morality" [2011, 10] or the analyses of moral concepts) from substantive moral theory. Meta-ethics in that sense "is a misconceived project" (2011, 166).

Dworkin's interpretation of morality—his own substantive theory—is inseparable from his interpretation of ethics, but "ethical" and "moral" are not, in contrast to common practice, simply synonymous ways to designate obligations pertinent to human decisions: "I use the terms 'ethical' and 'moral' in what might seem a special way. Moral standards prescribe how we ought to treat others; ethical standards, how we ought to live ourselves" (2011, 191).[7] Elsewhere, he asserts the same distinction: "Our ethical convictions define what we should count as a good life for ourselves; our moral principles define our obligations and responsibilities to other people" (2006, 21). Although the former define a good life for ourselves, Dworkin clarifies, our ethical responsibility is not to have that life but, rather, to strive for it—and he calls the latter living well. In his holistic interpretation, then, "we look for a conception of living well that can guide our interpretation of moral concepts. But we want, as part of the same project, a conception of morality that can guide our interpretation of living well" (2011, 193).

Our ethical responsibility is captured generally by two "fundamental requirements" (2011, 203), which "seem as categorical as our moral responsibilities" (2011, 213). One "is a principle of self-respect. Each person . . . must accept that it is a matter of importance that his life be a successful performance rather than a wasted opportunity" (2011, 203). The second "is a principle of authenticity. Each person has a special, personal responsibility for identifying what counts as success in his own life" (2011, 204). Indeed, this second principle is "the other side" of the first, because living well implies that one seek "a way of life that grips you as right for you and your circumstances" (2011, 209); one should "seek the right values" for one's life (2011, 213). "Together, the two principles offer a conception of human dignity: dignity requires self-respect and authenticity" (2011, 204).

The integration of ethics and morality occurs through an appropriation of Kant's ethics, which Dworkin calls "Kant's principle": "a proper form of self-respect... entails a parallel respect for the lives of all human beings" (2011, 255). Or, again: "The first principle of dignity, recast to make plain the objective value of any human life, becomes... Kant's principle" (2011, 260). The entailed respect for all becomes apparent, Dworkin argues, when one cannot find a reason for the special importance of one's own life—or, at least by implication, for any limited group of humans. "Someone who thought his special properties made his life particularly important would find it difficult to integrate that view with other responsible opinions" (2011, 257). In an earlier book, Dworkin formulates the point in what seems to be a rhetorical question: "Is there anything about you that could make it a matter of greater objective or cosmic importance how your life goes than how mine goes or anyone else's?" (2006, 15). In sum, he unites ethics and morality by so interpreting ethical responsibility that one's own dignity is violated by refusal to treat all human life similarly. "You must treat yourself as an end in yourself, and therefore, *out of self-respect*, you must treat all other people as ends in themselves as well" (2011, 265, emphasis added). Denial of human dignity generally is, in other words, denial of one's own.

If morality is, thereby, "essential to living well" (2011, 202), the two are integrated because the rights one claims in order to live well are what one affirms for others. Accordingly, one is not morally bound to act impartially toward all humans, as if one is immoral whenever one gives special attention to one's own interests or projects. For Dworkin, moreover, Kant intended no such conclusion. To the contrary, Kant's universalism is "less demanding... we must act in such a way that we can will the principle of our action to be universally embraced and followed" because, citing Kant, "'precisely the fitness of his [the agent's] maxims to make universal law... marks him out as an end in himself.'" Special attention to one's own life is permitted given the moral entailment thereof, namely, treatment of all other humans as persons who can do the same: "We claim no right in ourselves that we do not grant others and suppose no duty for them we do not accept for ourselves" (2011, 266).

This integration of ethics and morality informs Dworkin's account of politics and thus of religious freedom. Politics involves collective action through the state or government. "Political morality... studies what we all together owe others as individuals when we act in and on behalf of" (2011, 327–28) a "separate, artificial collective entity" (2011, 327). Applied to such action, dignity, inclusive of its Kantian entailment, defines justice: "Governments have a sovereign responsibility to treat each person in their power with equal concern and respect" (2011, 321), that is, "treat their fates as equally important and respect their individual responsibilities for their own lives" (2011, 330), and governments "achieve justice to the extent they succeed" (2011, 321). In another discussion, Dworkin argues that government is bound by two principles: "that each human life has a special kind of objective [or intrinsic] value" (2006, 9) and "that each person has a special responsibility for realizing the success of his own life, a responsibility that includes exercising his judgment about what kind of life would be successful for him" (2006, 10).

These two principles provide "the most abstract source of political rights," and among political rights, Dworkin differentiates from others those that "trump government's collective policies"—that is, "government has no moral authority to coerce anyone, even to improve the welfare or well-being or goodness of the community as a whole, unless it respects those two requirements [equal concern and respect] person by person" (2011, 330). Rights that are fundamental in this sense may be distinguished from legal rights, that is, political rights "properly enforceable on demand through adjudicative and coercive institutions without need for further legislation or other lawmaking activity" (2011, 407). Still, the fundamental rights may also be given legal status, typically by stipulation in a political constitution. Religious freedom is, at least in the United States, a trump right with constitutional status.

Because government should never fail to respect each individual's responsibility, Dworkin's interpretation of the First Amendment's religion clauses is not surprising: each individual has a fundamental right to ethical independence. Recalling his precept to define constitutional principles in terms of the basic rights they protect, we might say that, for him, the provision for religious freedom is rightly understood when "religious" is given a broad or extended sense, such that ethical freedom is protected. At least typically, however, Dworkin designates with "religion" a set of cosmological and evaluative affirmations, such that ethical beliefs are included within the latter.[8] The right to religious freedom, then, is a special case of the more general right to ethical freedom (see 2006, 61); as a constitutional principle, if I understand correctly, the former should be so understood as to represent the latter. All have the right to equal respect and thus equal freedom from coercion as each judges "what kind of life would be successful for him" (2006, 10). To be sure, this does not mean freedom to exercise just any "profound convictions about life and its responsibilities" (2013, 117); were that the case, any citizen could justly claim exemption from any law or governmental ordering whenever her or his profound convictions are contrary to it. In contrast, the right to ethical independence is, in accord with Kant's principle, equally possessed by all citizens, and accordingly, "government may not constrain foundational independence for any reason except when this is necessary to protect the life, security, or liberty of others" (2011, 369). I must "shape my definition of my own responsibility ... so that it is compatible with a like responsibility among other people because their lives are of equal importance to mine" (2006, 70).

Although the issue of proper political policy generally is not the focus of discussion in this chapter, one should not assume from Dworkin's limits on governmental constraint that his general political theory is libertarian, at least in the sense that counsels a policy of laissez-faire. To the contrary, treatment of all with equal concern as well as respect entails, on his interpretation, government's responsibility for the availability and fair distribution of resources in the community—including a right to adequate health care and a certain measure of economic security (see Dworkin 2000, chapter 4; 2011, chapter 25; 2013, 130--31). Nonetheless, respect for personal ethical responsibility confines government to the "fair distribution of means," thereby leaving "the choice of ends to its citizens one by one" (2011, 356)—although he also allows governmental constraint to protect "natural or artistic treasures" (2006, 71) or "natural wonders" (2013, 131), for instance, "great forests" (2013, 130).

On Dworkin's proposal, then, constitutional protection for ethical freedom, of which the right to religious freedom is an articulation, means this: "Government must never restrict freedom just because it assumes that one way for people to live their lives—one idea about what lives are worth living just in themselves—is intrinsically better than another, not because its consequences are better but because people who live that way are better people" (2013, 130). The right to ethical independence "limits the reasons government may offer for any constraint on a citizen's freedom at all" (2013, 133). Elsewhere, he formulates a similar point in terms of the justification without which government may not restrict people's freedom: government is prohibited from any "*personally judgmental* justification," one that "appeals to or presupposes a theory about what kinds of lives are intrinsically good or bad for the people who lead those lives" (2006, 70). All constraint requires some or other "*impersonally judgmental* justification," whereby government does not violate the "personal responsibility ... people have" for "their own convictions about why their life has intrinsic importance and what kind of life would best realize that value for them" (2006, 71).

DWORKIN'S INTERPRETATION: A CRITIQUE

Dworkin argues vigorously that interpretation of political principles is a truth-seeking practice because evaluative beliefs can be true. In keeping with this conclusion, he calls Hume's principle "itself a moral principle" or "a thesis about moral responsibility" (2011, 99, 122). Hume himself, we might note, apparently did not agree. "In moral deliberations," he wrote, "we must be acquainted beforehand with all the objects, and their relations to each other, and from a comparison of the whole fix our choice or approbation." Nonetheless, Hume continues, the "great difference between a . . . [matter] of *fact* and one of *right*" means that "after every circumstance, every relation is known, the understanding has no further room to operate, nor any object on which it could employ itself. The approbation . . . which then ensues, cannot be the work of judgment, but of the heart; and is not a speculative proposition or affirmation, but an active feeling or sentiment" (Hume, 290). For Hume, the great difference between a matter of fact and one of right is itself stated as factual and thus is not a moral assertion—choosing itself being not understood but, rather, the work of sentiment. Still, Dworkin is appropriating the principle, and thus his accounting of its character need not follow Hume's own.

For Dworkin, in any event, *that* there are moral truths "is an obvious, inescapable fact"—and this because "external skepticism" about morality (2011, 24), "which claims to argue from entirely nonmoral assumptions," is impossible (2011, 26, 24). "Morality and other departments of value are philosophically independent" (2011, 24), such that every denial of moral truth is itself a moral claim or is internal to moral theory. He does not thereby assert that some difference between moral and immoral, or morally better and worse, must be true. "The independence thesis leaves you free to conclude (if that is what seems right to you) that no one ever has any moral duties or responsibilities at all" (2011, 99). But this is itself a moral assertion. Moral skepticism is, in other words, always "internal skepticism" because "itself a moral position" (2011, 88, 40).

Moral truth is obvious and inescapable, Dworkin argues, because humans ask how to decide. "When people have decisions to make, the question of what decision they should make is inescapable, and it can be answered only by noticing reasons for acting one way or another; it can be answered only in that way because that is what the question, just as a matter of what it means, inescapably calls for" (2011, 24). Accordingly, a refusal "to make any moral claim at all" (2011, 42) cannot be distinguished from the moral assertion that all possible choices are morally permissible. The former cannot be asserted "without contradiction" (2011, 43) because both answer in the same way the question people ask when a decision is at hand; "external skepticism . . . contradicts itself" (2011, 46).[9]

On my accounting, Dworkin's conclusion about external skepticism is correct. But I am unsure whether his argument for it is fully convincing. To the best of my reasoning, a denial of moral truth cannot be impossible unless the following response to his conclusion is self-contradictory: the question that he supposes people inescapably ask when a decision is at hand is a meaningless or senseless question. At least some theorists for whom supposed moral utterances can be neither true nor false might accuse Dworkin of assuming what he needs to show—namely, that asking for reasons to act (and thus presupposing moral truth) is a genuine question. No doubt, those who deny this assumption deny what Dworkin calls "the ordinary view" of people's decision-making (2011, 26) —and, indeed, deny what most people throughout history have understood themselves to affirm. Still, external skepticism cannot be self-contradictory because most people reject it.[10] Dworkin's conclusion is not critically secure, then, unless the question about reasons for decision is itself explicitly redeemed.

We may approach completion or, at least, confirmation of Dworkin's argument for moral truth through underscoring that a person's decision making is conscious. Choice within a range of specific possibilities is distinctively subjective because alternative ends or actions are understood—and the decision is not itself understood unless these alternatives are consciously compared *with respect to choosing*. If inclusive of the latter, in other words, the comparison cannot designate solely how differing specific possibilities are descriptively similar and different; the decision is not conscious unless, in addition, alternatives are compared with respect to it—and this understanding, which follows all descriptive comparison, is evaluative, whereby distinctively subjective decision asserts that its chosen alternative is good. If decision itself is conscious, Aristotle was right: all human activities "aim at some good" (Aristotle 1962, 1094a2).

To be sure, one might allow a descriptive comparison of alternatives and yet deny a conscious decision between or among them. As we have seen, Hume apparently advanced that accounting. "In moral deliberations . . . all the circumstances of the case are supposed to be laid before us, ere we can fix any sentence," but then "the understanding has no further room to operate" (Hume 1975, 290). Conscious comparison of alternatives is, in other words, solely factual; evaluative comparison is impossible, so that decision itself cannot be understood. This accounting is, however, problematic because it claims to be true of people's decision-making as such, that is, claims to state how every person relates to her or his alternatives for choice. As Hume himself recognized, some people may, in fact, deny this claim to truth; they may understand their approbation or disapprobation as if it were bound by some or other criterion in terms of which alternatives may be truly evaluated. For Hume, then, these people choose among their specific possibilities with a false understanding of their decision-making, because, in truth, choice cannot occur with understanding. But that supposed truth is itself an understanding of all decision-making. The descriptive comparison of alternatives having been completed, so that all circumstances are "laid before us," the supposed absence of consciousness from choice can only be an understanding of the alternatives with respect to choosing. This is confirmed by the claim to truth for this understanding, which implies that all decisions ought to be consistent with it or ought not to be consistent with any false understanding of one's decision-making. Hume's denial that choice is understood is, against itself, a certain understanding of choosing as such, namely, an evaluative understanding on which there is no moral difference between or among the alternatives; all are equally good, so that each is morally permitted.

On my reading, this was Kant's insight—and is why he denied that all imperatives could be hypothetical or why he affirmed an a priori condition of practical reason. Every assertion about how subjective decision as such chooses among its available alternatives is a putative moral principle, precisely because, having taken it to be true, one implies that all decisions ought to be consistent with it. But if, with Kant, a person's decision-making cannot avoid an evaluative understanding of one's alternatives, the question about reasons for choosing is not senseless. It is, to the contrary, inescapably asked by every person who decides, and she or he then answers with a putative moral assertion—and Dworkin's conclusion, namely, that external skepticism is impossible, is indeed correct.

I am concerned to complete or confirm Dworkin's argument in order clearly to establish what his own formulation implies: moral thinking is inescapable because the reality of moral truth is a transcendental feature of subjective decision-making. Thus, his argument against external skepticism as inconsistent with such decision-making is, even if it needs completion, a transcendental argument. Here, the term "transcendental" means a necessary feature of subjectivity as such, whereby every denial of a transcendental feature is pragmatically self-refuting; that is, every act of denial implies what is denied. I do not say that Dworkin himself concedes, much less explicitly endorses, the transcendental character of moral truth. Nonetheless, it follows directly, given his insistence that external skepticism is impossible or self-contradictory (see 2011, 43, 46). Indeed, having endorsed Hume's principle, Dworkin can call that principle itself a moral thesis and thus assert that interpretive thinking about objective values constitutes, with science, "an embracing dualism of understanding" (2011, 123) only because moral truth is a necessary feature of human subjectivity as such.

This conclusion is important because one now has every reason to ask: Can moral truth be a transcendental feature of human subjectivity if the moral law itself is not transcendental? Here, "the moral law" means the most general principle (or set of principles) in terms of which moral and immoral (or, if all alternatives are equally good, merely morally permissible) choices as such are defined. Hence, the question now is whether one can avoid Kant's conclusion, namely, that his groundwork to reasoning about morals can be "nothing more than the investigation and establishment of *the supreme principle of morality*" (Kant, 8). And the question is pertinent because Dworkin seems to say (*a*), with Kant, *that* there is moral truth is implied by subjective decision-making as such, but (*b*), against Kant, *what* obligations bind subjective decisions can be explicated only by interpretive thinking that cannot, in the end, avoid a "kind of circularity" (2011, 101) among contingently held beliefs or that appeals to something like reflective equilibrium.

Committed implicitly to point *a* by virtue of his argument against external skepticism, Dworkin is apparently committed to point *b* by his account of evaluative or interpretive thinking, which rejects Kant's transcendental argument for the moral law. In his own way, Kant himself accepted something like Hume's principle, even gave a rigorous argument for it, by separating theoretical and practical reason: no theoretical statement, that is, statement about what is or is not the case, implies or is implied by a practical statement about what ought and ought not to be the case—and this separation is required because theoretical statements are about appearances, while practical statements are about what reason requires of a noumenal will. The latter requirement, Kant argued, is defined by a transcendental law of practical reason—because a person's thought about her or his own action "finds itself compelled" to assume what cannot be known, namely, freedom of the will, and "on the hypothesis ... of freedom of the will, morality with its principle follows from it by mere analysis of the conception" (Kant 1949, 75, 64). For Dworkin, however, this account is inseparable from Kant's "obscure ... metaphysics" (2011, 19). Kant's arguments for what have become "very influential principles are comparatively weak ... and the theories of freedom and reason he offered are opaque to almost all of those who are drawn to those principles." Accordingly, Dworkin proposes "a way of reading Kant ... that tracks the method I propose to follow here" (2011, 265), by which is meant, presumably, Dworkin's account of evaluative or interpretive thinking without any transcendental principle.

If the presence of moral truth itself is, for Dworkin, a transcendental feature of subjective decision-making, one has reason to wonder whether his interpretive account of substantive moral assertions violates his own denial of any separation between meta-ethics and substantive ethics; "'meta-ethics' is a misconceived project" (2011, 166). Although I may misunderstand, he seems, against this denial, implicitly to separate the meta-ethical assertion that subjective decision-making as such is inescapably moral from substantive moral truths, all of which are nontranscendental and defensible only by way of interpretation (in Dworkin's sense). But whatever Dworkin intends here, reason commends, I believe, both his account of moral truth and his refusal to separate meta-ethics from substantive morality.[11] The presence of moral truth as a necessary feature of subjectivity as such implies, with Kant, a necessary moral law, an implication that becomes apparent when we consider its denial.

If all substantive moral truths are said to be nontranscendental—for instance, if (*a*) that there is moral truth is transcendental, is said to imply (*b*) what decisions are moral rather than immoral has no transcendental principle—then this character of all substantive moral truths must itself be transcendental and, moreover, this character of all substantive moral truths defines a substantive moral law. As noted above, every assertion about how subjective decision as such chooses among its available alternatives is a putative moral principle, precisely because its supposed truth implies that all decisions ought to be consistent with it. To say that all substantive moral thinking is nontranscendental—is interpretive (in Dworkin's sense) or seeks reflective equilibrium or is contextual—itself prescribes in completely general terms what practical thought ought always to be.

That assertion, in other words, prescribes the kind of thinking by which all decisions should be informed and thus a comparison of alternatives for choice with respect to choosing: alternatives ought always to be compared in terms of an interpretation of subjective decisions and thus of moral beliefs, all of which are contingently held. If, as my discussion of Dworkin's argument intends to show, the denial of moral truth is pragmatically self-refuting, so, too, is the denial of a transcendental moral law. Given that conclusion, it follows that something is problematic in Dworkin's account of moral interpretation—precisely because it denies any transcendental principle of moral and immoral decisions and proposes what he calls an integrated moral epistemology, any instance of which involves a circularity of contingently held beliefs.

The problem is betrayed, I think, in his description of success within the truth-seeking practice of a given genre, for instance, in moral and ethical thinking: "A particular interpretation succeeds—it achieves truth about some object's meaning—when it best realizes, for that object, the purposes properly assigned to the interpretive practice properly identified as pertinent." Dworkin also makes clear that interpretation within any genre is, if only implicitly, interpretation of the practice in question and, specifically, its purpose: "When we interpret any particular object or event, therefore, we are also interpreting the practice of interpretation in the genre that we take ourselves to have joined; we interpret that genre by attributing to it what we take to be its proper purpose—the value that it does and ought to provide" (2011, 131). But, then, the term "properly" in the description of success can only itself mean a successful interpretation, such that his description may be reformulated: "a particular interpretation succeeds—it achieves truth about some object's meaning—when it best realizes, for that object, the purposes successfully interpreted as those assigned to the interpretive practice successfully interpreted as pertinent." Something seems amiss when interpretive success is defined in terms of interpretive success, and the emptiness of this definition becomes the more apparent when we state the supposed achievement of truth with respect to the purposes of a given genre: "an interpretation of the purposes assigned to a particular practice succeeds when it realizes a successful interpretation of the purposes assigned to that practice."

As far as I can see, Dworkin cannot escape an empty account of success in moral interpretation. Still, some may find the indictment here too facile because, they might say, it has not given due credit to what, for Dworkin, an integrated or holistic epistemology requires. Interpretive success in a given genre—for instance, moral thinking—may indeed be defined in terms of interpretive success, but he means overall success, that is, "an integration of background values and concrete interpretive insights" (2011, 131) that has integrity. Interpretation "knits values together," and we are "morally responsible" insofar as we achieve "overall integrity," whereby each of our evaluative convictions "supports the others in a network of value that we embrace authentically" (2011, 101).

But this response assumes what it seeks to defend, namely, Dworkin's interpretation of interpretive success—because his account of integrated or holistic moral or evaluative thinking can be itself only an interpretation whose success depends on his account of integrated success. Indeed, Dworkin's general theory of interpretation must itself exemplify an interpretive genre, with his own circularity of contingently held beliefs—because he purports to explicate in a thoroughly general way (and thus, by implication, in service to values as such) the independent or separated character of thinking in service to values. Hence, all other genres of interpretation (for instance, the moral and ethical and literary genres) are more specific instances serving more specific values.[12] In other words, interpretation is, as he asserts, "interpretive ... all the way down" (2011, 131). If that is so, there is no reason why one ought to accept as successful his interpretation of how moral responsibility is rightly understood or what proper moral thinking requires. As Dworkin says, "faced with someone who holds moral opinions radically different from my own, I cannot count on finding anything in my set of reasons and arguments that he would be irrational not to accept" (2011, 100)—and because interpretation goes "all the way down," this includes Dworkin's reasons for interpreting moral responsibility in the way he does.

Thus, someone who chooses to be eclectic in the values she or he affirms, deciding now for some and then for others, such that mutual support is absent, may be, for Dworkin, morally irresponsible. Similarly, someone who chooses to pursue solely her or his own physical pleasures may, for Dworkin, violate both ethical and moral responsibilities. In either case, however, the indictment is, by the implications of Dworkin's own theory, purely tendentious. Evaluative interpretations whose success depends on a simultaneous interpretation of interpretive success, such that no interpretation can avoid the circularity of contingently held beliefs, can never be anything more than mere assertions of their proponents. Even the insistence that a set of beliefs, all of which are said to be contingently held, should be internally consistent fails to imply any substantive evaluative conclusions—because internal inconsistency can be avoided by refusing either of two contradictory but contingently held beliefs. In the end, there can be no reason why alternatives for decision ought to be evaluated in one way rather than another, and moral truth or objective value is, by implication, denied. It may not be too much to say that Dworkin's proposal for moral thinking results, by implication, in external skepticism. The proposal denies the moral truth it asserts.

This consequence is confirmed in Dworkin's own moral theory. Proposing a difference between ethics and morality, he derives obligations to other people from the affirmation of one's own intrinsic value or dignity: given the latter, one has no basis on which to avoid generalizing the affirmation of dignity to all humans.[13] "We have a responsibility to live well," and by Kant's principle, all persons have an equal responsibility. If we ask why this responsibility falls to us—or, as Dworkin says, "responsibility to whom?"—he answers: "We are charged to live well by the bare fact of our existence as self-conscious creatures with lives to lead.... It is *important* that we live well; not important just to us or to anyone else, but just important" (2011, 196). But that response is mere assertion, not a reason for ethical responsibility: our lives are said to be objectively important because self-conscious life is objectively important. We may again conclude, in other words, that Dworkin's refusal of a transcendental moral law reduces ethical and moral principles to mere assertions. This criticism, we should note, does not deny that "each human life has a special kind of objective value" (2006, 9), so that living well "is an idea ... we almost all accept in the way we live but that is rarely explicitly formulated or acknowledged" (2011, 196). At stake, rather, is whether such common agreement—or, more generally, what Dworkin calls "the ordinary view" (2011, 26) of human decision-making—betrays a human condition Dworkin's account denies.

Given success in the above critique, one might appreciate the Kantian dictum, nothing is "more fatal to morality than that we should wish to derive it from examples" (Kant 1949, 26), that is, to derive moral obligation without a necessary or transcendental law of practical reason. To the best of my reading, Dworkin does not consider the reasoning behind this dictum. Kant's point is this: the exercise of subjective freedom always decides for some or other supreme principle in terms of which specific alternatives are evaluatively compared, and no such given principle can define what reason requires (good or right decision as such) if another can be chosen without pragmatic self-refutation. Hence, practical reason merely asserts its evaluative understanding in the absence of a practical law reason cannot consistently deny. On my accounting, this is simply another statement—or at least an implication—of what I earlier called Kant's insight. Because every assertion about how subjective decision as such chooses among its available alternatives is a putative moral principle, no such principle can be more than merely asserted unless it is transcendental.

TOWARD AN ALTERNATIVE INTERPRETATION

If Dworkin's ethical and moral theory fails because it fails fully to appropriate Kant's insight, his proposal may nonetheless be called broadly Kantian in a significant respect. I have here in mind not simply what Dworkin calls Kant's principle; more generally, I refer to the nonteleological character of Dworkin's ethical and moral interpretation. Here, "nonteleological" designates a theory whose principles are said to be independent of any good by which subjective purposes in their entirety ought to be directed or in terms of which subjective purposes should be inclusively evaluated. I will call a theory whose principles are said to depend on or to include such a good—that is, an inclusive telos for subjective purposes—a moral teleology. In contrast, all nonteleological theories propose instead moral and ethical principles that define constraints on subjective purposes. These principles are roughly analogous to grammatical constraints on speaking. Grammatical rules do not tell one what to say; that one seeks to say something is assumed, and grammar only restricts success in saying it. In a similar way, nonteleological moral and ethical principles assume that subjects have ends they pursue and then evaluate purposes in one or more but not all respects. For Kant himself, moral in distinction from immoral decision is defined as treatment of all persons, including oneself, as ends in themselves, never merely as means—and this moral law, he is clear, evaluates subjective purposes in one respect. Regard for "every rational nature" as "*an end in itself*" constitutes "the supreme limiting condition of all our subjective ends" or our purposes (Kant 1949, 48). Thus, rational nature "as an *independently* existing end ... is conceived only negatively, that is, as that which we must never act against" (Kant 1949, 54).

For Kant, on my reading, nonteleology follows from the transcendental character of the moral law. Were moral teleology possible, he reasons, some state of affairs or character of existence would define a transcendental telos, that is, a good to be pursued that is implicitly affirmed by every possible exercise of practical reason, so that no person could act in pursuit of anything at all without simultaneously affirming this transcendental good. But, then, nothing whose realization would be empirical or logically contingent—for instance, cosmopolitan democracy (as a state of affairs) or the happiness of all humans (as a character of existence)—can be this telos. An exercise of rational freedom could act against any such end without pragmatic self-refutation; for instance, neither cosmopolitan democracy nor the happiness of all humans is affirmed as a good to be pursued if one acts in pursuit of, say, some racial supremacy. Hence, moral teleology is inseparable from some necessary state of affairs or character of existence; the moral law could be teleological only if all purposes in their entirety were directed by a good pursued by purposes as such and thus implicitly affirmed by every possible exercise of practical reason—a telos that is metaphysical in the strict sense.

But metaphysical knowledge in that sense is, Kant believes, impossible, and thus moral theory must be nonteleological. A telos defined by reality as such, which we may call a comprehensive good, was endorsed by many ancient and medieval theorists, for whom Aquinas may be taken as exemplary. On their view, subjective decision-making—and religious belief—imply a final cause or divine telos and thus a comprehensive good constituting all things. Given Kant's denial of this tradition, his first critique, the *Critique of Pure Reason*, is a negative condition informing his analysis in the second critique, the *Critique of Practical Reason*, thereby separating theoretical from practical reason.

Although Dworkin's dualism of intellectual activity is, in its own way, a similar separation, his explication of evaluative thinking does not, as far as I can see, entail a nonteleological theory of our obligations. Because his account of interpretation implies, against his own intentions, that theories of morality become the mere assertions of their proponents, there can be no implied character for moral theory provided by that account. My hunch is that Dworkin is led to nonteleology, notwithstanding his refusal of what he calls Kant's "obscure" or "opaque" (2011, 19, 265) transcendental arguments, because Dworkin seeks to interpret morality in a manner consistent with Hume's empiricism. In other words, Dworkin is broadly Kantian, I suspect, because he credits, perhaps unwittingly, Kant's reading of moral teleology as inseparable from a metaphysical (in the strict sense) good to be pursued, and credits Kant's supposed discrediting of the presupposed metaphysics—and, thereby, endorses Hume's empiricism.

Be that as it may, Dworkin's principles of ethical and moral responsibility are indeed nonteleological. The "principle of self-respect" prescribes for each person acceptance as "a matter of importance that his life be a successful performance rather than a wasted opportunity," and the "principle of authenticity" prescribes that "each person has a special, personal responsibility for identifying what counts as success in his own life" (2011, 203, 204). If these "offer a conception of human dignity" (2011, 204), Dworkin neither asserts nor implies a character to the good life for which all persons ought to strive. What "is crucial is ... that you live in response to, rather than against the grain of, your situation and the values you find appropriate," and thus "living well means striving to create a good life, but only subject to certain constraints essential to human dignity" (2011, 210, 195). The two principles (of self-respect and authenticity), then, set limiting conditions on appropriate ethical values or the purposes each person is permitted to elect. Given that moral obligations universalize and, in that way, are essential to one's own ethical responsibility, they, too, can only be constraints on one's decisions.

Because one is charged to live as an end in itself, one is constrained to treat all other persons as ends in themselves; one ought not to define success in one's own life in a way that violates the equal dignity of all other persons.

Indeed, Dworkin's nonteleology seems both to require and be required by his difference between ethics and morality. The difference is required because what he calls Kant's principle depends on one's ethical responsibility to live well; having foregone a moral law necessary to practical reason as such, Dworkin derives the equal dignity of all from, or as an aspect of, the affirmation of one's own. The reading of Kant "begins . . . with ethical demands that match the two principles of dignity we have now recognized" (2011, 265). At the same time, Dworkin's difference between ethics and morality clearly requires nonteleology. Were there a character to the good life for which all subjects ought to strive—in the sense that, say, Aristotle and Aquinas proposed—the objective value of that character would define a good by which all of one's purposes in their entirety ought to be directed. The difference between living well and obligations within the human community would then collapse because all purposes in their entirety would include one's purposive relations to other people. A proper meaning of dignity and any principles prescribing human interaction could only be applications of or somehow derived from the inclusive good or telos.

The theory would become, in other words, a moral teleology. This is not to say that all such teleologies assert, as Aristotle and Aquinas perhaps do, one's own good life as the telos by which all of one's purposes in their entirety ought to be directed. To the contrary, that telos may be something other than one's own flourishing, even while it provides the meaning of "good" in terms of which one's own good life or flourishing is defined—as, for instance, in the utilitarian prescription always to pursue the greatest pleasure or happiness of the greatest number. What remains common to moral teleologies, then, is authorization of all other prescriptions for subjective decision by the inclusive teleological prescription. Against any such theory, to be repetitious, Dworkin's proposal is broadly Kantian.

Accordingly, Dworkin, as all nonteleologists, assumes individuals with purposes and thus separates constraints upon them from their inclusive reasons or ends. To be sure, he argues, as some nonteleologists do not, for ethical as well as moral constraints on such purposes and, thereby, for an integration of ethics and morality. But the basic separation remains, and with nonteleologists generally, it implies the priority of constraints to purposes—and, in Dworkin's case, the priority of moral constraints to or within living well. In one formulation, Dworkin makes the point metaphorically: "Morality . . .

defines the lanes that separate swimmers. It stipulates when one must cross lanes to help and what constitutes forbidden lane-crossing harm. Ethics governs how one must swim in one's own lane to have swum well" (2011, 371).

The point is repeated with specific reference to our public life: "morality must be treated as prior to ethics in politics" (2011, 371). Justice is morality applied to politics, and the demands of justice limit each citizen's permissible conceptions of a successful life. "Governments have a sovereign responsibility to treat each person in their power with equal concern and respect" (2011, 321). Thus, the state may and, presumably, should constrain citizens' purposes when, but only when, "this is necessary to protect the life, security, and liberty of others" (2011, 369). Insofar, proper governmental constraint is articulated in the fundamental rights of all people. Government's moral authority to coerce its citizens may never be in violation of those rights, that is, the requirements of equal concern and respect "person by person" (2011, 330).

We are now in a position to consider specifically Dworkin's account of religious freedom, because that constitutional principle articulates, as noted above, one such fundamental right. On the common or conventional understanding, religions, at least typically, assert or imply a telos for all reality and thus a comprehensive good—or, as we may also say, assert a religious teleology. Dworkin's nonteleology protects such religious adherence as a fundamental right by separating the principles of justice from all religions. Because a political constitution itself purports to be an articulation of justice, he separates it from religious teleology and restricts the latter to purposes of the adherents in question or, in his sense, to ethical purposes that moral principles are designed to constrain. As a constitutional provision, then, freedom to affirm a religious teleology is itself understood on grounds explicitly and implicitly independent of any such affirmation—and we may state his reasoning summarily: justice is independent of moral teleology; religious freedom is a principle of justice; hence, the express meaning of religious freedom is independent of any religious teleology. Accordingly, Dworkin understands religious freedom not as a special right peculiar to religious beliefs but, rather, as a special case of the general right to ethical freedom, a right government is always bound to respect. "We must understand the moral right to religious freedom . . . as a right to ethical independence" (2013, 133), the right and responsibility "each person has" to exercise "his judgment about what kind of life would be successful for him" (2006, 10).

But this accounting is problematic for the following reason: the adherent of a religious teleology denies Dworkin's nonteleological distinction between ethics and morality—and, indeed, denies any account, constitutional or otherwise, on which justice is separated from an evaluation of purposes in their entirety. Any such adherent believes that principles of morality and justice can be derived only from the comprehensive good. Hence, the constitutional principle of religious freedom, if it means explicitly the right to ethical freedom, in Dworkin's or any other nonteleological sense, is not a principle any such religious adherent can consistently accept—because it explicitly denies what she or he affirms.

It follows that any citizen who affirms a religious teleology cannot consistently be a good citizen. In saying this, I take a democratic constitution to stipulate the process through which governmental decisions should be taken and, therefore, a process or practice to which all citizens as members of "we the people" should adhere. If a political constitution stipulates that justice is independent of religion, a citizen's constitutional adherence can only mean her or his affirmation of that provision. This is precisely the stipulation Dworkin attributes to religious freedom as a constitutional principle, whereby any citizen who affirms a religious teleology is constitutionally bound simultaneously and inconsistently to affirm the separation of justice from her or his religious conviction. In sum, Dworkin's proposed understanding of that principle does not protect the religious freedom of any such citizen. To the contrary, the constitution imposes an affirmation in contradiction to her or his religious belief.

To avoid that imposition, the constitutional provision for religious freedom cannot explicitly deny religious teleology—or, indeed, any moral teleology. Toward an alternative to this effect, I return to Dworkin's precept that constitutional rights should be so understood as to make sense of democratic ideals. When he argues for religious freedom as a special case of ethical freedom, his conclusion, I noted in passing, might also be formulated in the following way: the term "religious" in the constitutional principle of religious freedom should be interpreted in a broad or extended sense, such that what is (on his account) protected is ethical freedom. Similarly, I now propose another broad or extended understanding of "religious" in that principle—namely, the term designates any explicit conviction about the ultimate terms of evaluation and, as typically is the case with or the implication of such convictions, about the ground authorizing those terms. With Dworkin, this constitutional principle should be so interpreted as to include within the protected class what are commonly or conventionally understood to be religions—and at least some religions in that sense formulate explicit beliefs about the most fundamental terms of evaluation. The broad meaning of "religious," then, extends the class to include any explicit convictions about such ultimate terms.

Perhaps use of "religion" in this broad or extended sense will seem to some inappropriately artificial. We may then learn from Dworkin and borrow his typical formulation: given that "religious" designates in something like its common or conventional sense, religious freedom is a special case of a general right properly protected by a democratic constitution, namely, freedom with respect to one's explicit conviction about the ultimate terms of evaluation and (at least by implication) the ground authorizing those terms. Hence, a constitutive provision for religious freedom should be understood as representing the general right.[14] On this reading, religious freedom constitutes a political process in which differences at the fundamental level of evaluation are legitimate. Moreover, protection of this broad class is essential if democracy means popular sovereignty. Government by "we the people" is incomplete if either the constitution or the state is ever permitted to stipulate how any citizen should evaluate any actual or proposed political decision. To the contrary, each citizen must be sovereign over her or his conviction about the ultimate terms of evaluation.

If religious freedom is so understood, democracy is also defined as government by the way of reason. Given a political process in which all differences at the fundamental level of evaluation are legitimate, there is no principled way to reach common decisions, that is, to determine activities of the state, except through full and free discourse. Any other principle for uniting the political community delegitimizes at least some of the differences. Accordingly, this proposal presupposes that all religious convictions, in both the broad and common or conventional senses, are open to argumentative validation or invalidation. Moreover, the constitution properly implies the way of reason in this respect: its legitimation of all explicit convictions about the ultimate terms of evaluation implies that all citizens should adhere to the political practice of full and free discourse.

On this alternative, a democratic constitution in its entirety properly stipulates nothing more and nothing less than the framework within which all claims to justice, including those of the constitution itself, are open to contestation by any member of "we the people" and, when contested, require discursive redemption. We may call such proper provisions formative in character, in distinction from any substantive claim to justice. A formative framework is one explicitly neutral to all political disagreements because it requires only adherence by those who disagree to resolution by the way of democratic discourse—including, because this is a political process, to a stipulated institutional decision-making procedure through which activities of the state are maximally informed by the discussion and debate. In contrast, adherence to any substantive claim takes sides within some possible political disagreement—and if a substantive claim is stipulated in the constitution, all citizens as political participants can adhere to it only by profession of it, whereby a citizen cannot consistently contest the claim.[15]

A critic may now object that politics constituted by the way of reason imposes an alien affirmation on some religious beliefs and thus contradicts religious freedom. Adherence to resolution by discourse can only mean a pledge to argumentative assessment as proper to one's political claims, and this commitment is inconsistent with any religious conviction that claims to be suprarational or immune to rational validation or invalidation. I will not seek here to defeat this objection but, instead, try to circumscribe consideration of it in the following way: the criticism cannot succeed unless the question about ultimate terms of evaluation is itself suprarational, that is, answers are not open to assessment in discourse because some suprarational answer is the valid one. In that case, as far as I can see, legitimating differences at the most fundamental level of evaluation does not permit a principled form of politics; if such differences cannot be civilized through full and free discourse, the possibilities are exhausted by accidental agreement (that is, a modus vivendi) and force.

But given that all beliefs about the character of justice as such and its authorization answer a rational question, the way of reason imposes nothing on any citizen she or he does not self-impose in making a claim for some or other ultimate terms of evaluation. If all such beliefs are open to validation or invalidation by way of argument, every citizen who claims validity for a religious conviction (in both broad and common or conventional senses) pledges, even if unwittingly, the possibility of assessment in discourse. Assuming that constitutional stipulation of nonteleology cannot consistently affirm religious freedom, we can reach at least the following hypothetical conclusion: religious freedom is a coherent political principle if but only if the question whose answers are thereby protected is rational.

To be sure, constituting politics by the way of reason does not explicitly deny nonteleological moral theory. Accordingly, a defense of it might be offered by withdrawing its separation of justice from the constitutionally implied meaning of religious freedom. On this revision, in other words, Kant was indeed correct in separating morality from an inclusive or comprehensive good. But the nonteleological character of justice is now said to be one view—although in some or other articulation, the valid one—advanced within democracy's full and free political discourse, which also welcomes moral teleologies. The explicit constitutional meaning of religious freedom, then, is consistent with the way of reason, and nonteleology is the truth about ultimate terms of evaluation successful discourse will confirm and apply to activities of the state.

This revision (that is, affirming the way of reason), we should underscore, is not Dworkin's position. The explicit meaning of religious freedom as a constitutional provision is, on his proposal, the protection of ethical independence. To the best of my reading, therefore, he never speaks of this provision constituting the political community because a diversity of convictions about the general character of justice might then engage in full and free discourse, through which the truth about ultimate terms of evaluation might inform activities of the state. In that sense, he never speaks of religious freedom as a positive contribution to the political process. For him, to the contrary, the constitutional principle asserts a liberty the political process may never act against and thus expressly names only a negative constraint on all actions by the state. Moreover, all other nonteleological accounts of democracy with which I am familiar, whether they reaffirm Kant's ethics or are in some other way broadly Kantian, also call, at least by implication, the separation of justice from inclusive ends or conceptions of the good the express meaning of religious freedom.[16]

To the best of my reasoning, in any event, nonteleology as a theory about the ultimate terms of evaluation cannot be rationally defended. Because it defines principles as constraints or limiting conditions on purposes subjects are assumed to have, nonteleology evaluates those purposes morally and politically in some respect or respects but not in their entirety. As far as I can see, that account is self-refuting. If decision with understanding is moral because alternatives for purpose are inescapably compared with respect to choosing, what are compared are possible purposes as whole things—because one's purpose cannot be chosen in part. Hume, I believe, stated the obvious: "all the circumstances of the case are supposed to be laid before us, ere we can fix any sentence" (Hume, 290). If the alternatives are then evaluated in terms of one or more aspects but not as whole things, the decision also asserts, by implication, that differences between or among alternatives in the respects not compared are morally indifferent. But that implication is a *moral* conclusion, thereby presupposing another moral principle in terms of which alternatives for purpose are compared in their entirety. Nonteleological principles, in other words, imply what they deny.[17]

Because constraining principles must assume subjects having purposes as whole things, the problem in nonteleology may be restated with specific reference to religious freedom. Let us suppose, as the revision suggests, democracy constituted by the way of reason, so that nonteleology is one among many claims about justice to be assessed by "we the people." To place any such theory within the full and free discourse has the following consequence: those who advocate nonteleology must then assume another kind of evaluative thinking in human decision-making—a nonpublic kind of thinking about purposes in their entirety or what Dworkin might call thinking about the good life. Thereby, those advocates concede to adherents of teleological beliefs possible validation by this alternative kind of thinking. To be sure, nonteleologists will insist that, on their account, such nonpublic thinking is irrelevant to justice because entirely specific to various circumstances of differing individuals and groups and thus concerned with ethics rather than morality. But this assumes rather than demonstrates the truth of nonteleology. Thus, adherents of a religious or other teleology may call this account a begging of the question because nonteleologists can only stipulate the irrelevance to justice of the teleological kind of thinking they themselves must posit.

Precisely because nonteleology itself assumes purposes as whole things, in other words, it becomes incoherent if placed within the public discussion and debate. On its own account, its attempted success in that context would entail a denial of the presupposition essential to democracy as politics by the way of reason, namely, that differing convictions about the ultimate terms of evaluation answer a rational question. Indeed, the objection we previously reviewed against the way of reason is now in force: the constitution involves an alien imposition on at least some religious claims; democracy fails to legitimize them because claims for their religious teleologies do not, so a nonteleological theory asserts, pledge validation or invalidation through discourse. This critique, on my understanding, simply repeats in its own way the previous one, namely, that nonteleological evaluation of purposes presupposes another principle in terms of which purposes are evaluated in their entirety, so that nonteleology could not be convincing in a full and free discourse. Denial of that presupposed principle is the concession of nonpublic evaluative thinking about the good.

Dworkin and other nonteleologists are, I believe, clearly or inchoately aware of this problem: were they to propose a constitution that implies only a full and free political discourse, public reason would thereby be subverted by a nonpublic kind of thinking they themselves require. Accordingly, they typically treat religious convictions, at least in the conventional sense of religion, as immune to argumentative assessment and, as mentioned above, define the constitutional principle of religious freedom as explicitly separating justice from conceptions of the good or the good life. Given their nonteleology, these theorists have reason to define the constitution in that way, even if it, too, fails to provide a coherent account of religious freedom.

Nothing in this summary critique of broadly Kantian accounts intends to abandon Kant's insight and thus a transcendental moral law. Given his insight—and allowing that extended argument would sustain the critique of nonteleology—we may then draw one additional conclusion: if religious freedom is not a coherent political principle unless the question whose answers are thereby protected is rational, religious freedom is not a coherent political principle unless the transcendental moral principle is teleological. If coherent, in other words, the way of reason implies moral teleology. To be sure, the antecedent in this statement remains—because the argument here for moral teleology is negative; that is, it seeks to show that nonteleology is not consistent with religious freedom. Accordingly, the way of reason cannot itself be successfully defended absent a positive argument for a teleological moral principle and, moreover, a teleology by which popular sovereignty is itself authorized.

Even then, we should underscore, the teleology in question must be solely implicit in a constitution that provides religious freedom. The explicit or express meaning of this provision can only be the right to any conviction about the ultimate terms of evaluation in their pertinence to state activities one takes to be true. Moreover, the activities thereby determined can never include a governmental stipulation that any such conviction is true or false. As far as the constitution properly provides, a nonteleological theory of justice is, like any other, thoroughly legitimate—because religious freedom protects the sovereignty of each citizen over her or his explicit conviction about the general character of justice and its authorization. If government with religious freedom makes sense, however, it implies transcendental teleology. And if that teleology requires—as Kant, I think rightly, believed—a good that is metaphysical in the strict sense, religious freedom cannot be a coherent religious principle unless it implies a telos defined by the ultimate nature of things.

7

ON RELIGIOUS FREEDOM AND ITS FREE EXERCISE

Especially during the past half century, the relation of democracy to religious convictions and communities has been the object of a protean and notably enduring discussion in both the academy and the larger public. That a democratic constitution provides religious freedom is, more often than not, affirmed or taken for granted, and thereby attention is directed to how politics properly relates to the diversity religious freedom protects.

On virtually all such proposals, religions in the relevant sense at least include comprehensive human convictions, that is, convictions about human life as such and thus about the ultimate terms for evaluating human activities as such. The later work of John Rawls, for instance, includes religious convictions among what he calls comprehensive doctrines, which "in the limit" apply "to all subjects universally" and "to our life as a whole" (Rawls 2005, 13). Again, Jürgen Habermas accepts that a religion is a "totalizing form of faith," which a person "taps into performatively to nurture her whole life" (Habermas 2008, 127). For instance, the Christian religion asserts, as many have said, the so-called Great Commandment, prescribing love of God without reservation and love of neighbor as oneself, as the proper basis for all evaluation of human activity—even if these ultimate terms must be interpreted and specified to differing situations. More generally, the view that religions include comprehensive convictions and thus such ultimate terms is, on my reading, uncontested in recent discussion of democracy with religious freedom.

I, too, will assume that religious convictions are at least among those "fully comprehensive," in Rawls's sense, or "totalizing," in Habermas's sense—and will so assume because I mean by "ultimate terms of evaluation" those a person implicitly or explicitly affirms as the basis for evaluating all human (including political) activities.[1] On the whole, perhaps, the recent discussion has called comprehensive convictions religious only when human life as such is defined by its relation to a transcendent reality, something beyond the contingent things of this world, and when I focus on this meaning, I will speak of religions in the conventional sense. In any event, a religion's political relevance consists in the ultimate terms of evaluation it provides because the political issue concerns a principle or principles for uniting a political community, notwithstanding a constitutional legitimation of whatever convictions about such terms religious freedom protects.

For many US citizens, past and present, religious freedom also includes a special right to exercise one's religious conviction, where this means that religious activities should not be substantially burdened by, and thus should be exempt from, laws of general applicability unless exemption is overruled through a compelling state interest test. The 1993 Religious Freedom Restoration Act, passed by the US Congress and signed by President Clinton, expressly endorsed this reading of the US Constitution's free exercise clause and stipulated exemptions (at least from federal laws) accordingly. Based on that legislation, in 2014 the US Supreme Court granted to Hobby Lobby and other "closely held" corporations exemption from a particular insurance regulation stipulated by the 2010 Affordable Care Act. Although the merit of free exercise exemptions is controversial and the controversy complex, my principal purpose here is to discuss their relation to the meaning of religious freedom.

For reasons that will become apparent, however, the issue of such exemptions cannot be clarified without first marking the political significance of religious freedom. Accordingly, I will first propose that democracy so constituted is politics by the way of reason, that is, political decisions through full and free discourse among "we the people," together as equals, and thus among answers to the religious or comprehensive question in their pertinence to activities of the state.[2] But this initial proposal is only background for the analysis of free exercise exemptions—and given democracy so understood, I will then argue the following: if such exemptions are proper, they should be stipulated by statutory law rather than constitutional provision, and the activities so exempted are rightly limited to those prescribed by a given religious or comprehensive conviction only for its adherents, in distinction from prescriptions for citizens generally. These assertions are, I recognize, terse. I mean here merely to state summarily what the following discussion seeks to clarify and defend.

That discussion is also limited in the following way: this chapter considers religious freedom, including the possibility of free exercise exemptions, theoretically or philosophically and thus does not intend an interpretation of US constitutional or statutory law. Although I will, when apparently helpful, make reference to US politics, this account will not interpret the religion clauses of the First Amendment or the Religious Freedom Restoration Act. Still, my discussion and US politics have the following in common: both claim to be democratic, and neither claim can be valid unless democracy with religious freedom makes sense. I will propose its coherence, but doing so requires the background argument for politics by the way of reason. Also, I recognize that democracy may depend on social and cultural preconditions (for instance, sufficient economic provision for citizens generally), and I will assume that such required circumstances, if there are any, obtain.

RECENT THEORIES

On my reading, virtually all recent theories of democracy with religious freedom posit or assume the following: at least some comprehensive convictions are immune to public assessment; that is, their claims to validity cannot be (or cannot be fully) validated or invalidated by public reason or by argument. In the end, it is said, the warrant for any conviction of this kind can only be something historically specific—an authoritative person or event or tradition or, in some other way, a circumscribed context. Perhaps some theories confine such immunity to conventional religions (or some of them), even while including secularistic convictions within the class protected by a democratic constitution. Still, if any comprehensive conviction is beyond reasoned assessment, the entire class must be—and in many proposals is—so defined. This follows because democracy, all agree, constitutes government through public discussion and debate, and public reason cannot assess comprehensive convictions if the true one may be among those public reason cannot establish.[3]

Given this accounting, virtually all theories of democracy with religious freedom require an express constitutional separation of some or all political principles from the diversity in question.[4] In the measure such separation occurs, the convictions protected by religious freedom are privatized—and with the separation, virtually all these proposals endorse, to borrow an apt term from Rawls, an "overlapping consensus" (Rawls 2005, 134) among comprehensive convictions on at least some principles of democratic justice. This reading of the theoretical discussion—namely, that virtually all proposals advance at least some principles of justice independent of any conviction protected by religious freedom—begs for extended defense. But I seek here briefly to present another proposal as background for attention to free exercise exemptions and thus will, in lieu of that defense, only assert how, on my readings, certain prominent thinkers illustrate this common pattern.

On John Courtney Murray's interpretation, for instance, religious freedom protects only religious convictions in something like the conventional sense, and he then distinguishes the suprarational truth about eternity, which is available only through special revelation, from the natural law with which temporal affairs should be consistent and that is accessible to public reason. Hence, he separates political principles from religious convictions about our relation to eternity, even while all citizens can share an overlapping consensus on the natural law (see Murray 1960). For the later Rawls, in contrast, religious freedom protects all "comprehensive doctrines," some of which may be secularistic, but he isolates the political domain from them by an account of public reason (at least about the "basic structure") that is "freestanding" because all citizens can join an overlapping consensus on the historically specific principles characterizing a modern democratic culture (see Rawls 2005). Habermas and Ronald Dworkin affirm universal principles of the right that are separated from any all-inclusive conception of the good, so that citizens can join an overlapping consensus on the priority of justice to such goods (see Habermas 2008; Dworkin 2011).

Naturally, these asserted readings are, for some, misreadings. I assert them, however, only to provide context for this critical point: taking religious freedom to mean an express constitutional separation of any principles of justice from the convictions protected is incoherent. Because adherence to a religious or comprehensive conviction claims for it truth or validity, this adherence affirms that *all* principles of justice depend on that conviction; they could not otherwise be valid, and thus their derivation from some contrary conviction is, at least in some respects, fallacious. To claim truth for a prescription applicable to all human practice is to deny that prescriptions for any human practice can be independent thereof. Any such claim, in other words, contradicts dependence on an overlapping consensus because the latter requires adherents of a given comprehensive conviction also to claim truth for the following: some or all principles of justice do not depend on the given comprehensive conviction.

It is to the point, then, that political principles separated from any given such conviction also require adherents of it to assert that differences within the overlapping consensus make no difference to politics. Given Murray's account, for instance, opposition to, say, same-sex marriage that relies on some or other distinctively religious reasons (that is, the opposition depends on one's suprarational beliefs about eternity) makes no difference to politics in competition with the contrary position on such marriages that relies on some or other differing religious conviction—so long as both religious views overlap on appeal to rational and universal principles, that is, to the natural law. Given Rawls's account, the same or similar disagreement about same-sex marriage makes no difference to politics—so long as both comprehensive doctrines overlap on historically specific or freestanding public reason. For Habermas and Dworkin, differences among views of same-sex marriage that rely on differing comprehensive conceptions of the good make no difference to politics, given only that citizens overlap on the priority of justice to these conceptions. In any of these or other cases, a conviction about the terms for strictly all evaluation that makes no difference to some given evaluation is an internally incoherent conviction—because any comprehensive conviction for which a claim to truth is made is thereby said to make all the difference in determining all principles of evaluation.[5] Hence, if religious freedom requires the express constitutional separation of any such principles from the beliefs it supposedly protects, every comprehensive conviction is thereby delegitimized.

To be sure, pursuit of an "incompletely theorized" (see Sunstein 1993) consensus on some more or less specific political outcome, that is, an agreement diverse parties join for differing fundamental reasons, may often be a wise counsel to democratic citizens. The time and capacities of humans are limited, and special demands are involved if critical reflection turns to the most fundamental convictions. These facts are pertinent in politics, where often a common decision is required in the more or less short term. Given extensive and profound pluralism, citizens may be well advised in many situations of discourse to abstract from basic disagreements insofar as possible and to seek more specific values and purposes each takes to be authorized by her or his comprehensive conviction. But incompletely theorized agreement cannot be a successful theory of politics with religious freedom. Taking the wise counsel to constitute the democratic way simply presents another separation of political principles from the diversity of comprehensive convictions, whose adherents are then called to join an overlapping consensus.

POLITICS BY THE WAY OF REASON

Some such separation of principles from comprehensive convictions must be expressly provided, I have asserted, whenever an account asserts or assumes constitutional protection for at least some comprehensive convictions immune to validation or invalidation by public reason. Warrant for any one of them, then, can only be some historically specific authority or justification. If all such separations are unsuccessful, democracy with religious freedom cannot be coherent unless that assertion or assumption is denied. I propose, then, that comprehensive convictions answer a rational question, that is, a question whose answers can be validated or invalidated in discourse. On this proposal, warrant for the true answer is not circumscribed by some special revelation or given tradition or context but, rather, includes thoroughly common human experience—although what is common to human experience may be understood only implicitly or inchoately, so that it may also be misinterpreted or denied.[6] Thereby, all humans have a common basis for assessment of comprehensive convictions by public reason.

With Rawls and others, a broad class of comprehensive beliefs is thereby constitutionally protected. The rational question asks for the character and ground of justice as such, and religious freedom, I propose, legitimizes all explicit convictions about the ultimate terms of evaluation—and thus the ultimate terms of political evaluation—and their ground. Any such conviction is legitimate in the sense that no citizen who decides for or adheres to it violates the constitution.[7] On this proposal, the term "religious" in "religious freedom" should be understood in a broad or extended sense, such that it designates inclusively the class of explicit comprehensive convictions or what Rawls calls comprehensive doctrines.[8] They answer a rational question, then, because they assert for humans differing explications of the encompassing truth about self-conscious life, including its proper commitment or orientation in practice, that all humans implicitly understand. All humans are, we can say, after the same thing, namely, to exist authentically, that is, to live without duplicity in that encompassing truth of which all are at least inchoately aware. As explications, the convictions religious freedom protects are for humans putative re-presentations of this truth. Each seeks to present again the ultimate terms of evaluation and their authorizing ground that are implicitly present to all people, and any such re-presentation claims to be important as an aid to decisions consistent with human authenticity.

Because any such conviction may be in greater or lesser measure a misinterpretation of common human experience, the point of validation or invalidation in political discourse is to determine the true terms for all political evaluation so that each activity of the state may be consistent with them. Given that comprehensive convictions answer a rational question, moreover, religious freedom is essential to democracy, at least if the latter is constituted as popular sovereignty. "We the people" can be the final ruling power only if each citizen is sovereign over her or his evaluation of every political claim; that is, she or he is free from any governmental stipulation with respect to political evaluation. Accordingly, each citizen must be free to endorse and advocate any ultimate terms of evaluation and their authorization she or he finds convincing—and thereby must be sovereign over her or his comprehensive conviction. All such convictions must be insofar legitimate.

Absent possible assessment of these convictions by public reason, in other words, popular sovereignty is impossible. If political contention at the most fundamental level of evaluation is immune to reasoned adjudication, conflict based on that disagreement cannot be civilized, since there is nothing more fundamental to which common appeal might be made. For conflicting parties, the only remaining alternatives are the accidental agreement of strategic aims (a modus vivendi) and force. In contrast, the potential for argumentative validation or invalidation of the most fundamental terms for evaluation allows "we the people," each of whom is sovereign over her or his assessment of every political claim, to unite as equals in a full and free political discourse.[9] Public reason is then defined by the comprehensive question in its pertinence to activities of the state—or, again, democratic government is constituted by the way of reason.[10]

Some may object that certain answers to this question, perhaps found especially among conventional religions, claim to transcend rational assessment, and thus the way of reason is in truth an alien imposition on adherents of those convictions, contradicting their legitimation. As discussed earlier, many democratic theories credit the claim and thus separate some or all principles of justice from whatever religious freedom is said to protect. But whether the way of reason is an alien imposition depends entirely on whether the question comprehensive convictions answer is or is not rational. The issue is not whether some answers *claim* to be validated by authority or tradition or specific context but, rather, whether they can be assessed in public discourse. If so, every citizen who claims truth for her or his religious or comprehensive conviction thereby pledges its redemption by reason, and the constitution imposes nothing on any citizen she or he does not self-impose in making the claim politically.[11]

If the relevant question is rational, constitutional provision for religious freedom is, we can say, itself religiously free because its stipulation is authorized by the pledge given politically when one claims truth for any answer. The way of reason, then, excludes no such conviction unless the comprehensive question is not rational. In that event, all answers are delegitimized because no answer can be assessed in public discourse, and government by "we the people" is, as mentioned, impossible. I will henceforth assume and thus not further defend the democratic possibility. Nonetheless, convictions about the ultimate terms of evaluation said to be suprarational are included within the class legitimized by a democratic constitution, and those who so believe are invited to argue for their claim, even if no argument of that kind can be successful.

Further, the way of reason protects comprehensive convictions on which popular sovereignty is said to be immoral or unjust. A democratic constitution requires that members of "we the people" adhere to it only in the following sense: they are to act in accord with, as distinct from endorse or profess, full and free political discourse. Hence, whether democracy can be vindicated and should be maintained are themselves questions to which "we the people" may seek the right answer and decide accordingly. In other words, constitutional stipulation that democracy accords with justice would contradict religious freedom, which grants to every citizen sovereignty over her or his assessment of every political claim, including a claim for "democracy is a just form of politics." Indeed, were that governmental form itself immunized against contestation, the political discourse could not establish what answer to the comprehensive question is true. The constitution would then confine comprehensive convictions to those consistent with democracy, but a discourse among those holding a specific class of such beliefs cannot establish which one is true unless it can establish that a true belief is within that class.[12] The question of whether the common character of the class is best—in this case, of democracy in distinction from, say, aristocracy or monarchy—is answered by mere stipulation.[13] Consider a discourse about which Kantian moral theory is true that cannot ask whether the true moral theory is Kantian.[14] If popular sovereignty seeks the true ultimate terms of political evaluation, all possible answers to the comprehensive question must be insofar legitimate.[15]

To be sure, a democratic constitution *implies* that democracy accords with justice, even as it also implies that comprehensive convictions answer a rational question. But these implications cannot be constitutionally stipulated because, if they were, they could not be contested within the full and free political discourse. To the best of my reasoning, then, the constitution of popular sovereignty properly stipulates no more and no less than (1) the rights that belong to each member of a political community as a potential and sometimes actual participant in discourse among "we the people," and (2) the institutions and associated practices of a decision-making procedure, so designed that the discourse maximally informs governing activities. So understood, a democratic constitution is, I will say, properly formative in character; that is, citizens as political participants can explicitly adhere to its prescriptions without professing them and thus without thereby taking sides in any possible political disagreement, including disagreement about whether the constitutional prescriptions themselves are morally valid.[16] As far as I can see, the one commitment explicitly neutral to any political disagreement, even disagreement about whether democracy accords with justice, is the commitment to debate or argument as the way to validate political claims. Thus, the rights of all citizens to equal membership in "we the people" and thus to freedom of speech and equal protection of the laws are properly included (although they do not exhaust) the rights stipulated by a formative constitution.[17]

So understood, formative prescriptions are distinguished from the substantive principles, laws, and policies for the political order, that is, prescriptions to which no citizen as a political participant can adhere without professing and thus explicitly taking sides in some possible political disagreement. A substantive law, in other words, stipulates something other than commitment to full and free discourse as the way to validate political claims. For instance, a prohibition on the manufacture, sale, and transportation of intoxicating liquors or a law restricting marriage to heterosexual couples is a substantive prescription. Adherence to either as a political participant is a profession of it and thus takes sides against those for whom it is unjust. Hence, neither should be constitutionally prescribed because, if it were, all political participants would be required to profess it, in contradiction to the sovereignty of each over her or his conviction about the ultimate terms of political evaluation. This contradiction becomes the more apparent, perhaps, if the constitution stipulates a religious or comprehensive conviction.[18]

To the contrary, then, religious freedom requires that substantive laws and policies should never be constitutionally provided and ought always to be statutory. To be sure, the obligations of citizens include (setting aside here the possibility of civil disobedience or rebellion) adherence to substantive laws and policies—but never as political participants. Citizens within the full and free political discourse are never bound to profess any such law or policy. Accordingly, statutory law should be constitutionally prohibited from teaching or supporting the teaching that any comprehensive conviction is true or is false because such activity would stipulate something about the ultimate terms of justice and, thereby, obligate citizens as political participants. It also follows that substantive laws should be limited to nonpolitical activity. They may regulate economic interaction, provide for education, require support for the state, relate the society to other societies, and so forth. But this legislated order of action and association may never expressly prescribe or proscribe any political evaluation.[19] In so doing, the government would violate the right of each citizen to assess all political claims. Summarily stated, then, religious freedom requires that substantive laws be statutory, noncomprehensive, and nonpolitical. Otherwise government, which is responsible to "we the people," would insofar stipulate their assessment of it.

On this account, no principle of justice, constitutional or otherwise, is separated from what is legitimized by religious freedom. To the contrary, the entire point of full and free political discourse is to clarify the true comprehensive conviction that authorizes both constitutional provisions and governmental activities. If we assume democracy's vindication, moreover, we can say that every citizen has a formative right to substantive justice, although the character of substantive justice cannot be constitutionally provided. The enduring full and free discourse seeks to mark the truth about ultimate terms of political evaluation in order that each substantive political decision may be consistent with them even while no such decision violates formative constitutional principles. Every democratic decision, then, will imply some or other ultimate terms of evaluation, and when the discourse has been successful, these will include the true conception of justice as such.

But if governing activities always imply some or other comprehensive conviction, this does not prevent them from being *explicitly* neutral to everything protected by religious freedom. Explicit neutrality is precisely the sense in which the pledge to argumentative assessment is the one commitment that does not take sides in any political disagreement. Moreover, explicit neutrality is what religious freedom must mean if the point of government by the people is to exemplify in laws and policies the true ultimate terms of evaluation and thus the character of justice as such. It then follows that explicit claims to truth for some or other understanding of those terms belong only within the discussion and debate among "we the people"—and this is just to repeat that substantive governmental prescriptions should never include teaching that any comprehensive conviction is true or is false and thus never prescribe or proscribe any political evaluation.

FREE EXERCISE EXEMPTIONS

Reading through the way of reason the terse opening of the First Amendment to the US Constitution—"Congress shall make no law respecting an establishment of religion, or prohibiting the free exercise thereof"—one might see in the previous section a long gloss on the first or nonestablishment clause, with the understanding that "religion" designates any comprehensive conviction and the ultimate terms of political evaluation it includes. Once this extended meaning of "religion" is in place, however, the foregoing might be seen to gloss the two clauses together. This could follow because "religion" and "religious" are so often assumed to designate in the conventional sense, as they doubtless did for framers and ratifiers of the First Amendment. If religious establishment in that sense is excluded by the first clause, it would, taken by itself, permit the state to teach or support the teaching of some nonreligious or secularistic comprehensive conviction. The free exercise clause, then, denies such permission by stipulating that religion is legitimate. Given the conventional meaning of "religion," in other words, the two clauses together, if read through the way of reason, prohibit the establishment of any comprehensive conviction and thus constitute the sovereignty of the people.

In US history, however, many have seen another meaning in the free exercise clause, namely, that religious activities cannot be substantially burdened by laws of general applicability unless so required by a compelling state interest that cannot be served in a less restrictive way. A free exercise claim in this sense was considered by the US Supreme Court in *Employment Division, Department of Human Resources of Oregon v. Smith* (494 U.S. 872 [1990]), which concerned the ritual use of peyote, a drug prohibited by the state of Oregon, by employees of that state in their Native American Church. Without invoking a compelling governmental interest, the Court denied the claim, finding that a state may accommodate religious practice contrary to generally applicable statutes but has no constitutional obligation to do so. Subsequently and in response, Congress passed and President Clinton signed, as mentioned earlier, the 1993 Religious Freedom Restoration Act, which stipulated free exercise exemptions (at least from federal law) under the conditions noted above—and based on this legislation, the Supreme Court, in *Burwell v. Hobby Lobby* (573 U.S. ___ [2014]), granted an exemption to the owners of Hobby Lobby and other "closely held" corporations from a certain requirement of the 2010 Affordable Care Act because those owners objected on religious grounds to certain contraceptive methods. In the Court's ruling, the government had ignored a less restrictive way to realize its interest (compelling or not) in providing contraceptive coverage for relevant women employees.

If democracy with religious freedom is incoherent except as government through full and free discourse, current debates about how generally applicable laws relate to religious activities counsel attention to what the way of reason implies for this issue. The matter is complicated because, as recent US discussion confirms, questions of free exercise exemptions may be asked about either constitutional or statutory law, and the way of reason may imply differing conclusions depending on which kind of law is in question. At the outset, however, one implication is clear: any exemption from generally applicable laws properly given to activities protected by religious freedom must apply to all convictions about the ultimate terms of evaluation. Were the exemption reserved for conventionally religious convictions, the state would take sides among answers to the comprehensive question, teaching that some answers merit special privileges. Thereby, the government would violate the neutrality it must evidence in order that all members of "we the people" may be together as equals in the democratic discourse. Denying free exercise exemptions to secularistic convictions is, Justice John Paul Stevens rightly wrote during a concurring opinion in *Boerne v. Flores*, "a 'law respecting the establishment of religion' that violates the First Amendment" because religious belief is thereby given "a legal weapon no atheist or agnostic can obtain" (*Boerne v. Flores*, 507 U.S. [1977] at 536--37).

Given that religious freedom implies the way of reason, I doubt that a constitutional provision for free exercise exemptions is permitted. As noted earlier, however, a widely held interpretation of the US Constitution asserts to the contrary. That fact commends asking whether any consideration, consistent with the way of reason, might support the provision. Its most compelling defense, as far as I can see, is this: protection for free exercise exemptions is implied by religious freedom and thus by popular sovereignty. If "we the people" are the final ruling power, freedom to choose ultimate terms of evaluation for the sake of public advocacy and assessment is useless absent a citizen's further opportunity to cultivate the orientation she or he has elected—and to do so in a way that informs more or less specific political evaluations.

In the present context, I use "cultivation" to mean the process through which one masters a comprehensive conviction—that is, increasingly attests, embodies, and becomes practically competent in relation to it. Such cultivation is, at least typically, a requisite preparation for participation in public discourse and hence for the generally applicable laws consequent on it. Moreover, the argument continues, this process of cultivation requires activities, typically within a community of like-minded people, through regular engagement in which each adherent more thoroughly believes or enacts the conviction and, thereby, becomes proficient in living and judging accordingly. Thus, the constitutional provision for religious freedom implies a corresponding freedom to cultivate comprehensive convictions.

Something like this implication, I mean to say, offers the strongest basis for why free exercise exemptions should be constitutionally provided. Still, whatever force the reasoning has does not, I think, warrant the conclusion. Religious freedom, on which the supposed provision depends, means that democracy's constitution should be entirely formative. The constitution should be explicitly neutral to all possible political disagreement, even disagreement about the justice of democracy as a form of political community. Only thereby is popular sovereignty constituted. Hence, constitutional provisions define a democratic ethic of citizenship no political participant is required to profess, even if all political participants should act in accord with it. The affirmation of free exercise exemptions constitutionally does not, to the best of my understanding, conform to this formative understanding, as I will now try to explain.

Because implied by democracy with religious freedom, a constitutional provision for such exemptions makes sense only given an explicit constitutional endorsement of democracy. But democracy itself cannot be vindicated by the democratic constitution. To the contrary, the latter stipulates a full and free discourse inclusive of citizens who advocate monarchical or aristocratic or, more generally, nondemocratic forms of government. In other words, constitutional provision for free exercise exemptions would depend on a substantive constitutional stipulation, namely, that democracy accords with justice. Thereby, all citizens would be required to profess popular sovereignty or to take sides in a possible political disagreement, namely, about whether popular sovereignty is morally valid, and the formative criterion would be violated.[20]

It then follows that constitutional provision for the exemptions in question is itself substantive and would also require all citizens to profess that very provision. If the constitution explicitly endorses democracy, any other constitutional provision dependent on that endorsement would also be substantive and could only be professed. Given a constitutional provision for free exercise exemptions, then, the ethics of citizenship would include taking sides against, say, democratic Kantians for whom the priority of morality and justice to ideals of the good life is unqualified. More widely, adherence to that provision would disagree with any citizen for whom generally applicable statutes, having constitutionally legitimate purposes approved by the people or their elected officials, should be obeyed by all members of the community, even if those laws have unfortunate but unintended effects on the cultivation of certain comprehensive convictions. Dissent from a constitutional provision for free exercise exemptions would, in other words, be illegitimate, and determination of its justice or injustice would not be accountable to the people.

Moreover, the supposed right to cultivate one's comprehensive conviction points toward a more general substantive issue in democratic politics. For many thinkers, equal membership in "we the people" is hollow or worthless unless citizens have the capacities needed to be active within the political process—and, plausibly, those capacities require not only cultivation of one's comprehensive conviction but also a certain measure of other economic and social resources, including education. Given that something like this argument is sound, it follows that a democratic constitution implies whatever political support is needed to ensure for all the worth of their citizenship. Accordingly, some have proposed that rights to these capacities or what they require should be stipulated constitutionally.

But what substantive conditions democratic participation requires is open to political disagreement within the discourse, even among citizens who are patriotic, that is, who do profess democracy. In fact, convictions range from severely libertarian to severely socialist ones and, in any event, could do so. Accordingly, a formative constitution cannot properly stipulate for all citizens any relevant such conditions, including the freedom to cultivate one's comprehensive conviction. As mentioned above, citizens have a formative right to substantive justice, but the character of substantive justice should not be defined by the constitution. To be sure, its own moral authorization is *implied* by a formative constitution. But it can only *anticipate* that full and free political discourse will continually vindicate popular sovereignty itself and will, at least in sufficient measure, result in laws prescribing for all citizens whatever substantive conditions equality in the political process requires. If government is indeed "by the people," everything depends on the people.

Reading the U.S. Constitution through this account of religious freedom leads one to agree with the decision in *Employment Division v. Smith* (494 U.S. 872 [1990]): the First Amendment does not provide a right to free exercise exemptions from generally applicable laws.[21] The above arguments for excluding such exemptions from a formative constitution may, I recognize, seem flawed or at least recondite. Even if the reasoning is sound, however, its conclusion leaves entirely open whether exemptions for the relevant activities, if they pass a compelling state interest test, should be provided by statutory law. Citizens as political participants are not bound to profess a substantive statutory law; to the contrary, its merit is subject to their ongoing evaluation of it in the political discourse. I have in mind here not only specific exemptions provided by some or other specific law, such as release for conscientious objection from a law mandating military conscription, but also a statute prescribing nonspecific free exercise exemptions, such as the Religious Freedom Restoration Act.[22]

A law stipulating a nonspecific right of this kind is the focus of the following discussion. Such a law might be enacted because "we the people" are persuaded that one's constitutional right to choose a comprehensive conviction implies the right to cultivate it. I will not seek to assess whether a law of that kind is convincing. In fact, however, statutes stipulating this right do exist in the United States, and their presence raises another question, which remains even for those who defend a constitutional rather than statutory provision of these exemptions: If religious activities that pass the compelling state interest test should not be substantially burdened by generally applicable laws, what activities are thereby exempted?

These activities cannot be just any prescribed by a comprehensive conviction because it provides terms for evaluating *all* human activities. To prescribe comprehensively is to deny that prescriptions for any human activity can be independent thereof.[23] If all politically relevant prescriptions dependent on a conviction protected by religious freedom were grounds for a free exercise claim, any citizen whose comprehensive conviction prescribes contrary to any generally applicable law could indeed claim exemption from it, at least if she or he takes the law's burden on that conviction to be substantial. Given that something like the Religious Freedom Restoration Act is so interpreted, in other words, any given statute save those in pursuit of some compelling state interest could be inapplicable to citizens who dissent from that law.[24]

If religious freedom implies the way of reason, however, the sovereignty of each citizen over the ultimate terms of evaluation is legitimized in order that generally applicable laws may be determined through a full and free political discourse and thus may, insofar as possible, be consistent with the true comprehensive conviction. This constitutional provision would be betrayed if each law applies only to citizens who, the compelling state interest test aside, agree with the given statute, or, at least, do not consider their comprehensive convictions substantially burdened by it. In contrast, a democratic constitution provides a different direction for dissent. Absent a basic constitutional change, popular sovereignty allows the ruled to be rulers, such that any who contest a given law are not required as political participants to profess it. Their membership in "we the people" is protected, and through the democratic process they may seek the law's repeal. Hence, providing by statute a right to free exercise exemptions cannot be consistent with democratic politics unless the relevant activities are in some way circumscribed.

Thus, the question returns: What activities might a statute stipulating that right exempt from generally applicable laws? We may approach an answer by recurring to the public assessment of comprehensive convictions. As previously discussed, democracy is possible because citizens, each of whom is sovereign over her or his evaluation of every political claim, have a common basis for assessment of their comprehensive differences, namely, their common human experience of, as we have called it, human authenticity. Religious freedom protects differing explications of that experience, each of which seeks to re-present the encompassing truth of which all humans are already aware, and true explications are important because they aid decision in accord with the encompassing truth about human life.

CONVICTIONS AND CONFESSIONS

This account, we should now add, implies that each such decision is complex, inclusive of two kinds. On the one hand, we humans take within the particular circumstances of our particular lives more or less specific decisions based on more or less specific understandings of the good—choices occurring in relation to private life or more intimate relationships or larger associational patterns—and each explication of human authenticity includes a conception of the good that is meant to aid deliberations about all of those specific decisions. On the other hand, each specific decision occurs through another at the innermost or implicit level of one's life with understanding, an encompassing decision for or against the authenticity of which we are always aware, and each explication of human authenticity is meant to aid this innermost, encompassing choice. These two kinds of decisions are inseparable because they influence each other. Choice for or against the encompassing truth informs the evaluation of specific alternatives, and a specific decision implies the decision about encompassing worth.[25]

That innermost decision to live in or against the encompassing truth is, we may say, for a person's comprehensive self-understanding, and the explication of a comprehensive conviction may include prescribed activities meant to aid that decision by mediating the given account of living in the truth. When activities of this kind occur, the explication typically takes the form of mediating symbols, including symbolic practices—and attention to or engagement in such expressions is prescribed in order to help evoke or persuade comprehensive self-understandings in accord with the given conviction. Toward clarifying this point, it will be useful to distinguish the content of a comprehensive conviction from the particular cultural formation of signs and symbols (that is, the language, including its metaphors and images, and the symbolic practices) with which a given individual or group cultivates its conviction about human authenticity. I will reserve the term "comprehensive conviction" for the content of any such supposed re-presentation of the encompassing truth and thus for what claims to be rightly affirmed by all humans. On this usage, in other words, two or more individuals or associations that participate in differing cultural formations may nonetheless affirm the same comprehensive conviction. In contrast, I will speak of a "comprehensive confession" when I mean the particular cultural formation that marks how a comprehensive conviction is re-presented by a given individual or group.

Religious freedom, then, which legitimizes all comprehensive convictions, protects all comprehensive confessions, and the moral and political prescriptions authorized by a conviction are also authorized by any confession of it—so that, with respect to political laws and policies, the difference between the two is insofar inconsequential. Still, individuals and groups may adhere to their comprehensive confession because its cultural formation is given by or derives from a particular person or historical context taken to be a decisive disclosure of the encompassing truth about human life. Moreover, the difference between a comprehensive conviction and its confession is important because mediating symbols, including symbolic practices, belong to a confession. The confession and its mediating expressions are inseparable because the expressions are born with what is taken to be the decisive disclosure.

The purpose of attention to or engagement in mediating expressions is, I will say, a confession's direct—rather than indirect—cultivation. When the distinct activity prescribed by a given such confession is for its mediation (or is necessary to such mediation), the cultivation is direct; for instance, the worship of a religious community (or as necessary thereto, the provision of a place where the community gathers for worship and the teaching that enhances understanding of what worship mediates) directly cultivates. When the distinct activity prescribed by the confession is for something else, the cultivation is indirect; for instance, the advocacy of political laws and policies prescribed by the confession indirectly cultivates it. Hence, activities of direct and indirect cultivation may be distinguished as those whose distinct purpose is, on the one hand, to aid decision for a comprehensive self-understanding and, on the other, to aid some or other specific decision. This distinction is effective even if that specific decision is about what explication of human authenticity to affirm (as, for instance, when discourse asks about the true comprehensive conviction or when one is deciding in what community of worship to participate). Moreover, the concept of direct cultivation provides the limitation on activities for which free exercise exemptions might properly be claimed—as I will now seek to clarify.

Given the way of reason, the symbols, including symbolic practices, through which an individual or association directly cultivates a comprehensive conviction is not the same as the conviction's content thereby given mediating expression. Mediating expressions are one thing, the conviction about human authenticity thereby mediated is something else. The conviction claims to explicate the truth present in common human experience and thus to prescribe (or to authorize prescriptions) universally. Hence, the prescriptions claim to be valid for all members of the political community. Mediating expressions are dependent on some particular person or historical context—and, accordingly, the relevant prescriptions for adherents of that confession need not make or imply any such universal claim. For instance, the activities of baptism and the eucharist prescribed for Christians are mediating practices born with the response to Jesus and may be distinguished from the conviction about ultimate purpose and thus the ultimate terms of evaluation mediated through the Christian confession—and that conviction can be publicly explained and advocated without essential reference to those activities.

Accordingly, those who directly cultivate a given comprehensive confession have reason to allow that another individual or association of citizens may directly cultivate the same conviction through symbols dependent on some other historical context—and no such expressions can rightly claim to be indispensable for mediating a true account of human authenticity. Direct cultivation, in other words, permits adherents of a given confession to distinguish prescriptions for their own mediation from the conviction about human authenticity they claim to be prescribed (or to authorize prescriptions) for all humans. If Christians, to focus further on this example, claim truth for what is disclosed in Jesus as the Christ and mediate this understanding through participation in Christian worship and other activities dependent on the response to him, common human experience of the encompassing truth allows recognition that others may mediate the same conviction through expressions dependent on a differing historical context. Hence, activities prescribed by Christianity for the sake of direct cultivation cannot rightly claim exclusivity. Even if the Christian conviction about human authenticity is true, Christians have reason to distinguish activities through which they mediate that conviction from their advocacy of laws and policies prescribed by their religion for the political community. Through the latter activities, their religion is indirectly cultivated.

Democracy has an interest in the mediation of comprehensive confessions whenever adherents of any given one allow that other confessions may directly cultivate the same account of human authenticity: this proviso at least implies that every comprehensive conviction is open to validation or invalidation by reasons appealing to common human experience. With the proviso, we can say, the claim to truth for the conviction a given comprehensive confession mediates occurs with a religious or comprehensive reservation, that is, an affirmation of fallibility and, therefore, a pledge to public assessment. In contrast, any citizen whose claim to truth for her or his religious or comprehensive conviction appeals solely to some specific authority and thus to some historical disclosure denies common human experience of authenticity and thus denies the possibility of public assessment. Thereby, this citizen implies that no human has access to the encompassing truth except through the same historical context—so that all direct cultivation of that truth occurs only through the same mediating expressions.

Here, then, is a proposal for the activities that might be exempted from generally applicable laws: the relevant activities are those through which adherents of a given comprehensive confession directly cultivate it. This is because dissent, even conscientious dissent, is not itself proper grounds for exemptions from a legitimate enactment (a comprehensive conviction warrants evaluation of all political claims). Such mediating activities may be distinguished from political advocacy as follows: when a given comprehensive confession prescribes only for its adherents (as may occur, for instance, with a prescription for worship in a religious community or for what is necessary thereto), the prescribed activity is a candidate for a free exercise exemption; when a given comprehensive confession prescribes laws or policies for the political community, the advocacy of them is not a candidate for a free exercise exemption.

Or again, we may summarize the distinction this way: candidate activities cannot include those whose distinct purpose is to contest or express opposition to the law from which one seeks an exemption—and this precisely because candidate activities are those prescribed only for adherents of the confession in question. To be sure, these adherents cultivate living and judging in accord with their confession when they advocate its prescribed political laws and policies. But doing so indirectly cultivates the confession—as one can see because such advocacy prescribes for all citizens, including those who affirm differing comprehensive confessions or convictions. This proposal, then, accords with the following intuitive recognition: a claim to exemption from some generally applicable law does not disagree with the law in question;

to the contrary, general applicability is not thereby questioned. In contrast, opposition to a democratically determined statute contests the law's validity. To immediate appearances, therefore, claims to free exercise exemptions make sense only if the candidate activities do not express dissent from the law.

On the assumption that a relevant statute is applicable and the activity in question passes the compelling interest test, use of peyote in worship ceremonies or the drinking of wine in certain eucharistic celebrations or a certain personal appearance in the military or in prison might be exempt from generally applicable laws or legal policies prohibiting such activities—*if* in each case the activity is prescribed only for those who confess this form of mediation. Perhaps such direct cultivation is likely found for the most part in some conventionally religious communities, and if so, we should repeat that any free exercise statute should provide exemptions for any explicit conviction about the ultimate terms of evaluation.[26] In contrast, opposing or advocating political laws or policies because one's comprehensive conviction so prescribes cannot be relevant to release from generally applicable laws—because these prescriptions are not limited to adherents of that confession. If a statute endorsing free exercise exemptions is valid, they are meant, given the way of reason, to enhance cultivation for public advocacy, not as compensation when one's advocacy does not prevail.

In *Employment Division v. Smith* (494 U.S. 872 [1990]), Justice Antonin Scalia's decision for the Court dismissed the notion that a right to free exercise exemption should apply only when a given activity is "central" to a given religious belief. That criterion would, he argued, inappropriately require judges to determine what religious activities are central to the given religion (see *Employment Division v. Smith* at 886--87). With that conclusion, Justice Sandra O'Connor, in her concurring opinion, agreed (see *Employment Division v. Smith* at 906--907). On these grounds, if I understand correctly, the Court has rightly refused to decide whether a given religion has been substantially burdened. The difference here stated between direct and indirect cultivation, let us underscore, does not require any judge to decide whether activities purporting to be exempt are of one kind or another. To the contrary, the claimants themselves are required to draw the distinction. On their own account, the distinct activity for which they seek an exemption must be prescribed only for adherents of the comprehensive confession in question and, therefore, must not contest or express opposition to the generally applicable law. Accordingly, any citizens who successfully claim a free exercise exemption will at least imply the difference between mediating expression and public advocacy of their conviction. Their claims will have merit, in other words, only because the direct cultivation for which they seek an exemption includes mediation of a religious or comprehensive reservation.

Against this accounting, some may argue, a given confession legitimized by religious freedom could insist that advocacy of certain clearly political prescriptions functions directly to cultivate that confession. This is so, the objection holds, when a given political advocacy is said to be entailed by, and thus to be a tenet of how, human authenticity is expressed. So-called peace churches, for instance, may take complete pacifism or, at least, opposition to all wars between or among nations to be itself a religious tenet, an aspect of God's abiding will. Similarly, opposition to abortion may be for some religious adherents a distinctively religious belief. When affirmed in this way, the objection explains, the advocacy belongs to the religious confession itself and thus directly cultivates it. Accordingly, the argument concludes, the activity cannot be excluded from those relevant to free exercise claims.

This argument is unconvincing. If opposition to, say, a declaration of war or legal permission for abortion is called a distinctively religious belief, this dissent from the law may entail a claim against the state—but not for exemption from a generally applicable law. The relevant claim indicts the government for a supposed violation of nonestablishment, that is, of explicit neutrality toward all comprehensive convictions. On this claim, the very applicability of the law is denied because the law is said to be unconstitutional—having taught, say, that pacifism or opposition to abortion as a religious tenet is false. But that indictment, too, is unconvincing. If religious freedom legitimizes any ultimate terms of political evaluation a citizen elects, the state cannot teach anything about true and false such beliefs without restricting full and free discourse by somehow stipulating a basic evaluation from which citizens as political participants should deliberate. Absent such teaching, the law is, in truth, explicitly neutral to all comprehensive convictions and confessions. A statutory declaration of war or statute permitting abortion does not stipulate a political evaluation but, rather, leaves all citizens, including the religious adherents in question, free to contest every political claim in public discourse.

Hence, a generally applicable statute said by some to contravene a religious tenet may imply, but does not teach, its falsity. Given the way of reason, in other words, the establishment issue is not whether certain religions *claim* a violation of religious freedom but whether the law, in truth, fails to be noncomprehensive because it explicitly asserts or teaches something about ultimate terms of political evaluation—and the relevant test is whether an enactment restricts full and free political discourse. Still, nothing said here denies that religious freedom legitimizes and invites into the continuing political discourse any political prescriptions taken by their adherents to be tenets of their religious or comprehensive confessions.

Religious freedom also legitimizes any comprehensive confession whose prescribed activities that clearly and directly cultivate it are, at least by implication, also prescribed for all in the political community; that is, the symbolic mediation is said to be necessary for access to the ultimate terms of evaluation. That appears to be the point, for instance, whenever Christians deny salvation "outside the church." But a claim to exclusivity for some direct cultivation of a comprehensive confession is, at least by implication, a denial of popular sovereignty or democracy with religious freedom, precisely because a common human experience of authenticity is denied. This claim to exclusivity, in other words, implies a form of government consistent with the constitutional establishment of that confession. Although its adherents are free to argue for it, their claim can only mean that no activity the given confession prescribes is a candidate for a free exercise exemption. To the contrary, all people ought to be adherents of that confession, and thus no distinction is drawn between activities prescribed in the political community and those for adherents alone. As mentioned, such exemption is improper unless adherents, on their own accounting, distinguish prescriptions applicable only to them from prescriptions applicable to the political community. Unless they affirm this difference, adherents of a religious or comprehensive confession withdraw any claim to free exercise exemptions because they withdraw their adherence to full and free political discourse.

If the Religious Freedom Restoration Act is read through the account proposed here, one is led to disagree with the Supreme Court's decision in *Burwell v. Hobby Lobby* (573 U.S. ___ [2014]). Quite apart from whether a corporation or its owners as they manage it are properly subjects of a free exercise claim or whether a less restrictive way is open for the government to ensure contraceptive coverage, granting exemption from the Affordable Care Act to Hobby Lobby's owners is misguided because they did not appeal to religious prescriptions applicable only to adherents of their confession. To the contrary, their objection to abortion and, supposedly on this basis, to certain methods of birth control is prescribed for the political community and thus for all citizens—and this because the distinct activity for which they claimed exemption (refusal to participate in support of what they take to be forms of abortion) expresses their opposition to an aspect of the law. On the account of religious freedom commended in this chapter, the owners of "closely held" corporations are not exempt from the Affordable Care Act because on religious or comprehensive grounds they take it to be, at least in certain respects, a bad law.

In contrast to this proposal, currently widespread opinion seems to sanction, subject to the compelling interest test, free exercise exemptions for dissent from any generally applicable law, in distinction from activities prescribed only for members of a given comprehensive confession. The fact that public debate about *Burwell v. Hobby Lobby* has focused on whether a corporation or its owners are properly subjects of free exercise claims is a testimony to this view. This opinion results, I suspect, from assuming that religious (in the conventional sense) convictions about the ultimate terms of evaluation depend on suprarational grounds and thus cannot be validated except by some authoritative disclosure. Given that premise, no distinction between prescriptions applicable only to adherents and those applicable to the political community is possible. Given the premise, in other words, a democratic constitution that affirms popular sovereignty is denied. This is, then, the same assumption that prompts many recent theories of democracy to separate at least some principles of justice from the diversity religious freedom protects.[27]

In any event, the present accounting depends on the way of reason. Because a democratic constitution is properly formative, that is, does nothing more and nothing less than establish a full and free political discourse, free exercise exemptions should not be provided constitutionally but, rather, only by statute. If statutory enactment of a nonspecific right to such exemptions is valid, the way of reason requires a difference among the prescriptions dependent on a given religious or comprehensive confession: prescriptions for attention to or engagement with certain symbols function to mediate the corresponding conviction or cultivate it directly and are prescribed only for adherents of the given confession; in contrast, political prescriptions are for all citizens. Given a relevant statute, claims to free exercise exemptions are rightly limited to activities prescribed by a comprehensive confession only for its adherents. In contrast, opposition to a generally applicable law properly belongs to the political discourse of "we the people."

8

THE REVOLUTION'S PROMISE

In 1787, Article VII of the proposed United States Constitution stipulated that ratification should occur through a constitutional convention in each of the several states and, further, that ratification by nine states would be sufficient to constitute among those nine the "more perfect Union" those states would enter.[1] Still, the Preamble to this document also proposed that "we the people of the United States" are the final ruling power by which the Constitution is or would be ordained and established. In contrast, ratification through conventions in each of the several states seems to imply that each of the thirteen was at the time an independent people. Hence, the question: Why did the Constitutional Convention propose this ratification procedure?

The plausible alternative to what Article VII stipulated was a single convention, representing collectively people in all of the states. To be sure, something like this national form of ratification was proposed by Gouverneur Morris in the Constitutional Convention and "found no support" (Beer 1993, 333). But that fact alone fails to clarify *why* that proposal was quickly dismissed. At least in retrospect, a single convention appears plausible because, as Samuel H. Beer notes, the Constitution itself projected, as part of the federal legislature, a single House of Representatives to which people in the several states would elect members (see Beer 1993, 333–34)— and the more plausible, perhaps, if this convention included a substantially larger company than either the Constitutional Convention or the envisioned

House of Representatives. Hence, the question remains: if "we the people of the United States . . . ordain and establish" the Constitution, why should ratification or its refusal be assigned to each state, at least suggesting thereby that each was an independent people and must decide whether to enter the new federated republic? Was this a gap in the Convention's reasoning (cf. Beer 1993, 313--17)?[2]

This apparent puzzle may seem a mere curiosity in US history—although a "gap" in the Convention's reasoning could provoke the question of whether the Constitution was, in fact, duly ratified. Be that as it may, justifying Article VII is the more demanding because, as I hope to show, doing so requires an attempted resolution of the enduring debate in US politics between those for whom the Union is a creation of previously sovereign states and those for whom the states were created with the Union—between those who affirm the so-called states' rights view and those who affirm the so-called national view. As is well known, this debate is seared into US history by the country's ruinous Civil War, when secession embodied the states' rights view, as advocated earlier by John C. Calhoun, and the Union embodied the national view, as advocated especially by Abraham Lincoln. As many have said, however, the war's outcome in 1865 did not settle the debate, and each of the two views has been consequential within subsequent accounts of US politics (see Jaffa 1999, 2000).

To be sure, one might well ask why the contention between these two views needs an attempted resolution in order to justify Article VII. My answer is this: absent the national view, the US political tradition, defined by its commitment to popular sovereignty, is not possible. On the states' rights view, I will argue, that tradition is impossible because that view is internally inconsistent: the states' rights view implies that ratification of the US Constitution is not a moral claim and, thereby, contradicts its own affirmation of popular sovereignty. The contradiction occurs because government by the people depends on the practice of argument or discourse about every asserted political decision and thus depends on each such decision being a claim to moral validity.

Clearly, the history of US politics is important to a resolution of this debate, but I have little relevant historical knowledge—and while I will, at appropriate points, offer some historical claims, they are, I expect, noncontroversial. This is, then, primarily a theoretical chapter because I judge that a theoretical point about constitutional ratification, leading to a discussion of constitutional authority, will aid the discussion. More specifically, the debate between states' rights and national views occurs within a common commitment to popular sovereignty, and a national public must have preceded constitutional ratification as the discourse in which claims for ratification were made—and making this point elicits a question about the authorization for government by the people. In the end, I will also argue, the states' rights view is inconsistent because it implies subjectivism. The moral law is transcendental to human decision as such,[3] and thus a moral law could be absent anywhere only if absent everywhere. Hence, every denial of the moral law finally asserts that all human decisions are merely arbitrary. If so, I will argue, a US Constitution[4] that authoritatively defines and structures institutionally popular sovereignty and, thereby, the US political tradition is impossible. In contrast to the states' rights view, the national view allows one, I think, to make sense of why the proposed Constitution provided for its own ratification in the manner stipulated by Article VII.

POPULAR SOVEREIGNTY

The difference between states' rights and national views may be formulated as a disagreement about what the Declaration of Independence declared independent. On the states' rights view, the Continental Congress in 1776 declared thirteen states or political communities independent and thus sovereign. This view can appeal to the Declaration's final paragraph, wherein the colonies are said to be, "and of right ought to be, FREE AND INDEPENDENT STATES," which "have full power to levy war, conclude peace, contract alliances, establish commerce, and do all other acts and things which independent states may of right do." The states thereby created, we are told by this view, then entered a treaty structured institutionally by The Articles of Confederation and Perpetual Union. "Treaty" here means an alliance accepted by each party in view of its own interests alone and, therefore, from which each party may withdraw if and when its interests so counsel (recognizing that one such interest may counsel honoring treaties). Accordingly, these thirteen independent peoples created the United States, first with the Articles of Confederation, on which the sovereignty of each was reaffirmed, and subsequently, on the view's strongest version, with the Constitution. "By the doctrine of John C. Calhoun ... when the thirteen colonies became independent of Great Britain in 1776, they each became sovereign states, and independent of each other as of the British Crown.... Thus to the secessionists in 1861, their lawful political obligation was primarily to their states" (Jaffa 2000, 365–66).

On the national view, in contrast, the Declaration declared a single people or political community sovereign, and it simultaneously created the states as members of the Union. This view can appeal to the Declaration's first paragraph, which speaks of "one people" separating themselves from "the political bands which have connected them with another," and to the same final paragraph, wherein, as James Wilson argued in 1785: "This act declares that '*these United Colonies*' (not enumerating them separately) 'are, and of right ought to be, free and independent states'" (Wilson 2000, 1:66). This single people, which I will call "we the people" or national public, first structured relations to each other institutionally through the Articles of Confederation and, subsequently, through the Constitution. As Abraham Lincoln said, "the original [states] ... passed into the Union even *before* they cast off their British colonial dependence.... [T]he Declaration of Independence ... [did not] declare their independence of *one another*, or of the Union" (Lincoln 1946, 603).[5]

But if the two views differ about what the Declaration of Independence declared independent, they nonetheless agree on this: the political communities or community so declared were or was characterized by self-government, which was itself asserted as morally valid. To be sure, most of the Declaration submits "to a candid world" the "history of repeated injuries and usurpations" by "the present King of Great Britain" and the history of colonial attempts to be treated justly by "our British brethren." In addition, the opening paragraph announces why this submission is made, and the final paragraph explicitly declares independence. But the second paragraph is eminently clear on the prescription for self-government: "all men are created equal and endowed by their creator with certain inalienable rights," among which are "life, liberty, and the pursuit of happiness," and to secure which "governments are instituted among men," so that governments receive their "just powers" from "the consent of the governed" and for their "safety and happiness."

Moreover, the consent affirmed by the Declaration was *actual*, in distinction from the *virtual* consent to which theorists in Great Britain appealed. Actual consent means "that all members of the community have access by virtue or grace to the truth about the common good and that, therefore, the ruled consent because they already agree with what the rulers require of them" (Beer 1993, 53).[6] In contrast, virtual consent means that "the governed consent to government, not because they understand the truth and goodness of the law, but because they recognize the authority of the law-giver.... Their consent is the passive consent of deference, not the active consent of self-government" (Beer 1993, 56). On Samuel H. Beer's reading, this distinction made the conflict between England and its thirteen colonies intractable (see

Beer 1993, 146–53). As it happens, "self-government" is also the term that Lincoln, in objecting to Stephen Douglas's view of "popular sovereignty" for the territories, chose to express his point: "no man is good enough to govern another man, *without that other's consent*. I say this is the leading principle—the sheet anchor of American republicanism.... Allow ALL the governed an equal voice in the government, and that, and that only, is self-government" (Lincoln 1946, 304).

The affirmation of self-government is also rightly called a commitment to popular sovereignty; that is, the people (whether this means thirteen differing peoples or a single "we the people") are the final ruling power. Popular sovereignty is not possible unless each adult member of the political community may engage all of the others in or through public reason. Any given member of the sovereign people must be able to assert any politically relevant decision, so that governmental activities, in which the people act-as-one, are determined through a full and free discussion and debate, a full and free political discourse. Here, "full" means that every political claim is open to contestation, and "free" means that every adult member of the community is an equal political participant—and "political discourse" means the way of reason.

But asserted political decisions cannot be objects of public reason unless they are *moral* claims to validity. Hence, the people cannot be the final ruling power unless "political claim" means any claim for the justice of some actual or proposed governing activity (including an activity in which government refrains from legislating with respect to a certain issue) or for the validity of any norm or principle of justice—a claim that pledges its possible validation or invalidation by the way of reason. Were some or all asserted decisions not claims to moral validity and thus merely expressions of arbitrary preference, public discussion of them would be a cacophony of mere assertions, such that sufficiently important and conflicting preferences could only fight. In other words, public reason could not determine what action-as-one should occur, that is, could not lead to political decisions and, thereby, governmental activities.

The Constitution, then, is entirely to the point when its First Amendment guarantees religious freedom. I take this provision to mean that each citizen is free to affirm whatever ultimate terms of evaluation—and, at least typically, their ground in reality—she or he finds convincing. In other words, any such conviction a citizen takes to be true is legitimate. Because self-government requires a full and free political discourse among moral claims about governmental activities, each adult member of the community must be free to assess all political claims, including claims for the terms in which all actual or proposed governing activities should be evaluated. The religion clauses of the Constitution's First Amendment guarantee precisely that freedom; each member of the people may affirm any conviction about those ultimate terms—of which all other political claims are either implications or, alternatively, specifications—she or he takes to be valid.

Religion, I recognize, is often understood in a more conventional sense, whereby it designates a certain class of convictions about the ultimate terms of evaluation and their ground—namely, those beliefs said to base evaluation on some reality beyond the contingent things of this world. Religious beliefs are then distinguished from secularistic ones, those for which no such reality but solely the world exists. In contrast to any such conventional meaning, "religious" in "religious freedom" should, on the reading here, be understood in an extended sense, whereby it designates any explicit conviction about those ultimate terms of evaluation. As far as I can see, only religious freedom in this extended sense is itself consistent with popular sovereignty. Without religious freedom in that sense, citizens cannot be the final ruling power because freedom with respect to the ultimate terms of evaluation is then subject to some or other constitutional or governmental constraint.[7]

In July 1776, the Continental Congress asserted that government by actual consent of the governed is, at least in the political communities or community then declared independent, authorized by "the laws of nature and nature's God." This statement expressed the signers' conviction that self-government is morally valid because it is prescribed or permitted by the providential moral law. In other words, the Declaration of Independence is at least consistent with the view that popular sovereignty is possible because every asserted political decision is a moral claim addressed to a public that properly proceeds by the way of reason. Hence, actual consent of the governed and, therefore, religious freedom presuppose "that all [adult] members of the community have access to" (Beer 1993, 53), or have common experience of, the truth about the ultimate terms of evaluation. Full and free discourse seeks to make readily apparent something all citizens inchoately know, and the people can then determine governmental activities accordingly.

To be sure, speaking of popular sovereignty and thus religious freedom as the defining character of politics in each of or among the thirteen former colonies seems improper once the establishment of some given religion in one or more of the eighteenth-century states is noted. The religion clauses of the First Amendment (as its following clauses) initially applied solely to the federal Congress (or, perhaps, federal government) created by the Constitution. Perhaps "Congress shall make no law *respecting* an establishment of religion" (emphasis added) otherwise assigned the relation between religion and politics to the several states, whereby the right of a given state to establish some or other religion is preserved. But whether this assignment makes sense is at least doubtful. If a given state established a religion, all of its citizens were in some way required to support and insofar endorse it—and given that a religion includes some conviction about the ultimate terms of evaluation, this endorsement carried over into national politics.

Be that as it may, even more problematic is the eighteenth-century exclusion of many persons from whatever peoples or people the Declaration declared independent. Above all, slavery was present in most states to which the Declaration referred and, further, was explicitly accepted by the Constitution, even while the latter named slavery euphemistically. In addition, the Constitution assigned to the several states decisions about who is qualified to be a political participant. The states' practice subsequent to the Revolution excluded almost entirely African Americans, Native Americans, and women (indeed, even virtual consent appeared in the supposition that enfranchised citizens were almost entirely male)—and, at least often, the poor (although in some states, differing measures of property were, among other qualifications, attached to voting for differing offices). Further, most of these exclusions extended for most of the nation's history.

If the commitment to self-government identifies the US political tradition, this character must be present at the outset of that tradition, and the exclusions present then, along with the absence of complete religious freedom, may give reasons to question whether actual consent of the governed does indeed mark U.S. politics. Over the course of its political history, the United States has, largely through constitutional amendment, sought to correct at least some of these exclusions. African American males, Native Americans (by act of Congress in 1924), women, the poor, and those between eighteen and twenty-one years of age have been included. But such inclusions have been resisted and delayed, have often followed atrocity and bloodshed, and in the 1860s, cost horrific carnage—and even with the changes, cause remains to doubt whether "we the people" are yet adequately defined. Moreover, this pattern throws into stark relief the exclusions of the eighteenth century.

Indeed, the Revolution may have succeeded in part because colonial revolutionaries played up British efforts to secure support from African Americans and Native Americans and played down the participation of both in the fight for independence, seeking to exploit the fears of white colonists and thereby unite the colonies in a common cause.

> For patriot political and publicity leaders ... [the] actions taken by dozens of British agents and thousands of Indians and African Americans, also provided a golden opportunity. The patriots worked assiduously to make this the foundation of why colonists should support resistance and, eventually, independence. The common cause appeal was, then, the merging of both these interpretations: it simultaneously valorized white citizen soldiers for defending freedom and castigated those who opposed it....
>
> The cement of the union was catastrophically thin.... Though thousands of Indians and African Americans did support the patriot side, they were never a part of the common cause appeal. (Parkinson 2016, 664–65)

Still, the pattern of delayed inclusion also allows one to see in US politics an *ideal* present at the outset and continually worked out, even when one deplores the resistance to and obstruction of the corrections. The changes, however arrested, have marked a more or less obvious trajectory. Since 1787, formal amendments to the Constitution have, with relatively few exceptions, either sought to make governmental officials more responsive to the people or erased previous exclusions from membership therein—and, as Akil Reed Amar observes, "no amendment has ever cut back on prior voting rights or rights of equal inclusion" (Amar 2005, 19). The ideal of popular sovereignty, I propose, has been from the outset essential to the US political tradition, notwithstanding the compromises the tradition has suffered—so that its identity may be stated: the pursuit of popular sovereignty, or the perfecting of government by the people. As something to be achieved, that ideal is attested by the trajectory of change reviewed summarily above. As an ideal characterizing the US political tradition, one may further note, popular sovereignty perhaps remains consistent with the absence of full religious freedom in the eighteenth-century states. The several religious establishments died in the early nineteenth century (in 1833, Massachusetts was the last state to abolish an official religion)—and while limited initially to the federal government, the First Amendment provision for religious freedom was itself applied to the states in the Supreme Court decision incorporating many rights within the Bill of Rights.

Moreover, at least some participants in the 1787 Convention were aware of popular sovereignty as a perfection-to-be-pursued, at least in this respect: they insisted that neither monarchy nor aristocracy, neither rule by the one nor by the few but solely rule by the many, properly marks the nation created by the Constitution. "We may define a republic to be," wrote James Madison in *The Federalist*, "a government which derives all of its powers directly or indirectly from the great body of the people" (Hamilton, Madison, and Jay 1998, 182). Again, James Wilson wrote in 1804: "the *vital* principle... which diffuses animation and vigour through all the others... [is] that the supreme or sovereign power of the society resides in the citizens at large" (Wilson 2000, 1:440--41). Above all, however, this ideal was given expression in the Declaration of Independence: "all men are created equal"—where "men" can be understood, at least in retrospect, as generic for "humans," and "created equal" means, whatever else it may mean, created politically equal. Lincoln's formulation of the point, referring specifically to the presence of slavery in the states, has application beyond that reference: the Declaration's authors "meant simply to declare the *right* [to equality], so that the *enforcement* of it might follow as fast as circumstances should permit. They meant to set up a standard maxim for free society" (Lincoln 1946, 361).

The Revolution's leaders, wrote Alexander Hamilton, "reared the fabrics of governments which have no model on the face of the globe... [and] which it is incumbent on their successors to improve and perpetuate" (Hamilton, Madison, and Jay 1998, 64). Some founders, wrote William M. Wiecek in 1972, "expected the concept of republican government to change over time, hopefully perfecting the experiment begun by the Revolution" (cited in Amar 2012, 85)—and with this sentiment, some African Americans, Native Americans, women, and the poor may well have agreed. Still, I do not say that eighteenth-century founders or citizens of the Republic having the franchise typically saw an inconsistency between the ideal of popular sovereignty and the exclusions they endorsed. Liberty was widely thought to require the independence that only propertied white males were widely thought to enjoy, and political inclusion was widely thought to require such liberty (see McPherson 1991, 48--50).

Be that as it may, what character defines a tradition need not be recognized by all participants in that tradition. In contrast to eighteenth-century people, we today can see in popular sovereignty an ideal with which their exclusions were inconsistent. Moreover, the concept of this ideal was present at the nation's outset because the logic of government by the many, that is, the alternative to monarchy and aristocracy, precludes denial to any adult citizen of her or his right to participate in self-government. Any such denial—of African Americans, Native Americans, women, or those without significant property—is, in effect, the endorsement of some aristocracy, one defined by color or national origin or gender or wealth. Each is, in the words of James

Wilson, a "quality independent of the choice of the people" (Wilson 2007, 1:278). Rule by the many, in distinction from rule by the one or the few, drives to full inclusion.

THE STATES' RIGHTS VIEW

On the states' rights view, the ideal of popular sovereignty initially defined thirteen independent states, which subsequently created the Union. As if to underscore this sequence, their first agreement was not the Constitution but, rather, the Articles of Confederation, which are, we are told by that view, rightly understood as a treaty: each of the thirteen peoples remained independent and thus sovereign and entered an alliance with the other twelve for certain designated purposes (for instance, common defense). The document articulating this agreement (the Articles of Confederation) is itself a witness to their mere alliance because Article XIII stipulates that no change in the agreement can be made without the consent of all thirteen. In 1787–88, then, ratification of the proposed Constitution by eleven (and later thirteen) of these independent states either (1) created a "more perfect Union" and thus a new, national public, wherein each state somehow maintained its sovereign independence, or (2) effected a two-step process, in which each of these peoples first gave up its independence and, as a second step, joined the new people of the United States, thereby entering a federated Union (see Amar 1987, 1459–60). In either case, "we the people," designated in the Constitution's Preamble, were created with or did not exist prior to the Constitution's ratification.

With this conclusion, however, the states' rights view is left with a problem: although a national public is said not to exist prior to 1787–88, its prior presence is presupposed given the acknowledged commitment, shared by the states' rights and national views, to popular sovereignty, to the peoples or people as the final ruling power. Popular sovereignty (or what comes to the same thing, government with religious freedom, in the extended sense) can be a form of political community only if asserted political decisions are moral claims purporting to be an implication or, alternatively, specification of the true ultimate terms of evaluation or moral law. Ratification is itself an asserted political decision which claims moral validity for the Constitution—and this claim could not be advocated among the people supposedly created by ratification because the discourse in question was about whether that public should be created, that is, whether ratification of the Constitution is best. The prior discourse, then, seeks action-as-one by the way of reason. Hence, whatever exclusions from the peoples or people may have been taken for granted in the eighteenth century, some national public apparently must be present in order for any state to make a ratifying claim to consistency with the (true) ultimate terms of evaluation, because it must occur within a discourse through which the people determine action-as-one.

But the Declaration of Independence, some may object, itself makes a political claim to moral validity, notwithstanding that so declaring could not have presupposed the prior presence of a sovereign peoples or people because the Declaration began the peoples or people declared independent. In the same way, the objection goes, the national people was created by the states in 1787–88. This reasoning is not convincing given, as the objection allows, the unique kind of political claim the Declaration exemplifies. As many have noted, the Declaration was not itself ratified. Perhaps less noted is the following: submitting it to the people would ask whether the colonists (1) approved being independent and sovereign (either as thirteen peoples or a single people), or (2) approved continuing deference politically to Great Britain—and to this question, the second answer would imply the absence of whatever peoples or people made ratification necessary. In this sense, ratification was pointless because there was no sovereign peoples or people until the Declaration declared independence—or, better, until independence was sustained by the Revolution[8]—and thus peoples or a people to which a claim might be addressed were or was created. In the absence of independence, a claim for its moral validity could only be declared, as the Declaration said, in order to respect "the opinions of mankind."[9] But whether the Declaration declared separate states or "we the people" sovereign, independence had, by 1787–88, been achieved. Given popular sovereignty, then, the proposed Constitution could be submitted for ratification, and a question about the deciding public to which a state's ratifying claim to moral validity was addressed is entirely proper.

Perhaps we will be told that each state addressed this claim (that is, the claim to moral validity for constitutional ratification) internally or to its own public; that is, the people who could contest and thus seek to validate or invalidate the claim were within the state in question. This reply has the advantage of presenting, at least in one version, the states' rights view of constitutional ratification—namely, that it consisted in the acceptance of a treaty among thirteen independent peoples. Each of the sovereign parties entered this alliance solely in terms of its own interests—even if these interests were defined with respect to the longer run, and even if they included what the party in question took to be its obedience to moral norms. The mark of a treaty, as previously mentioned, is judgment by each party thereto in view of its own interests alone, and thus each party has the freedom to withdraw if and when, in its own judgment, those interests so counsel.

Any party to a treaty that assigns sovereignty to the people, then, has every reason to consider its own people the proper public to which a claim for ratification is addressed. Moreover, nothing about these circumstances prevents a given state from claiming moral validity for a treaty, that is, claiming consistency with the ultimate terms of evaluation. The treaty will be good, at least for that state, if its own interests serve the maximal good—and this can be assessed only by, assuming a commitment to popular sovereignty, the people of the state in question. If some party makes a claim to moral validity for all interests the alliance serves, that claim can only be made in view of the moral terms the given party affirms (or on which several parties agree), even if these result from an internal contestation, and thus the claim is made in order to respect the "opinions of mankind."

Nonetheless, this attempt to substitute a given state's people for a national public, and thereby, to make of constitutional ratification the endorsement of a treaty, can surely be turned aside. Given that it assigned extensive power to a central government and thus created a new political order among the states, the Constitution, to all appearances, could not be ratified or accepted by states so pervasively committed to popular sovereignty without a national public whose (actual) consent alone gives reason for the exercise of those powers—that is, without a national public as the final ruling power. But even if that consideration is insufficient to the states' rights view, the following question is conclusive: if constitutional ratification was acceptance of a treaty, how did the Constitution assign sovereignty with respect to the central government for which extensive powers were created? Was the assignment in this respect autocratic or aristocratic? To that question, there is no answer because, in truth, constitutional ratification was not the acceptance of a treaty. Rather, "we the people" ordained and established the Constitution. In sum, the states' commitment to popular sovereignty *required* a national public. But if the affirmation of popular sovereignty required a single discourse, it must have preexisted constitutional ratification as the public to which a ratifying claim to moral validity was addressed.

The ratifying process itself, in other words, must have occurred within "we the people" as named in the Constitution's Preamble. Constitutional ratification waited on whether the prior people to whom the claim was addressed were persuaded of the new Union's moral validity. It is worth noting, then, that ratification by each state, at least before the ninth, could not possibly create this national public because whether the Constitution should be ratified was what the public in question should determine. For the same reason, then, even the ninth state could not consistently claim moral validity or goodness for the creation of "we the people" without presupposing the prior existence of a discourse unless the previous eight had made the same claim, and the previous eight, absent a prior national public, could not make the claim.[10]

It might be objected that a moral claim for the Constitution is not addressed to a prior national public but, rather, to the indefinite "argumentation-community" (Apel 1979, 335) or to "the opinions of mankind" and, in that sense, to the rational capacity of subjects generally. Accordingly, a moral claim for ratification of the Constitution need not presuppose a prior national public because no such public is addressed. As this objection implies, a favorable determination within some or other *actual* political discourse that is full and free does not establish the validity of a moral claim; only a sound argument and thus the indefinite argumentation-community can do so—even if the actual discourse of a political community might be sufficient to the legitimacy of that determination. At the same time, a more extensive discourse is, other things equal, more likely to overcome error—and arguments presented therein for the validity of a moral claim may indeed be sound.

Still, the prior national public is presupposed for the following reason: the Constitution purported to define and structure institutionally the relations among a limited company of citizens, namely, the company included in the thirteen states previously governed by the Articles of Confederation. Because a sovereign political community is itself responsible for discerning or deciding in some way or other its own definition and structure, popular sovereignty means address to *this* company of citizens as a public that should assess the Constitution's implied claim to be good. Although no actual discourse can guarantee a valid decision, the point of popular sovereignty is to embody insofar as possible the way of reason within the independent political community. It remains, then, that a moral claim for the ratifying decision presupposes a prior deciding and thus national public.

Even Amar, to whose scholarship on the Constitution I am immensely indebted,[11] nonetheless sees the Articles of Confederation as "merely a 'league of friendship,' a multilateral treaty among the thirteen sovereigns" (Amar 2012, 57; see 2005, 25) and thus understands (indeed, perhaps initially presented) ratification of the Constitution as the "two-step" process mentioned earlier:

> It was by these very acts [of ratification] that previously separate state Peoples agreed to "consolidate" themselves into a single continental People. Before ratification, the People of each state were indeed

sovereign—and for that very reason could not be bound by the new Constitution if they chose not to ratify, no matter what any of the other sovereign states chose to do.... The ratifications themselves thus formed the basic social compact by which formerly distinct sovereign Peoples, each acting in convention, agreed to reconstitute themselves into one common sovereignty. (Amar 1987, 1459–60)[12]

Still, Amar also says: "In America, the supreme lawmaker would be the American people themselves, who were being asked by the Philadelphia framers to ordain and enact the supreme law of the Constitution," and he speaks of the ratification process during 1787–88 as "America's Great Debate" (Amar 2012, 529, note 1). Because *America* had this debate, we have, I think, every right to conclude that a single American people must have been present prior to the debate's outcome. Hence, "we the people" as mentioned by the Constitution cannot be what the ratification process created—even while, as I will discuss later, that Constitution, as the Articles of Confederation previously, structured "we the people" institutionally.

THE NATIONAL VIEW

If this critique of the states' rights view is sound (namely, approval of the Constitution could not create because its claim to moral validity presupposes the prior presence of a national public), we might then ask: When did "we the people" as the Union's final ruling power begin? Still, whether the critique is sound might be doubted absent the answer to another question: Why has the states' rights view endured? If that view is, in the manner argued above, self-refuting (because its affirmation of popular sovereignty means that a national public preceded constitutional ratification), a critique to that effect has a responsibility to explain why the states' rights view has continually attracted advocates. Perhaps the considerable mind of John C. Calhoun should be discredited because he sought to defend slavery. But the Civil War did not settle the debate—which has lived on until the present time, even among those who denounce the Confederacy. If the above critique is sound, why has the debate about the nation's beginning so persisted in US politics? This question requires a convincing answer—the absence of which would be cause to reconsider the reasoning against the states' rights view.

Accordingly, I propose the following: the states' rights view has endured because the premise it implies is so widely affirmed (indeed, is often accepted even by those who take the opposing view), namely, that ratification of the Constitution by nine or more states is alone the source of its authority in US politics; that is, constitutional authority to define and structure institutionally the US political tradition depends solely on the Constitution's ratification. Thus, Amar, for whom constitutional ratification effected a two-step process through which each state *gave up* its sovereignty (and thus "the original Constitution emphatically denies state authority to unilaterally secede" [Amar 2012, 85; see 2005, 35–39]), apparently agrees: "The Preamble's language prominently directs readers to the ratification process as the very foundation of the entire document's legal authority" (Amar 2012, 63, see also 77, 256; Amar 2005, 21).

Given its commitment to popular sovereignty, in any event, the states' rights view implies the premise that ratification alone grounds the Constitution's authority because the national public or its single people was created by the ratifying process. That process alone must authorize the Constitution, in other words, because popular sovereignty in the nation did not exist and thus could not be a source of authority prior to ratification. Moreover, the premise and the states' rights view imply each other. Given the ratifying process as the sole source of the Constitution's authority, the Declaration must have declared thirteen sovereign states as independent of each other as each was from Great Britain, because "we the people" could not exist prior to the Constitution's ratification. But if the ratifying process can occur only within the prior presence of "we the people," constitutional authority depends also on a prior source, namely, whatever authorizes "we the people" as the final ruling power.

In other words, the mutual implication between the states' rights view and ratification as the sole source of constitutional authority is what the above discussion found problematic—and as far as I can see, thinkers who assert the national view and take ratification alone to authorize the Constitution contradict themselves. Only because something else prior to 1787–88 created and authorized "we the people" as the final ruling power could ratifying the Constitution constitute a "more perfect Union." Notwithstanding how widely ratification alone is said to be the necessary and sufficient condition of how the Constitution constitutes US politics, an exercise of popular approval cannot authorize popular sovereignty—because the former does not extend beyond the people who give their approval, and popular sovereignty is an ideal characterizing a political tradition. The Constitution's authority also depends on something else. Pursuit of that something else will, I hope to show, also serve to mark the beginning of "we the people."[13]

The authority in question, we should note, is not merely de facto but, rather, de jure. I have in mind the following distinction: De facto authority means that individuals subject to it in fact attribute to some other individual or group or document the right to command in relevant respects their beliefs and related actions—and de facto authority is what the exercise of popular approval alone confers. De jure authority means that this individual or group or document legitimately so commands; that is, relevant individuals *should* attribute to it the right to command in relevant respects their beliefs and related actions—whether in fact they do so or not (see DeGeorge 1985). For instance, US citizens who affirm the US judicial system should attribute to the judge in a particular US trial (subject to the system's process of appeal), rather than any other person or group, authority to regulate the trial; those who affirm the Christian religion as true and salutary for their lives should attribute to the apostolic witness, rather than any other conflicting witness within the Christian tradition, authority to command their religious beliefs and related actions.

Similarly, US adults subsequent to the Constitution who affirm the US political tradition as morally valid should attribute to the Constitution, rather than any conflicting document or expression, authority to define and structure institutionally their beliefs and related actions as political participants. I will call US citizens who do so affirm *patriotic*—and it may well be that most patriotic US citizens *do* attribute to the Constitution authority over the definition and institutional structure of the politics in which they participate. For those citizens, in other words, the Constitution *does* constitute the US political tradition, identified by its ideal of popular sovereignty, whereby the Constitution also has insofar de facto authority in US politics. But its authority is not merely de facto because it does not depend on that fact; to the contrary, its authority is de jure, that is, all patriotic US citizens should attribute authority to it, rather than to any conflicting expression—for instance, the conflicting account of some religion or the conflicting pronouncements of a given charismatic person or the statement that US politics has no abiding character or identity at all.

That a de jure authority legitimately commands in relevant respects the beliefs and related actions of relevant individuals does not mean that one can establish what beliefs are true or what actions are good by appeal to any authority. To the contrary, what beliefs are true can be established only by, as Alfred North Whitehead writes, the reason "individual to each, to which all authority must bow" (Whitehead 1961, 162), and what actions are good can be established only in terms of the moral law, that is, the ultimate terms of evaluation. Hence, individuals are not subject to a de jure authority unless they have affirmed that for which it is authoritative as true or good. If, for instance, the apostolic witness is de jure authoritative for the Christian tradition, only those who affirm Christian faith as true and salutary for their lives are subject to that authority or should attribute to it the right to command their beliefs and related actions. But *whether* the Christian faith is true cannot be determined by appeal to the apostolic witness or any other authority.[14]

Similarly, one cannot establish whether the US political tradition, identified by its ideal of popular sovereignty, is good by appeal to the Constitution's authority, notwithstanding that it defines and structures institutionally US politics. Still, a political tradition must be defined and structured institutionally by some authority, and because one cannot establish by appeal to it the moral validity of that tradition, popular sovereignty then means that any citizen can question whether the tradition is good. That question is not about the Constitution's authority but, rather, about whether the ideal of popular sovereignty is morally valid. Hence, the affirmation of its moral validity by patriotic citizens is essential to the Constitution's legitimate command of their relevant beliefs and related actions.

Accordingly, the Constitution's authority does not mean that all US citizens ought to be patriotic, that is, are constitutionally bound to profess US politics, defined by its ideal of popular sovereignty, as good. Likely, the US political tradition would not long endure unless most US citizens so profess and thus are indeed patriotic. But if "we the people" are truly the final ruling power and thus "ordain and establish" even the Constitution as well as constitutionally enacted statutory law, the Preamble's assignment of sovereignty to the people is itself a political claim over which the people are sovereign. Government by the people is itself something the people rightly evaluate. If, for James Wilson, "the *vital* principle ... which diffuses animation and vigour through all the others ... [is] that the supreme or sovereign power of the society resides in the citizens at large," the citizens, he also concluded, "always retain the right of abolishing, altering, or amending their constitution, at whatever time, and in whatever manner, they shall deem it expedient" (Wilson 2007, 1:440–41).[15]

The US commitment to religious freedom, in other words, cannot exclude a belief that monarchical or aristocratic government is prescribed by the ultimate terms of evaluation. A belief of that kind is also legitimate—even if, as I think, false—and citizens for whom any such account is persuasive are free to embrace and advocate it. If "we the people" have the final ruling power, they have the power to abolish religious freedom and thus popular sovereignty, and were the Constitution to stipulate that all citizens should affirm democracy, the Constitution would insofar be sovereign and would contradict the popular sovereignty it asserts. Hence, both constitutional and statutory law can be determined only through full and free public discourse. On my accounting, then, the Constitution constitutes US politics only in the sense that all adult citizens should *adhere* to, that is, act in accord with, the conditions of that discourse, namely, the equal rights of all other adult citizens and the decision-making procedures constitutionally stipulated. But whether the people should be the final ruling power can itself be questioned and some other assignment of sovereignty publicly advocated. Only patriotic citizens are bound to *profess* the people's sovereignty, that is, are subject to the Constitution's authority in relevant respects over their *beliefs* and related actions.

But adherence, some may object, is itself an action that must be authoritatively prescribed by the Constitution, even if the profession of democracy is not. At least in this respect, the objection continues, popular sovereignty must be qualified—because, if unqualified, whether such adherence is good could itself be questioned, so that even this adherence could not be obligatory for all US citizens. On my accounting, however, the one commitment explicitly neutral to strictly all political disagreements, including disagreement about the ultimate terms of political evaluation, is commitment to validation and invalidation of political claims, if contested, in full and free discourse—even if the person making a political claim is not able to provide the argument by which it may be validated. Absent this commitment, constitutional provision of religious freedom could not be, as the provision itself requires, religiously free (or explicitly neutral to all convictions about the ultimate terms of evaluation). In other words, adherence to such discourse is, at least wherever popular sovereignty occurs, self-prescribed in making any political claim. This commitment, therefore, does not itself depend on the Constitution's authority but is, rather, a self-imposed moral prescription of any and all engagement in US politics, even if one asserts politically that one is not committed to political discourse.[16]

On the above critique, in any event, ratification alone cannot authorize the Constitution because, given popular sovereignty, the claim for a ratifying decision as morally valid or consistent with the ultimate terms of evaluation presupposes the prior presence and confirmation of a national public to which this claim is addressed. Ratifying claims occurred within this public—and agreement therein on the Constitution's moral validity by nine or more states may be called a source of the Constitution's authority. The question, then, is whether this prior national public authorizes itself or whether its authority is derived from some previous source. A given source of authority, we should note, may itself be authorized by some authority prior to that source. For instance, the judge's authority to regulate a given trial (subject to the judicial system's process of appeal) is authorized by the legislature's authority, and that, in turn, is authorized by the Constitution's authority. But the regress of authorities cannot be indefinite because a political tradition must have a historical beginning. Something must be the primary or originating authority defining that tradition, and its authorizing source may be called the original or primal *source* of all authority.[17] No tradition can persist, to be repetitious, unless some subsequent inheritors of it take it to be morally valid—in the present case, unless some subsequent US citizens are patriotic. But if so, the tradition must somehow be defined by some primary authority. In the case of US politics, then, we may ask for that original authority and, behind it, for the primal authorizing source.

Let us consider, then, whether the national public presupposed by the Constitution's ratification must have been present prior to the Articles of Confederation. Several historians have argued, with Amar, that the Articles themselves are properly understood as a treaty or alliance among thirteen sovereign states (see Ellis 2015; Jensen 1970; Morgan 1988). But the difficulty facing that account is how "we the people" could have become a reality prior to the Constitution in order that America's "great debate" over constitutional ratification could occur. To the contrary, the Articles as a treaty or alliance seems to imply, as one of the above historians (Edward S. Morgan) has it, that "Madison was *inventing* a sovereign American people to overcome the sovereign states" or was "calling" a "new people ... into existence" (Morgan 1988, 267, 270)—that is, existence under the Articles of Confederation could be existence under a treaty if and only if "we the people" were solely the consequence of constitutional ratification. How, then, did "we the people" have a prior existence as a discourse to which claims for ratification of the Constitution could be addressed?

In any event, Madison and those who advocated as he did at the Constitutional Convention were eminently clear about the original source of authority for "we the people," namely, the promise (or promises, or principles) of the American Revolution (see Maier 2010, 2, 4, 6). I have already cited Madison's definition of a republic or republican government: "a government which derives all of its powers directly or indirectly from the great body of the people" (Hamilton, Madison, and Jay 1998, 182). In addition, Madison, writing in *The Federalist*, associates republican government with the Revolution: "The first question ... is, whether the general form and aspect of the government be strictly republican? It is evident that no other form would be reconcilable with . . . the fundamental principles of the revolution" (Hamilton, Madison, and Jay 1998, 181).

There is, moreover, grounds to assume that appeal to the Revolution was widespread (see Maier 2010, 2, 4, 6). Prior to sending the Articles of Confederation to the several state legislatures for their approval, the Continental Congress pursued a considerable debate between those who favored "a New Nation" or "single people" (Ellis 2015, 8, 11) and those who thought any central government should be thoroughly subordinated to independent states—and the latter group claimed to be in concert with the Revolution. According to Joseph J. Ellis, those opposed to being a single people (he cites principally Roger Sherman of Connecticut) appealed to the "core values" of the Revolution as inconsistent with a "distant government" (Ellis 2015, 139)—and according to Merrill Jensen, Thomas Burke of North Carolina, also opposed to any central government with significant power, "placed before Congress the basic constitutional issue of the revolution" (Jensen 1970, 175).[18] Because the Revolution was itself a "common cause," there is reason to affirm it as the primal source of authority for popular sovereignty and thus for "we the people."

Still, the Revolution itself did not clearly identify its significance, and thus it required authoritative expression. That expression occurred in the Continental Congress and, specifically, its July 1776 Declaration, most especially its second paragraph: government is by "consent of the governed" and for their "safety and happiness." Hence, we can conclude this: the sovereignty of "we the people" as "the *vital* principle" (Wilson 2007, 440) defining US politics was authorized by the Revolution's promise as this was understood by those who, acting together, first expressed it in the Declaration of Independence. That Declaration is, in other words, the primary authority of the US political tradition and was itself authorized by the primal source of authority, the Revolution's promise. The ideal of popular sovereignty defines US politics because it was the reason for, the significance of, the Revolution.[19]

This does not make the Declaration a part of the Constitution, as some theorists of US politics have said. Rather, the Declaration is the primary authority for the Constitution's expression of popular sovereignty, and, as the primary authority, the Declaration authorizes "we the people" as the immediately prior national public to which claims for constitutional ratification were addressed.[20] Ratification then becomes a thoroughly *necessary*—although not *sufficient*—condition of the Constitution's authority, of both the 1787 document and later amendments or changes to it. This follows because the Revolution's authorization of popular sovereignty assigns to the people the decision about how their politics will be structured institutionally, and thus the Declaration did not articulate the institutional structure through which the political community acts-as-one. That task fell first to the Articles of Confederation and, when those were found wanting, to the Constitution.

But the Revolution's promise, expressed by the Declaration, did authorize government by (actual) consent of the governed, government by the people. Hence, an institutional articulation must be consistent with their sovereignty, the only political test for which is ratification or approval by "we the people." In that sense, ratification, both of the Articles and the Constitution, is a necessary condition of their authority—necessary but not sufficient because, as noted above, an exercise of popular approval cannot authorize popular sovereignty. As a necessary condition, however, ratification by the people is, in the US political tradition, (de jure) authoritative until altered by the people because the ideal of popular sovereignty defines that tradition. It is true that "we the people" could decide to assign sovereignty elsewhere—for instance, to a monarch or aristocracy—even if, on my accounting, that decision would be inconsistent with the ultimate terms of evaluation. But with that decision, at least if it were not contested, the US political tradition would cease.

CONSEQUENCES OF THE REVOLUTION

Nothing above intends to say that a company of people cannot begin a political tradition and thereby authorize its identity. Indeed, there is a clear sense in which people who inhabited what had been America's thirteen British colonies authorized the Constitution—but "the people" in question are not solely those who ratified the 1787 proposal issued by the Constitutional Convention. Rather, the authority of popular sovereignty as an ideal defining US politics depends originally on the people who, in distinction from loyalists, engaged in or supported the Revolution and communicated the reason for their collective activity to the Continental Congress, where expression in the Declaration of Independence became the primary authority for "we the people" as the final ruling power. As previously mentioned, in other words, a national public began with the Revolution, the common cause, and the states were created only as the United States. In that sense, the Declaration of Independence never declared the states independent of one another or implied the possibility of a state outside the Union—however debased that beginning was by racism (again, see Parkinson 2016, 664–65). "Great ideas," wrote

Whitehead, "enter into history with evil associates and disgusting alliances" (Whitehead 1961, 18).

The national view (namely, the Declaration declared a single people or political community sovereign, and it simultaneously created the states as peoples within or members of the Union) is thereby vindicated. A defense of that view has here turned on supposing that each state's ratification of the Constitution (and, previously, of the Articles of Confederation) made a moral claim for how the Revolution's promise relates to a central government of the several states. Consistency with the focus of both states' rights and national views on the principle of popular sovereignty requires that every asserted political decision makes a moral claim to be assessed by the way of reason—so that ratification presupposes the prior presence of "we the people."

Still, if defense of the national view depends on ratification's claim to moral validity, there is, at least formally, an alternative: in its ratification of the Constitution (and, previously, the Articles) a state did *not* claim moral validity for its decision. On that description, the political decision was merely strategic or prudential, that is, taken only in service to whatever the state arbitrarily wanted because taken without any moral obligation—and the prior presence of a national public to which the ratifying claim is addressed is avoided. In addition, the states' rights view might then warrant secession in 1860: the Constitution was itself created by sovereign states, and our federated Union is, in effect, a mere treaty among them—"mere" because the federated Union as proposed and thus ratification of the Constitution makes no claim to moral validity.

Given that description, however, the Constitution's authority becomes merely de facto. Ratification would then express nothing more than a decision of those who considered the Convention's proposal in 1787–88 and attributed to it authority over their politics, and its authority would not extend beyond that fact. This is because, absent a moral claim for the Constitution, it becomes solely what nine or eleven or thirteen states, each calculating strategically from its solely preferential interests, accidentally wanted in common—and there is no reason why subsequent citizens should consider themselves bound by the agreement reached in 1787–88. Moreover, merely de facto authority would also characterize amendments enacted in accord with Article V and decisions of the Supreme Court or lesser courts stipulated in Article III. Absent a moral claim for the Constitution, in other words, it cannot constitute—define and structure institutionally or have (de jure) authority over—the US political tradition. Hence, no US citizen can be patriotic, such that she or he affirms the moral validity of popular sovereignty as an ideal and thus *should* attribute to the Constitution the right to command in relevant respects her or his beliefs and related actions.

On my accounting, constitutional ratification does make a claim to moral validity because the moral law is universal and transcendental to human decision as such. The moral law is, in the broad sense, a metaphysical feature of human decision. "Anyone who is interested philosophically in grounding the basic norm is able to appreciate through transcendental reflection that he is already presupposing this norm" (Apel 1980, 296, note 103). This is because humans as such decide with understanding, and the decision cannot be understood unless its alternatives are compared *with respect to choosing* and, thereby, evaluated. To be sure, some have asserted that alternatives can be compared only with respect to their descriptive similarities and differences, such that no decision among them can be understood, and choice among the alternatives is merely arbitrary or subjectivist. Something like this was, on my reading, David Hume's view (see Hume 1975, 290).

But *that* assertion is itself an understanding of alternatives for decision that belongs to the class denied. This is because, as Hume rightly allowed, an individual might misunderstand the supposedly proper understanding of alternatives for decision (namely, that understanding is limited to their descriptive similarities and differences)—for instance, by thinking some of them to be morally prescribed. Hence, the supposed limitation cannot itself be a comparison of descriptive similarities and differences but is, in truth, a completely general understanding of alternatives with respect to choosing. This comparison, in other words, evaluates alternatives as such and thus purports to be the moral law because the assertion implies that every human decision *ought* never to consider certain alternatives better or worse. For this reason, Kant argued that every theory of practical reason as such, including the theory that understanding cannot evaluate alternatives, is a moral theory.

I recognize that moral thought in the Western tradition, perhaps especially in its modern expressions, has often denied any universal terms of morality and asserted some or other account of goodness and rightness that is in all respects relative to context. Given that religious freedom as stipulated in the First Amendment legitimizes all possible convictions about the ultimate terms of evaluation, moral relativism is included. Nonetheless, any moral relativism, one may argue within the public discourse, is self-refuting. It implies, against itself, a comparison of contexts universally, of *all* contexts, in order to warrant the assertion that moral evaluation is in all cases entirely peculiar to context. A universal law absent anywhere is absent everywhere, and asserting the latter is a universal statement. Moreover, this universal comparison must be itself moral or, at least, must imply moral content. Otherwise, it could not warrant the moral conclusion. What Karl-Otto Apel says about reason in general applies to moral reason in particular, namely, it cannot function "merely as an object and no longer as the subject of critique" (Apel 1998, 164). A claim to moral validity, then, is a claim to consistency with a universal moral law.

Others assert that universal moral principles are applicable only when humans as such take a certain kind or kinds of decision—for instance, when a person's decisions affect the purposes of other people (for instance, promises should be kept, or one ought to tell the truth)—where purposes themselves are merely chosen and thus not the objects of moral evaluation. On this proposal, its adherents might agree that all asserted political decisions are moral claims, so that government through discussion and debate among the people governed is possible, because all asserted political decisions inescapably affect the merely chosen purposes of other people. But the moral theory articulating this proposal is also self-refuting, implying, against itself, a moral principle applicable to *all* human decisions. A distinction between moral and nonmoral kinds of decision implies a comparison of all decisions, that is, a variable the two kinds of decision are said to specify, and this comparative variable cannot be solely nonmoral because moral kinds of decision cannot specify a nonmoral variable. Hence, the comparison must itself be moral or, at least, imply moral content, so that all human decisions are bound by the moral law. In sum, the assertion that some kind or kinds of human decision are morally indifferent is itself a moral conclusion, requiring a moral principle applicable to human decision as such—and supposed moral indifference is always the assertion that alternatives for decision are insofar morally equal or equally good. Indeed, denial of a moral law universal to human decision as such is, in its own way, a version of relativism, even if one asserts that moral and immoral decision is relative to a certain universal kind or kinds of human decision.[21]

The implication of popular sovereignty (namely, it implies that every asserted political decision is a claim to moral validity whose validation or invalidation can be pursued by the way of reason) follows because asserted political decisions are subject to this moral law. A political decision, in other words, could refuse to claim moral validity only by denying any such law. Ratification of the Constitution, then, could refuse to be a moral claim only by denying the transcendental principle of moral validity—and the decision to ratify then asserts, at least by implication, that all supposed moral utterances are merely subjective: no supposed statement about better and worse alternatives is either valid or invalid; it is merely an exercise of will or is merely "emotive." Because it can deny the prior presence of "we the people" only by refusing a moral claim for the ratifying decision, the states' rights view, given its affirmation of popular sovereignty, is nonetheless thoroughly subjectivist with respect to evaluation. With Thomas Hobbes: "Good, evil, and contemptible are ever used in relation to the person who useth them; there being nothing simply or absolutely so; nor any common rule of good and evil to be taken from the objects themselves" (Hobbes 1962, 48–49).

This implied subjectivism is the underlying reason why the states' rights view contradicts its own affirmation of popular sovereignty and entails the absence of constitutional authority with respect to US politics.[22] Accordingly, the Constitution, which purports to constitute and thus to be (de jure) authoritative for the US political tradition, implies a claim to moral validity for its definition of US politics by the ideal of popular sovereignty and for the institutional structure provided. In contrast to the states' rights view, then, the national view is at least consistent with saying, as popular sovereignty requires, that every asserted political decision makes a moral claim, and thus US politics can be so constituted. In other words, the preceding discussion has sought to present the states' rights view and its commitment to popular sovereignty with a dilemma: either ratification of the Constitution does or does not make a claim to moral validity: if ratification does, it presupposes the prior presence and authorization of "we the people" (the national view) as the final ruling power; if ratification makes no such claim, the states' rights view reduces to subjectivism with respect to moral evaluation and denies the Constitution's authority over, including its definition of popular sovereignty as the ideal of, US politics.

The moral claims essential to popular sovereignty, whether for constitutional or statutory law, should always be distinguished from the moral law or the ultimate terms of evaluation—because the latter are universal to human decision as such and a claim to moral validity is always historically particular. This difference allows every asserted political decision to be contested and subsequently assessed by the way of reason. Indeed, the moral law's transcendental nature is finally what permits popular sovereignty, that is, government through a full and free discourse about the claim to moral validity made by every asserted political decision. Because they are universal to human decision as such, the ultimate terms of evaluation are commonly experienced by humans as such, so that a political community with religious freedom is possible because all humans, as mentioned in passing above, have access to those ultimate terms. Moreover, the moral law's transcendental nature implies that it and subjectivism exhaust the alternatives for understanding human decisions, in the following sense: the moral law and subjectivism are both implied by every denial of the former's transcendental character. Moral relativism, on which the moral law is specific to context or to a certain kind or kinds of universal human decisions, is self-refuting for the same reason—and subjectivism may be understood as relativism in which "good, evil, and contemptible" are relative to the self-conscious decision in question.

I will not here seek further to address the transcendental issue, but the following considerations may be pertinent to US citizens. First: if the states' rights view implies subjectivism with respect to supposedly moral statements, it also denies the thoroughly apparent moral claim made by all drafters and ratifiers in 1787--88, namely, the Constitution provides the institutional structure for popular sovereignty and thus constitutes, until altered or abolished, all subsequent US politics, being thereby authoritative for all patriotic US citizens. Second: if no political decision can be morally valid, the Constitution's provision for religious freedom legitimizes a plurality of substantially differing convictions about the ultimate terms of evaluation that must be excluded from the public's determinations because those who affirm one or another such conviction cannot engage in discourse. Relations among such citizens, then, can be based on nothing other than solely strategic deliberation, and, at least if the political decision is sufficiently important, such deliberation marks the occasion to fight. The political community is then a civil war waiting to happen, and civil peace is never more than a modus vivendi. This second consideration is simply another way to assert that popular sovereignty as the ideal marking US politics is impossible on the states' rights view. In any event, perhaps the implied denial of the Preamble and the First Amendment to the Constitution will be enough to commend the national view.

On that national view, the Declaration's expression was, in effect, a promissory note—precisely because a political tradition requires an authoritative set of political practices or institutions. In other words, "we the people" awaited articulation in some institutional structure. The Articles of Confederation were a first attempt to provide that structure, in which the "sovereignty, freedom, and independence" of each state (Article II) were underscored. Because the Revolution promised popular sovereignty, it was necessary to the Articles' articulation that they be ratified—and it is reasonable that ratification took a form modeled on the kind of Union proposed. Such ratification, in other words, should occur through the legislatures of the thirteen peoples because the institutional structure assigned extensive independence to each state. This assignment and thus the institutional structure articulated was, no doubt, greatly influenced by convictions within each state that granting to a "distant government" significant power (for instance, the power of taxation) would contradict the meaning of republican representation for which the Revolution was being fought. Nonetheless, given that "we the people" began with the Revolution, the Articles should be understood as a proposal to be ratified through the several states by the single people of the United States.

Still, if the Articles of Confederation were a first attempt by "we the people" to make good on the Declaration's promissory note, the Constitution is rightly understood to be a correction in that institutional structure. Finding woeful fault in the earlier articulation, the one people of the United States recognized that those Articles did not, in fact, institutionalize the Revolution's promise, so that a revision of the institutional structure was required. The initial attempt was renounced as inadequate to the promise, and thus another attempt to make good on the significance of the Revolution was effected, even while the US political tradition, defined by the final ruling power of a single people, endured.

With this conclusion, we can justify Article VII of the 1787 Constitution, which stipulated that ratification should occur through a convention within each state.[23] "We the people" could renounce as inadequate their own former attempt to articulate institutionally the Revolution's promise only with the recognition that, as sovereign, they had ratified the former attempt. Had "we the people" not ratified the Articles, they would not be bound by its decision-making procedure, but having done so, that procedure now structured authoritatively the renunciation of it. The Articles stipulated a procedure in accord with which the single people of the United States would make political decisions, and a change in that procedure, because it was authoritative, must be decided in accord with it. For the same reason, namely, a decision-making procedure ratified by "we the people" as an articulation of the Revolution's promise, any future change in the procedure stipulated by the Constitution (for instance, abolition of the electoral college) can be decided consistent with popular sovereignty only in accord with Article V of the Constitution, which stipulates how amendments are effected.

Given how the Articles of Confederation defined the procedure for decisions of the people as the final ruling power, in other words, the Constitution, with its substantial changes in that procedure, required ratification by appropriate bodies within each state. The earlier ratification stipulated a structural imperative for the Revolution's promise of popular sovereignty, which promise the proposed Constitution itself claimed to articulate. Thus, it could be itself consistent with that promise and with its own Preamble only if the Constitution prescribed ratification through the conventions for which Article VII provided.

NOTES

Introduction

1. The phrase "the future as such in its strictly metaphysical respect" may be redundant. Perhaps only metaphysical features could characterize (or, at least, could be understood to characterize) the very distant future. If so, the redundancy is useful because it underscores that "good" is defined metaphysically in the strict sense and that immorality defines "good" in some other way when a subject decides, at least in some undue measure, for its own future or the future of some community or group to which it is attached.

2. As I will discuss in chapter 5, the moral law is transcendental to subjectivity notwithstanding that existence with understanding does not become a subject without learning. This is because a telos, for which decision necessarily occurs, is strictly metaphysical and thus transcendental even to states that are nonmoral, and pursuit of this telos becomes a moral obligation when actualities become activities.

Chapter 1

1. See the distinction between individuals and activities in the introduction.

2. Kant famously asserted that "existence" is not a predicate because, were it so, the concept of something and the concept of its existence would not be the same concept. For this reason, some have suggested that existential statements are "systematically misleading expressions" (Alston 1993, 169). If I understand Kant's phrase correctly, I disagree. I doubt that, for Kant, "existence" is never rightly used as a predicate, principally because "existence" is, for Kant, a category, which he often used without noting that he then spoke in a misleading way. I take Kant to mean that "existence" is never *entailed* by the concept of a given thing and, thereby, is never a predicate implied by the essence of that thing. Accordingly, Kant meant to deny that any given thing exists necessarily. On my accounting, he assumed that "exists" designates a fully concrete thing or particular, and he rightly denied that a concept ever implies one of

its exemplifications. Still, I disagree with Kant because the existence of something should be distinguished from the various states in which that something is actualized, such that "x exists" means that x (designated by a concept) is now actualized in some particular state or other; x is actualized somehow, where actualities are the fully concrete things and are properly said to occur. For instance, a person or a stone or a hundred dollars in one's pocket, whether it exists or not, is indeed an abstraction, designated by a concept that might (or might not) be actualized in differing states. If this is so, a concept that entails its existence is no longer problematic; the distinction between existence and actualization means that no concept implies any given one of its exemplifications. Thus, Charles Hartshorne has said that *mode of existence* is indeed a predicate entailed by whatever concept is said to designate some existent; for instance, contingent existence is the predicate of most concepts designating a given existent, even while necessary existence is, for Hartshorne, the mode of one concept of an existent, namely, the divine individual (see Hartshorne 1962b).

3. "Nothing exists" is self-contradictory, rather than impossible in the sense of being hopelessly vague or mere gibberish, because the term "nothing" and the term "exists" can be used in statements that are possibly true—for instance, "nothing that is a dinosaur exists."

4. Some existential *denials* are necessarily true even while they are not implied by all existential statements and their denials, for instance, "something that is a married bachelor does not exist." This is because some statements about existence are necessarily true on condition; for instance, "if a bachelor exists, he is unmarried." In contrast, the necessarily true existential statements this chapter defends are necessarily true without condition; for instance, "something exists." Even necessarily true statements about existence that are conditional, moreover, imply existential statements that are necessarily true without condition because, as I will argue, "nothing exists" is not possibly true. Hence, all necessarily true existential denials imply statements designating the features of "something" in its most general sense.

5. More precisely formulated: the affirmation of "'nothing exists' is possibly true" implies the denial of "'something that knows some existential statement or statements exists' is possibly true."

6. For Hume, no existential statement is necessarily true because "whatever we conceive as existent, we can also conceive as non-existent," so that "the words ... *necessary existence* have no meaning" (Hume 1955, 58, 59).

7. Apel further distinguishes what he calls "dialectical strategic rationality" (Apel 1979, 338, emphasis deleted), which, in its own way, depends on scientific, hermeneutical, and ethical rationality.

8. As reviewed above, Nagel is one of these thinkers: "something existing" of which we cannot have "a conception" (Nagel 1986, 97) is something designated only by negation.

9. This notation designates the *Summa Contra Gentiles*, book 3, part I, the thirty-ninth chapter, the first paragraph. My citation is from Aquinas 1975. Also I will

subsequently designate citations from the *Summa Theologiae*, as, for instance, S.T. I. 1. 1. and, thereby, mean book I, the first question, the first article—and, within that article, Aquinas's answer to the question at hand. My citations are from Aquinas 1973.

10. To be sure, one might well ask how Aquinas could possibly know what is necessarily implied by a divine essence he cannot know.

11. A defense of Aquinas's demonstration might argue as follows: both existential statements about the world and the statement "no thing exists" imply God's existence because "not all beings are merely possible . . . [and] we cannot but admit the existence of some being having of itself its own necessity"—what Aquinas calls the third way to prove the existence of God (S.T. I. 2. 3). But if the God whose existence is supposedly implied is said to be designated only by negation, this argument is unconvincing—because such designation cannot be distinguished from "no thing exists."

12. This last statement, some may assert, expresses our condition precisely: we can only posit our existence and the world's existence in terms of some or other historically circumscribed lifeworld we inherit. But this assertion about our condition implies that it, too, must be only posited, thereby confirming that any positive existential statement can be only the mere assertion of the subject or subjects who assert it.

13. Perhaps this is why, although I am not confident that I understand his meaning, Nagel speaks of our "natural realism" (Nagel 1986, 74).

14. That Nagel does assert or assume the possible truth of "nothing exists" is also apparent when he reviews Bede Rundle's book, *Why there is Something rather than Nothing*, in which Rundle argues for the necessity of something—and Nagel concludes: "Though it is likely to make you giddy, it is hard to cast off the thought that there might have been nothing at all—not even space and time—that nothing might have been the case, ever. It is not a thought of how things might have been. It is not the thought of an empty universe. Nevertheless, it seems an alternative both to the actual universe and to all other possible universes that might have existence instead" (Nagel 2010, 30).

15. The pragmatic self-refutation in the assertion of "nothing exists" leads to another argument against "'nothing exists' is possibly true": The statement could be true if and only if the existence of subjects were impossible. But subjects cannot be impossible because they do, in fact, exist. Still, there is one supposed condition, given which the statement "nothing exists' could be true, namely, were it *necessarily* true. Only in that case would subjects be impossible (were "nothing exists" necessarily true, in other words, the existence of something with features and thus of subjects would be impossible). But the statement cannot be necessarily true because something (including subjects) does exist. For the sake of argument, however, I judge that one may credit a difference between (1) a self-refutation in the assertion of "nothing exists" and (2) a self-refutation in the assertion of "'nothing exists' could be true"—even if, given the existence of subjects, the latter could be true only were it necessarily true.

16. Pragmatically self-refuting statements that could nonetheless be (semantically) true (that is, are not self-contradictory) deny the designations of one or more

conditions *specific* to subjective existence as such, for instance, a denial of the existential statement "something that understands itself exists." Because no subject may exist, the denial is possibly true notwithstanding that an existing subject cannot believe or assert the denial because the statement is then pragmatically self-refuting. But "'nothing exists' is possibly true" does not deny a designation of one or more conditions specific to subjective existence as such. To the contrary, this statement purports that *all* existential statements can be denied without self-contradiction and that denies all designation of conditions *general* to existence as such. In other words, "'nothing exists' is possibly true" denies that "something exists" is necessarily true.

17. I take this fact about any true such assignment to be noncontroversial. Still, if that fact is contested, perhaps the following argument for it will suffice: a true statement is merely possibly true (that is, possibly but not necessarily true) if its being true depends on conditions; a true statement is necessarily true if its being true is independent of conditions. Were the merely possible or, as the case may be, necessary truth of a true statement itself merely possibly true, a true statement that is merely possibly true would, given certain conditions, be not merely possibly true, that is, would be necessarily true—and a true statement that is necessarily true would, given certain conditions, be not necessarily true, that is, would be merely possibly true. Hence, the truth of a merely possibly true statement or a necessarily true statement both would and would not depend on conditions. Stating that the truth of a true statement both depends on and does not depend on conditions is self-contradictory.

18. That "nothing exists" is self-contradictory can, I think, be argued more directly: the statement "nothing exists" cannot be distinguished from a putative statement "something that is x exists" that is merely putative because it is self-contradictory. The statement that some existent has self-contradictory features—for instance, "a colorless yellow thing exists"—attributes existence to something designated by a grammatical subject defined as "not-x and nothing other than x" and thus something designated only by negation. For instance, a colorless thing is not a yellow thing, and a yellow thing is nothing other than a yellow thing; "something that is not a yellow thing and nothing other than a yellow thing" defines the thing only by negation. Because complete negation cannot be distinguished from complete negation, the statement "nothing exists" cannot be distinguished from a self-contradictory existential statement. Hence, "nothing exists" is self-contradictory. But if this argument is sound, it remains, on my reading, that a dominant consensus in recent philosophy so discredits transcendental metaphysics that many take its futility for granted—even while participants in this consensus typically endorse in some way or other the pursuit of scientific and moral knowledge. In this context, I judge, showing first how those pursuits are inconsistent with the dictum in question may better serve a general reconsideration of metaphysical necessity.

19. That positive designation can be distinguished only from another positive designation is true even if one of the two designates a strictly metaphysical feature, such that "something that is x exists" is necessarily true. Given that temporality is a

strictly metaphysical feature, for instance, designation of something as temporal can be distinguished from designation of the same thing in terms of some nonmetaphysical feature, for instance, as a subject. Thus, strictly metaphysical features are distinguished from the contingent features of some actual or possible thing.

20. For instance, statements about the features specifically necessary to existence with developed understanding, such that it is distinguished from other existence, each imply all of the others; but those statements also imply metaphysical statements, and the latter do not imply the former.

21. I do not imply that Whitehead affirmed the transcendental character of metaphysics. I doubt that he did so explicitly, and whether he did so implicitly is controversial.

22. Moreover, the distinction between necessary and contingent features is itself a necessary or metaphysical feature of every possible something that exists. *That* every possible existent exemplifies some or other contingent features is itself a necessary feature of it.

23. See, for instance, Whitehead; Hartshorne; Ogden. I have sought to outline a metaphysics of this kind in Gamwell 2011, chapter 3.

Chapter 2

1. In general, the view that speaking of God is not possible independently of the Christian community and its discourse is, I hold, unconvincing—at least if this means that whether one speaks of God is independent of all philosophical assessment. Here, philosophy is critical reflection that asks about the most general features of human existence and thus asks about what is, if anything, common to all human experience. To the best of my reasoning, the view in question implies the absence of any common human experience of God, and the critical statement that common human experience excludes an experience of God is itself philosophical. Some who defend the view in question may then assert that even this statement (namely: "there is no common human experience of God") is warranted by the discourse of a particular religious community. Those who thereby separate Christian theology from philosophy, however, are bound to say something stronger, namely, that *only* the discourse of a particular religious community warrants the statement in question; that is, the statement cannot be warranted philosophically. But if the statement is true, it can also be established by appeal to the most general features of human existence. What can be established is, in other words, the absence within common human experience of any experience of God—or, perhaps, what can be established is the absence of any common human experience at all. Hence, the statement implies something about human existence that philosophy can assess.

2. This notation refers to the *Summa Theologiae*, the first part, the second question, the first article, and within that article, to the answer Aquinas gives. Henceforth, I will follow this notation in references to this work. When the reference is to a reply

Aquinas gives to one or another objection, I will supplement the reference with "ad1," "ad2," and so forth, depending on the number of the objection in question. I will also refer to the *Summa Contra Gentiles* (S.C.G.), citing the book, the chapter, and the paragraph, as, for example, S.C.G. 1.1.1. The translations from which I cite are given in "Works Cited."

3. The term here translated "properly" (*proprie*) may also be translated "literally." For this reason, some may conclude that Aquinas here qualifies the assertion that "univocal predication is impossible between God and creatures" (S.T. 1.13.5). But it seems clear in the third article of S.T. 1.13 that speaking "properly" or "literally" of God is distinguished from speaking metaphorically (cf. Alston 1993, 147; Kretzmann 1997, 179–80). Thus, speaking "properly" includes speaking univocally and speaking analogically. To speak univocally of God is to speak "through negations," and in speaking positively of God and creatures, speaking properly is speaking analogically.

4. The importance of "healthy" as an example is its illustration of predication in different senses "through a relation to some one thing," a characteristic also found in analogical names applied to God and creatures. In other ways, however, the example fails adequately to illustrate theistic analogies. For instance, Aquinas distinguishes between analogical speaking according to which "many things have reference to something one" and such speaking according to which "the order or reference of two things is not to something else but to one of them" (S.C.G. 1.34.2,3). On my understanding, this distinction serves to differentiate analogical names applied to God, which exemplify the latter, from at least some others, including "healthy," which applies to medicine and urine by reference to an animal body. More important, theistic analogies, or at least some of them, designate perfections with respect to which there is a likeness between God and creatures, such that what is in God is also in the creature less eminently. By contrast, one would not say that the health in an animal body is in the medicine less eminently. Rather, medicine is called healthy solely as the cause of animal health. But Aquinas explicitly rejects the assertion that positive names applied to God mean only that God is the cause of what is found in creatures (S.T. 1.13.2), and this denial expresses his affirmation that God is the *first cause* of all things other than God. In an essay to which I am indebted, William Alston makes this point by saying that causality in the divine case "is of such a sort as to involve transmission of form (perfection) from cause to effect" (Alston 1993, 157, emphasis deleted). The distinction between what is signified and the mode of signification that characterizes analogical names of God and creatures also serves to protect this limitation on the illustration of "healthy." Once this limitation is clarified, one might conclude that theistic analogies exemplify for Aquinas what has traditionally been called "analogy of attribution." If I understand him rightly, Alston himself comes to this conclusion, in contrast to the classic interpretation of Thomas Cajetan, "according to which commonality of intrinsic property is found only in the analogy of proportionality" (Alston 1993, 158). In contrast to analogies in which

"names predicated of many ... all are predicated through a relation to some one thing" (S.T. 1.13.6), an analogy of proportionality designates a likeness between two or more relations. For instance, "rule" is applied analogically in saying that reason rules the passions as the king rules the city. E. J. Ashworth concludes, "Thirteenth-century logicians simply do not seem to be interested in proportionality; and this in turn suggests to me that it is a mistake to suppose that Aquinas is talking about proportionality, or the comparison of two proportions, except in those places where he says explicitly that that is what he is doing" (Ashworth 1992, 122–23; see also Wippel 1992, 290–97). Ralph McInerny has argued, against Cajetan, that "there is no distinction between analogy of attribution and analogy of proportionality in St. Thomas Aquinas" (McInerny 1996, 12). In this chapter, I present and discuss analogical names for God and creatures as examples of analogy of attribution. In the end, however, the validity of my conclusions does not rest on showing that, for Aquinas, this is the relevant kind of analogy. I will argue that Aquinas implicitly excludes a conception of the relation between God and creatures essential to the distinction between analogical and merely equivocal names and does so because he excludes a conception of God. Because the latter exclusion occasions the basic problem, the reasoning could be presented mutatis mutandis should predication of God and creatures be taken in terms of the analogy of proportionality.

5. Because it is central to Aquinas's account of theistic analogies, his distinction between the *res significata* and the *modus significandi* is itself the object of extensive discussion and varied interpretations. I understand it and have presented it as differentiating a real or ontological order of priority and posteriority from an order of priority and posteriority in our understanding.

6. As all premises, the statement that assertions about something inconceivable are not meaningful might be and has been contested. At least by implication, both Stephan Körner and Richard Rorty assert that statements about what is inconceivable may be meaningful (see Körner 1969, 215; Rorty 1979, 82–83). Although I cannot see how one could show that any statement about what is inconceivable is so much as possibly true, I will not seek to defend that statement here—except to say that designation of something as inconceivable designates it solely by negation (see chapter 1, "A Defense of Metaphysical Necessity," in this book, and Gamwell 1990, chapter 4).

7. It is at least debatable whether the sense in which "being" is analogical (and thus nonunivocal) with respect to, say, substance and accident or concrete and abstract is the same sense in which "being" is analogical (and thus nonunivocal) in all speaking that is positive of God and creatures. That analogy has a valid use in the first case does not imply its validity in all positive naming of the difference between God and creatures. I am assuming, then, that Aquinas intends the analogical sense of "being" in speaking positively of God and creatures as similar to the sense in which "wisdom" or "living" is analogical in speaking positively of God and creatures—that is, such that we cannot know God's essence.

8. Norman Kretzman defends one of Aquinas's arguments for the existence of a first cause, which is found in chapter 15 of the *Summa Contra Gentiles*. On Kretzman's reading, Aquinas there shows that an "explanation of the most familiar kind of actual existence" (Kretzman 1997, 96), in the sense of its sustaining rather than generating cause, requires that we "posit a first necessary being, which is necessary through itself" (S.C.G. 1.15.5). But even if we credit the argument in the sense Kretzman does, I cannot see how it could demonstrate or contribute to demonstrating the existence of a God whose essence we cannot know—because thereby both "cause" (whether sustaining or generating) and "being," as all other positive names, apply to God only analogically, and if the above argument is sound, analogical names for God cannot be distinguished from purely equivocal ones.

9. My attention to Burrell will focus on his argument in the former of these two works, which, as he himself says, gives the "fuller treatment of analogy" (Burrell 1979, 176; preface, n. 3). The later work, an interpretation of Aquinas, does not, as far as I can see, substantially revise the earlier account of what is involved in speaking analogically of God.

10. Burrell notes the similarities between this interpretation of Aquinas and the constructive formulations of Paul Tillich, but Burrell also recognizes important differences between the two (see Burrell 1973, 129, 132–33). For instance, Tillich typically calls all positive theistic predication symbolic, and the relevant meaning of "symbol" is roughly equivalent to what Aquinas designates as metaphorical predication. Thus, Tillich does not systematically distinguish, as Aquinas does, between symbolic or metaphorical and analogical speaking of God. Moreover, some argue, this difference exhibits differing understandings of the divine reality (see Ford 1966). At least with respect to the character of theistic predication, however, one might conclude, as Burrell seems to suggest, that the similarities between Aquinas and Tillich are more impressive than their differences. Both assert that only by negation can the divine reality be named in terms that apply to God and creatures without equivocation or, in that sense, designate literally. To be sure, Tillich famously said "God is being-itself is a non-symbolic statement" (Tillich 1951, 238), but even this designation is negative because it is equivalent to the statement "God is not a being." On my reading, this common conviction that nonanalogical and nonsymbolic speaking of God must be negative is what makes the two accounts, whatever their differences, fundamentally alike. If this is so, then one has some initial reason to think that success in the present criticism of Aquinas should give pause to any philosophical account of theistic symbols that is dependent on Tillich.

11. On my accounting, the question is not meaningful because it presupposes that being nothing at all is a meaningful thought, and as I discuss briefly below, I do not think that this is the case. In the end, I believe, Burrell's proposal is, at least by implication, properly included among those for which speaking of God is not possible independently of the Christian (or some other religious) community and its discourse. In his later book, Burrell argues that Aquinas explicates "the grammar of

divinity" in a manner "designed to make plausible the formula 'the beginning and end of all things and of reasoning creatures especially'" (Burrell 1979, 2). If this formula can be employed to speak of what is inconceivable, such speaking must be solely dependent on the discourse of a religious community—and I suspect that Burrell agrees with this view (see Burrell 1979, chaps. 5 and 6, esp. 88–89). I will not seek here to reach a decision about that view (but see note 1 in this chapter).

12. Nor can it be said that this is solely an epistemic conclusion, so that, notwithstanding our incapacity to distinguish it, some complete negation may still be possible. That statement purports to distinguish what cannot be distinguished, namely a complete negation from no object at all. In the end, I believe, the principle of prior actuality in this sense implies and is implied by the assumption mentioned in the conclusion of section II above, that is, that assertions about something inconceivable are philosophically impossible. An assertion of this kind can purport to designate only a complete negation. Given the principle, then, every such assertion is senseless. Conversely, if the inconceivable is simply inconceivable, no meaningful assertion can be free of positive implications. The required philosophical conclusion is, then, not only epistemic but also ontological.

13. Instead, see Hartshorne 1970, especially chapter 8; Ogden 2018; and the outline of metaphysics in Gamwell 2011, chapter 3.

14. Since I have mentioned Alston's denial of divine simplicity, it is worth noting that he has proposed a metaphysical conception of God that is formulated in explicit contrast to that of Hartshorne. This proposal asserts, with Hartshorne, that "relativity," "potentiality," "contingency," and "complexity" apply univocally to God and creatures. But, Alston argues, Hartshorne has failed to show that these affirmations are inconsistent with saying, as Aquinas does, that God is nontemporal, immutable, omnipotent, incorporeal, absolutely perfect, and creator ex nihilo. Thus, Alston's essay is titled "Hartshorne and Aquinas: A Via Media" (Alston 1984). I cannot here pursue the detailed assessment Alston's essay merits. I will only mention that I do not find his proposal convincing because it requires a metaphysical conception of God that is independent of God's relativity, that is, a positive conception of God consistent with the possibility that God does not relate to a world, and I do not think that Alston has presented such a conception. The possibilities he offers, "a being with an infinite specious present" (Alston 1984, 91) and Whitehead's conception of God "as a single infinite actual entity" (Alston 1984, 93), both imply relativity. For an argument against the consistency of asserting that a God who is really related to a world might not be really related to a world, see Ogden 1991, 54–56.

15. In his own way, Hartshorne himself affirms analogical speaking of God that is distinct from both literal and symbolic predication, although Hartshorne holds that such analogical speaking would not make sense were literal speaking of God and creatures impossible (see Hartshorne 1962a, 133–47). I am convinced by the critique of Ogden that Hartshorne's own attempt to differentiate analogical and symbolic predication of God is also unsuccessful (see Ogden 1984).

Chapter 3

1. I mean by "relation" a positive relation. Some might take separation to be, in its own way, a relation, but I use the term such that independence is the absence of a relation and thus ask what relation there is, *if any*, between Schleiermacher's achievement and transcendental philosophy.

2. References to sections of Schleiermacher's *The Christian Faith* (1989) will be included parenthetically in the text.

3. As dogmatic, in other words, the statement that dogmatics is separate from philosophy would supposedly express the meaning of Christian faith; but philosophy might then have the possibility of asking whether the meaning of Christian faith (including this statement) makes sense philosophically.

4. Some who defend the view in question may then assert that even this statement (namely: "there is no common human experience of God") is warranted by the Christian experience of Jesus. Those who so separate Christian dogmatics from philosophy, however, are bound to say something stronger, namely, that *only* that experience warrants the statement in question; that is, the statement cannot be warranted philosophically. But if the statement is true, it can also be established by appeal to general or common human experience—and the statement implies something about human existence that philosophy can assess.

5. To be sure, self-conscious existence is, in the terms I have used in the introduction to this book, not necessarily subjective, on the one hand, and subjects are not necessarily human, on the other—so that everything essential to human nature may not be essential to self-conscious creatures or to subjects. A subject, on my account, is self-conscious both of the self in its given activity and of the self as an individual of which that activity is a part. But some nonhuman animals may be, at specific moments, self-conscious without understanding the individual of which that moment is a part, and some individuals, either other nonhuman animals or individuals on other planets, may understand themselves or be subjects without depending on a distinctively human body. As far as I can see, however, Schleiermacher does not distinguish between self-conscious existence, human existence, and subjective existence. In any event, the features he mentions that I take to be transcendental to human existence are entirely shared with any other individuals whose self-consciousness includes an understanding of the individual in question and thus are subjects.

6. I refer to Schleiermacher's assertion that every object on which one is partially dependent is also partially influenced by one's freedom, even if only in trivial measure (see § 4.2), an account apparently connected to his conception of a "universal nature-system" (§ 34.1). On my accounting, that conception implies determinism. Or, what finally comes to the same thing, the assertion of reciprocity with all objects in the world misconstrues the nature of time. In truth, the present is influenced by the past and influences only the future, and thus there are some others on which we are partially dependent that we do not affect.

7. In speaking of an intentional object that depends on concepts, I do not imply that it is necessarily dependent on language, such that the subject in question must have a linguistic representation of the object. To the best of my reading, Proudfoot equates dependence on concepts with dependence on language (see, e.g., Proudfoot 1985, xiv). But his critique of Schleiermacher's feeling of absolute dependence does not require this equation.

8. "Prior" here does not mean temporally prior but, rather, prior in constituting the subject, in the sense of being presupposed by reflective consciousness and thus by theoretical and practical reason.

9. Again, I mean by "relation" a positive relation (see note 1 in this chapter). One might say that experience of God as simply "not the world" is an experience of God in relation to the world, but I so use "relation" that relation is absent in this description of God.

10. This notation refers to the *Summa Contra Gentiles*, the third book, the thirty-ninth chapter, and the first paragraph. I will also refer to the *Summa Theologiae*, citing the part, the question, and the article, and within that article, the answer Aquinas gives—for instance, S.T. 1.1.1. The translations from which I cite are in the Works Cited.

11. Indeed, I am tempted to say that Schleiermacher's account of dogmatics is, in an instructive way, similar to the later Martin Heidegger's account of understanding. In each case, truthful thought about ourselves within the world as a whole becomes possible by virtue of a particular disclosure of what cannot be thought positively as such. In Schleiermacher's case, the disclosure occurs when feeling of the infinite so combines with the sensible self-consciousness as to found a particular religious community, and for Heidegger, the disclosure occurs through a concealing/unconcealing event in the history of Being. To be sure, Schleiermacher, at least on the reading I propose, holds that this very account of our existence within the world is itself a transcendental understanding of subjectivity—and, for that reason, dogmatics is not philosophy. Perhaps, in *Being and Time*, Heidegger also sought a transcendental account. If so, that project was abandoned, and his later work more or less clearly insisted that meaning and truth in philosophy itself is circumscribed within an epoch in the history of Being. Still, we can say that, mutatis mutandis, Schleiermacher's feeling of absolute dependence occupies in his thought what Dasein's "being held out into the Nothing" occupies in that of Heidegger (see, e.g., Heidegger 1993, 103; see also Gamwell 2011, chapter 2).

12. Tillich famously writes: "The statement that God is being-itself is a non-symbolic statement.... after this has been said, nothing else can be said about God as God which is not symbolic" (Tillich 1951, 238–39)—thereby implying one positive statement about God that is nonsymbolic. As far as I can see, however, the statement "God is being-itself" is, for Tillich, equivalent to "God is not a being"—and strictly nothing positive can be said literally about being-itself because it is not a being.

13. It follows that Schleiermacher credits Kant's assertion that "noumena exist"—even if Schleiermacher, unlike Kant, holds that relation to a noumenon

232 NOTES

(namely, God) can be found in the feeling of absolute dependence, so that religions can symbolize God's relation to the world and, therefore, theoretical truth.

14. See chapter 1, "A Defense of Metaphysical Necessity" in this book.

Chapter 4

1. In this section, all references by page number alone are to this text.

2. I grant that Augustine is here explicating his statement "only something that is seen can incite the will to act" (121); that is, he intends to explain why turning away from God is an alternative. Still something more is at stake precisely because the serpent's suggestion not only offers sin as an alternative but, rather, presents the *allure* of inferior things, just as the devil's awareness of self includes presenting impiety as pleasing.

3. Henceforth, all references by page number alone are to this text.

4. An account of temptation as caused by socially prior sin might imply the temporal mystery of how temptation got started in the human adventure itself. But that cannot be the sense of mystery Niebuhr has in mind because he would thereby be led back to Adam in a historical sense, that is, Adam as standing for a (mysterious) historical beginning by which all subsequent humans are somehow affected, in contrast to Niebuhr's explication of Adam as "representative man" (261).

5. I recognize that Niebuhr sometimes speaks as if humans are tempted because anxiety as the occasion for sin follows from being both finite and free and thus is necessary to self-awareness. So, for instance, he writes: "The temptation to sin lies ... in the human situation itself. The situation is that man as spirit transcends the temporal and natural process in which he is involved and also transcends himself.... Since he is involved in the contingencies and necessities of the natural process on the one hand, and since, on the other, he stands outside of them and foresees their caprices and perils, he is anxious" (251). As my explication has sought to express, however, I take his considered position to be more circumspectly formulated in the following: "The situation of finiteness and freedom in which man stands becomes a source of temptation only when it is falsely interpreted. This false interpretation is not purely the product of the human imagination. It is suggested to man by a force of evil which precedes his own sin. Perhaps the best description or definition of this mystery is the statement that sin posits itself" (180–81). Temptation cannot be necessary to self-awareness, Niebuhr believes, because God as Creator would thereby be the cause of an evil. Thus "the temptation to sin lies ... in the human situation itself" only if that situation is understood to include the mysterious "bias toward sin" so that self-awareness foresees the "caprices and perils" of "the natural process" through the "defect of the will" (251, 249, 251, 242).

6. On my reading of Niebuhr, his understanding of the divine ground does not permit this distinction because, for him, God is a completely eternal reality. Accordingly, one cannot speak of God except by way of negation or by way of symbolic or

mythological statement. Every existential understanding of God is, then, an understanding of totality "coloured" by "finite perspectives drawn from ... [one's] own immediate situation (182)," and the logic of Niebuhr's position makes sin necessary because fragmentary consciousness cannot have a true understanding of its authentic alternative for original freedom.

CHAPTER 5

1. If infinite indetermination in all respects can be designated only by negation, we may anticipate subsequent discussion by noting that designation only by negation does not follow from the infinity of past (because every actuality relates to previous actualities) and future (because every more or less immediate future possibility specifies some possibilities further in the future). In other words, designation only by negation does not follow from the metaphysical necessity of "something exists." This is because the necessity of "something exists" means "something that is now actualized exists" whereby a limit to future possibility is created—and the infinite past and future can be designated positively as the infinity of metaphysically final actualities and possibilities therefor. Hence, this is the difference between an absolute distinction (which is, in fact, impossible because one side of the distinction is designated only by negating the other side) and an infinite distinction between necessarily true and contingently true existential statements.

2. Merely numerical difference—as, I think, Aquinas may imply with respect to individuals (humans aside) of a given species—is not a difference; were it so, the supposed difference would be designated only by negation.

3. On a proper use of terms, I expect, only aggregates exist; their actualities, in contrast, occur. Still, one may speak of metaphysics in the strict sense explicating existence as such (that is, explicating necessarily true existential statements) because every actuality, through internal relation to the past, belongs to some aggregate or aggregates, however brief its or their duration, and every existing aggregate must be actualized somehow.

4. As far as I can see, extraordinary or all-inclusive actualities occupy all space, so that every ordinary actuality may be understood as a localization of the divine.

5. Some readings of Kant may affirm his moral theory because, for them, the formal universality of reason is completely independent of any matter or purpose. I do not think that Kant so intended. This is principally because his affirmation of the "absolute worth" of "any rational being" (Kant 1949, 45), such that rational freedom is "the supreme limiting condition" we should never "act against," (Kant 1949, 48 54), implies that chosen purposes or material ends are rightly evaluated in part.

6. To be sure, there is another sense in which one may choose an alternative in part. Consider, for instance, the alternatives (1) pursuit of one's own success (however understood), and (2) the devotion to one's family—where these two define competitive pursuits. One might aim at success in some lesser measure in order to spend more

time with one's family—and in that way, pursue each alternative in part. But, then, there are really three alternatives: (1) pursuit of one's own success; (2) devotion to one's family; and (3) a compromise in which each is sacrificed in some measure in order to pursue the other (or there are many alternatives, depending on the measure in which each of the first two is compromised). None of these three (or these many) can be chosen in part. Similarly, any set of alternatives, one or more of which may be chosen in part is, in truth, a larger set of alternatives, none of which can be chosen in part.

7. To be sure, I hold that two or more alternatives for purpose, and thus two or more telé that define those alternatives, may be *equally* good. The strictly metaphysical feature "good" is maximally abstract, so that more specific conditions may yield telé in which that abstract feature is equally exemplified. Still, this circumstance requires a definition of "good" exemplified as a variable, else there could be no decision between moral and immoral.

8. The phrase "the future as such in its strictly metaphysical respect" may be redundant. Perhaps only metaphysical features could characterize (or at least could be understood to characterize) the very distant future. If so, the redundancy is useful because it underscores that "good" is defined metaphysically in a strict sense and that immorality defines "good" in some other way when a subject decides for, at least in undue measure, its own future or the future of some community or group to which it is attached.

9. Absent this question about what future is good, I suspect, there is no credible answer to a vexing question about immoral choice—namely: why would one be attracted to, or take any interest in deciding for, a false original decision when one is aware of the truth; why would one be *tempted* to lie to oneself by choosing a lesser good when one is aware of the truly good? The answer depends, I think, on the individual's fragmentary understanding of the future—specifically, the individual's more concrete appreciation of its own future and that of groups or communities to which it is attached. I have sought to address this question in chapter 4 of this book; see also Gamwell 2000, chapter 2.

10. Summarily stated, this is because a subjective activity cannot understand a particularity—and the range of possibility given to an activity by its relations to the past must be particular to it, else there could be two identical activities. In other words, understanding is consciousness of universals—and there is no universal exemplified in attention to one's own particularity alone. Hence, it is not possible for a subjective activity to understand its own range of possibility; its decision can be only for some telos subsequent to the activity, in pursuit of which it becomes determinate within the range of possibility given.

11. I owe this discussion to a problem with teleology identified by Brian Barry's *Justice as Impartiality* (1995), although he may disagree with my resolution of that problem.

12. Even if very small children are not subjects, I hold nonetheless that subjects' rights extend to such children because they are, perhaps unlike some nonhuman animals, at least potentially subjects. For a discussion of how this point relates to the issue of abortion, see Gamwell 2005, 131–43.

13. Some may object that a principle of subjects' rights cannot be, strictly speaking, transcendental because a subjective activity that does not affect another subjective activity is, at least, conceivable. Hence, a principle of subjects' rights could be only a specification of the transcendental moral law to conditions in which such affects occur—as is, for instance, a specification of the moral law to conditions in which a subjective activity belongs to a US citizen. To the contrary, I believe, the principle of subjects' rights is indeed implied by subjectivity as such because every subjective activity does affect other subjective activities, even if the latter will occur solely within the subjective individual in question. Indeed, this is the very meaning of self-expression, that is, of unification for the sake of future realization. Moreover, the difference between a subjective individual and a community of such individuals is itself implied by subjects as such—so that, in this sense, subjective activity is intersubjective: the existence of subjective individuals occurs in the plural, as the learning without which an individual cannot become a subject testifies. Even the last activity of the last subjective individual on earth implies a community of subjective individuals from which it became a subject and implies a principle for the effect of individuals in that community on the subject in question.

14. I have discussed the address to this criticism at greater length in Gamwell 2011, see 115–26.

Chapter 6

1. In this discussion, I will cite these three books parenthetically in the text and, respectively, as simply 2006, 2011, and 2013.

2. This precept has two possible meanings—and, correspondingly, "important basic right" has two meanings. First, those religion clauses should be so interpreted as to make sense of the role assigned to them in politics defined by the US Constitution. Thereby, religious freedom should be understood in service to, for instance, popular sovereignty—if government "by the people" is taken as the fundamental principle of that constitution. Second, those religion clauses should be so interpreted as to make the best sense of them morally and politically, that is, in terms of valid principles of justice. Which of the two Dworkin has in mind is not completely clear to me. In his books *Law's Empire* (1986) and *Freedom's Law: The Moral Reading of the American Constitution* (1996), Dworkin seems to intend the second meaning, although it is qualified by a prescription to make best sense of the history of constitutional interpretation. In any event, I agree with the precept on its first but not its second meaning. What form of politics is defined by the US Constitution and what form of politics is best or in conformity with justice are different questions—even if the US Constitution is, in fact, just.

3. Dworkin includes in this class a proposal he himself once advanced, namely: "Religions attempt to answer the deeper existential question by connecting individual human lives to a transcendent objective value" (2013, 121).

4. Because a substantive definition of "religion" is what I will subsequently offer, I should here respond to this criticism. Without a definition of "religion," as far as I can see, the constitutional provision of religious freedom cannot be interpreted—because, absent that definition, courts cannot decide from what citizens are free. Dworkin's critique of substantive definitions, namely, that "questions of fundamental value are a matter of individual . . . choice" (2013, 123), depends on *his* understanding of religious freedom.

5. For Dworkin, the cosmological part of religion does not necessarily include belief in a transcendent or divine reality. In *Religion without God*, he so defines religion that an atheist may be religious. Hence, the "religious attitude" is said to include "two central judgments about value": (*a*) "that human life has objective meaning or importance," and thus "each person has an innate and inescapable responsibility" to live well, and (*b*) "that what we call 'nature'—the universe as a whole and in all its parts—is not just a matter of fact but is itself sublime" (2013, 10). Because evaluative truth is separated from truth about what there is, these value judgments can, if I understand correctly, be affirmed whether or not one's cosmology includes belief in a transcendent or divine reality. But whatever "religion" means for Dworkin, he does not interpret the political principle of religious freedom as protection for religious beliefs alone.

6. Given his inheritance from Hume and Kant, moreover, Dworkin apparently dismisses that metaphysical project without a hearing as a kind of supposed thinking no longer in need of refutation. He does, at one point, reject a theistic basis for morality because it cannot escape the supposed choice first stated in Plato's *Euthyphro*—namely, if God is good, an independent definition of good is presupposed; if no independent definition of good is presupposed, God's will or command is merely an arbitrary exercise of power. Dworkin endorses the former choice—although in doing so, he says, he "is taking sides in an ancient theological controversy" (2011, 341), and he does so because a theistic basis for morality violates Hume's principle (see 2011, 341–42). Thus, Hume's principle controls his conclusion to the supposed dilemma. Thereby, Dworkin ignores the possibility that a comprehensive good can be defined only metaphysically in the strict sense, such that God is the metaphysical individual whose will implies and is implied by every other feature of God's necessary nature. Hence, neither an independent definition of good nor an arbitrary exercise of power is implied, and the supposed two sides of this ancient controversy do not exhaust the alternatives.

7. I am not clear that Dworkin's use of "moral" in *Justice for Hedgehogs* should always be understood as distinct from "ethical." In the earlier part of the book, he speaks of moral truth and responsibility in ways seemingly inclusive of ethical truth and responsibility. If I understand correctly, however, the earlier discussion concerns the object of moral theories generally, recognizing that some of them may not include Dworkin's interpretation of the difference between morality and ethics; accordingly, that discussion intends, at least implicitly, to abstract from his own proposal, to which the distinction, introduced later, is essential.

8. See note 5 in this chapter. In contrast to a meaning of "cosmological affirmation" that allows atheism to be a religion, Dworkin sometimes speaks of religion in a still more specific sense, such that its cosmological affirmation includes belief in a transcendent or divine reality—and, thereby, "religion" means what he takes to be commonly or conventionally understood by the term. But he is not, on my reading, confusing; the context clarifies the relevant designation of the term.

9. In this argument, Dworkin may seem to violate his endorsement of Hume's principle: from the fact of human decision-making, he seems to derive the conclusion that supposedly external skepticism is a moral claim. But this criticism perhaps misunderstands what Dworkin means by "scientific and metaphysical" facts, from which, according to Hume's principle, moral claims are logically independent. Elsewhere, Dworkin differentiates statements from a perspective "outside an agent's ordinary sense of his situation" and statements "within the brackets of an ordinary life lived from a personal perspective" (2011, 229). On my understanding, "scientific and metaphysical" facts in the sense relevant to Hume's principle are designated by statements from the former or impersonal perspective, while the question asked and answered in all human decision-making occurs within the latter or personal perspective. In other words, this dualism of perspectives is what warrants the "embracing dualism of understanding" (2011, 123). At the same time, as far as I can see, Dworkin does not ask or, at least, does not tell us from what perspective the dualism of perspectives is itself understood.

10. On my reading, moreover, Dworkin would be inconsistent to argue from the ordinary view to the reality of moral truth. Most people throughout history have also taken their choices to determine what is otherwise undetermined, namely, which among more than one alternative will be realized. Against this belief, however, Dworkin credits the possible truth of so-called compatibilism, on which human choices are consistent with "every one . . . [being] fully determined by processes and events that precede it and lie outside the control of the decider" (2011, 220). He defends this possibility notwithstanding his simultaneous assertion that choices have moral criteria because each is asserted from a different perspective. "The causal principle views the question of responsibility from outside an agent's own ordinary sense of his situation. . . . The capacity principle, on the contrary, locates responsibility within the brackets of an ordinary life lived from a personal perspective" (2011, 229). In sum: "The universe may know what we will decide, but we do not" (2011, 230).

11. As far as I can see, that supposed separation could obtain only if all substantive moral utterances were neither true nor false because, if taken as assertions, they answer a senseless question. Only then could a meta-ethical statement to this effect, that is, the statement about all substantive moral utterances, be independent of any one.

12. As far as I can see, moreover, Dworkin's separation of science and interpretation must itself be an interpretive conclusion. This follows from calling Hume's principle itself a moral principle; that is, understanding the "embracing dualism of understanding" (2011, 123) cannot itself be a scientific understanding. Dworkin

seems to imply this reading in saying that we should "understand truth [including scientific truth] as an interpretive concept. We should reformulate the different theories of truth that philosophers have proposed, so far as we can, by treating them as interpretive claims" (2011, 173). Perhaps this is consistent with the circularity Dworkin asserts of interpretation generally, but the proposal gives no reason to call that account of Hume's principle true—much less "obviously true" (2011, 44).

13. The alternatives Dworkin considers appear to be (*a*) intrinsic value in one's own life (or the lives of members of one's group) alone, and (*b*) intrinsic value in the lives of all humans. But we are not told why these exhaust the possibilities. Some thinkers assert the intrinsic value of all living creatures—or, for that matter, strictly all things. Even if more expansive accounts of intrinsic value require some way to conceive the relative value of differing kinds of things, it remains that Dworkin does not allow such accounts as alternatives to (*a*) above.

14. Extending the class of protected convictions and, thereby, the meaning of "religious" in "religious freedom" might seem to be a revision, rather than an interpretation, of the US Constitution's First Amendment. Still, the broad meaning of "religious" might be defended as an interpretation in the following way: along with all other principles in the United States Constitution, the religion clauses are properly interpreted, if possible, in relation to the Constitution's defining purpose, namely, to constitute a political community in which, as the Preamble makes apparent, sovereignty is assigned (as the ideal to be pursued) to "we the people." Because government by the people requires the freedom of each citizen to decide for any conviction about the ultimate terms of evaluation, we may credit the founding generation with this intent notwithstanding its expression of the point with the term "religious liberty" or "religious freedom." This is because virtually all citizens at the time affirmed some or other religious belief in the conventional sense. Accordingly, the term "religious" is today properly extended; that is, the First Amendment's protection of religious freedom may now be so interpreted as to be consistent with popular sovereignty.

15. Although I will not pursue extended discussion of it here, Dworkin's assertion that government may never coerce anyone for personally judgmental reasons is, I think, a substantive political claim and thus does not belong in a democratic constitution. The matter is somewhat complicated because, on my accounting, a properly democratic constitution does prohibit any law that denies rights belonging to all citizens as equal members of a full and free political discourse, that is, equal members of "we the people." Such rights are, I think, formative rights. But I doubt that every governmental proscription based on the judgment that people who engage in a given activity are, quite apart from its communal consequences, simply worse people fails to respect properly constitutional rights. For instance, statutory (not constitutional) proscription of alcohol consumption, even if enacted for personally judgmental reasons, would not be unconstitutional—nor would a law against suicide enacted because "we the people" judge that taking one's own life, quite independent of communal consequences, is bad. I am not here advocating governmental proscription of either

but, rather, merely doubting that Dworkin's assertion belongs in a democratic constitution. Because that assertion is a substantive political claim, in other words, it should be enacted, if at all, as statutory law, so that citizens as political participants may contest it without simultaneous profession of it.

16. Here, I have especially in mind thinkers such as Alan Gewirth, Jürgen Habermas, and John Rawls. See Gewirth 1996; Habermas 1993 and 2008; and Rawls 2005.

17. Because their understanding is fragmentary, it may well be that subjects cannot understand and thus cannot evaluate alternatives in their entirety. If so, the argument in this paragraph implies that respects in which alternatives are not understood are, by implication, understood to be morally indifferent and thus equally good. In comparing alternatives with respect to choosing, in other words, the moral principle applied is a comprehensive purpose.

Chapter 7

1. On my accounting, even the view that people in differing historical contexts necessarily evaluate human activities in thoroughly differing ways, or that differing kinds of human activity are rightly evaluated in terms entirely specific to them, itself provides a set of terms applicable to all human activities.

2. Because I have defended this account previously, the argument for it here will be relatively condensed, although I hope to say enough that my earlier presentations need not be consulted. The latter include Gamwell 2005 and 2015, chapters 1–4.

3. When that possibility is allowed, no such conviction can be rationally validated or invalidated: if any given one could be validated by public reason, all contrary others (including those supposedly immune to public reason) would thereby be proven false, and if any given one could be invalidated by public reason, the criterion for assessment would be rational. As far as I can see, in other words, the issue is whether or not comprehensive convictions answer a rational question, that is, a question answers to which can be rationally validated and invalidated. If the true answer might be nonrational or suprarational, the question itself must be nonrational or suprarational.

4. On my intention, the constitution of democracy with religious freedom stipulates the conditions to which every citizen as a political participant should explicitly adhere because they constitute or define politics in the given community. These conditions are immunized against contestation—or, better, changing them is bound by a more demanding standard than majority rule—because they constitute the form of political interaction within which discussion and debate occurs. Virtually all recent theories of democracy, then, assert or imply a constitution stipulating that justice is, at least in some respect, independent of any one or any specific type within the legitimized diversity of comprehensive convictions.

5. Perhaps some find in Jeffrey Stout's proposal (see Stout 2004) a relevant alternative to all of the above because it welcomes comprehensive convictions or "visions"

into a secularized but not secularistic public discourse. On my reading, however, his account still separates some principles of justice from any such vision, all of which are said to be "final vocabularies," such that, in each case, public reason is limited to criticizing the internal consistency or inconsistency of beliefs none of which is necessary to human life. Thereby, the principles or "presuppositions" stipulated by a democratic constitution, on which differing religious or secularistic convictions must overlap, are separated from any given one or type thereof (see Stout 2004, 175, 184). Democracy is affirmed as a tradition independent of the visions it welcomes (and whatever traditions they involve). Accordingly, democracy is and must be posited as just, and that evaluation is separated from convictions about the ultimate terms of all evaluation. If Stout thereby endorses an exchange of internal criticism among contrary positions on, say, same-sex marriage, there can be no exchange of reasons about democracy itself and thus the application of its constitutional principles (for instance, the principle of equality in the exchange of reasons or the principle of equal protection of the laws) to that or other issues. I have sought to summarize and criticize Stout's proposal in Gamwell 2011, chapters 5–6.

6. "Common human experience" does not mean a separate experience that occurs at some time or other in all or virtually all human lives (for instance, an experience of the sun) but, rather, an experience that occurs whenever anything else is experienced. What is common is, in Reinhold Niebuhr's metaphor, "an overtone ... in all experience" (Niebuhr 1941–43, 127). That such common experience is *human* means that all human activities are implicitly aware of it or understand it; as Niebuhr writes, it "impinges upon" a "soul which reaches the outermost rims of its own consciousness" (Niebuhr 1941–43, 127). Strictly speaking, I intend what is at least implicitly understood by all humans who understand themselves as individuals, and I do not contest that some aspects of such common human experience require learning. For instance, a human individual becomes and remains aware that her or his experiences depend on her or his own body and that she or he will die when this body dies only because, I expect, they are at some point learned—notwithstanding that these are ever-present aspects of each experience from our earliest days and even if the learning typically occurs early in a human's life. Still, learned aspects of such common human experience should be distinguished from those aspects understood, at least inchoately, whenever anything is understood—for instance, that the activity is aware of itself with others within the all-inclusive whole. On my belief, a telos by which any decision with understanding is directed and that becomes a moral law when a human life understands itself as an individual is included within common human experience.

7. The term "citizen" here and throughout this discussion designates an adult citizen and, thereby, a member of "we the people."

8. On my reading, both Thomas Jefferson and James Madison (and perhaps other US thinkers at the nation's origin) thought of religion in the conventional sense and, nonetheless, included any citizen who did not affirm a conventional religion when they spoke of "religious liberty." They might be excused for so speaking,

moreover, because affirmation of a transcendent reality was more or less universal throughout the eighteenth-century United States.

9. Equality in the discourse follows from religious freedom because inequality is itself something that would require evaluation.

10. For some, perhaps, one or more of the thinkers previously reviewed (Murray, Rawls, and so forth) intends his theory as a contribution to full and free discourse about justice. But this cannot consistently be the case. As noted above, each theory in its own way (and, on my reading, virtually every recent theory) takes at least some religious or comprehensive convictions to be immune from public assessment and, accordingly, must so define the entire class (see n. 3, this chapter). In other words, each theory asserts, at least by implication, that the comprehensive question is *not* rational. Accordingly, each denies that comprehensive convictions can be objects of public debate—and, thereby, must assert an express constitutional separation of justice, at least in some respect, from the convictions constitutionally protected by religious freedom.

11. If the comprehensive question is rational, in other words, claiming truth for one's answer politically is relevantly analogous to making a promise. In each case, a person decides to join a social practice defined by its norm. Promising is a pledge to keep one's promise, and if the content promised is an action one cannot perform, one's act is pragmatically self-refuting. Given a democratic community, claiming truth for one's comprehensive conviction politically pledges its redemption in full and free political discourse—pledges, in other words, that it can be so redeemed, irrespective of whether the person making the claim can herself or himself provide the argument—and if the conviction includes its authoritative or solely contextual validation, one's act is pragmatically self-refuting.

12. An earlier endnote asserted that constitutional conditions are immunized against contestation (see note 4, this chapter), and I have now said that democracy cannot itself be constitutionally stipulated because democracy itself must be open to contestation. This appears both to proscribe and the prescribe constitutional contestation and thus to be self-contradictory. But both statements are, I think, true. Constitutional conditions are immunized against contestation because all political participants should adhere to them, but constitutional provisions cannot be immune to contestation because the constitution may contradict itself—and citizens cannot adhere to a contradictory framework. The constitution of democracy as popular sovereignty becomes contradictory whenever it includes, to cite a distinction introduced in the text subsequently, a substantive rather than formative provision—and the constitutional stipulation of democracy is a substantive provision. Because popular sovereignty means that "we the people" are the constituent as well as statutory sovereign, the solution is to include constitutionally the provision for constitutional changes in accord with a more demanding standard than majority rule, and citizens rightly appeal to this standard when they seek to make the constitution formative.

13. To be sure, one might stipulate democracy (on some definition thereof) and ask a question consistent with this stipulation, for instance, about proper institutionalization of a democratic political community. But one does not thereby establish that democracy is the best form of politics.

14. Indeed, this discourse could not even establish which Kantian moral theory is best because better and worse Kantian theories could be defined only in terms of the truth about our moral obligations.

15. I am fond of some words from Thomas Jefferson's First Inaugural: "If there be any among us who would wish to dissolve this Union or to change its republican form, let them stand undisturbed as monuments to the safety with which error of opinion may be tolerated where reason is left free to combat it" (Jefferson 1999, 174). These words echoed the singular formulation in his Bill for Establishing Religious Freedom in Virginia: "Truth is great and will prevail if left to herself... she is the proper and sufficient antagonist to error, and has nothing to fear from the conflict unless by human interposition disarmed of her natural weapons, free argument and debate" (Jefferson 1999, 391).

16. A democratic constitution must stipulate the institutions and associated practices of a decision-making procedure because the full and free discourse established is *political*, that is, constituted to determine the governing activities. Given stipulations through which decisions are maximally informed by the discourse, the procedure is formative: citizens can adhere to its prescriptions without explicitly taking sides in any political disagreement, including disagreement about those prescriptions. One may adhere to the decision-making procedure even while one contests its merit and seeks its revision because participation in a formative procedure is entirely consistent in seeking through it a decision to alter that very procedure.

17. A formative constitution is, we can say, self-democratizing; it prescribes an ethics of citizenship to which "we the people" can adhere without professing and is ordained by them because it preserves their sovereignty. In a cryptic statement about what he called the American and, by implication, constitutional consensus, John Courtney Murray once wrote: "We hold certain truths; therefore we can argue about them" (Murray 1960, 10). Whatever Murray himself may have meant or may have included within such truths, something very like that statement can be crafted to capture the formative character of a properly democratic constitution, namely "we adhere to this constitution, therefore we can argue about it."

18. To be sure, all political prescriptions are, on another use of the term, "substantive," in the sense that each prescribes something contrary to its denials and thus can be acted against. But that use of "substantive" then requires, at least on the account I seek to commend, a distinction between formative and nonformative such prescriptions, that is, between political prescriptions to which political participants *can* adhere without professing and those to which political participants *cannot* adhere without professing. I here propose so to use terms that only nonformative political prescriptions are substantive.

19. The state may never, for instance, proscribe criticism of Congress, as in the US Sedition Act of 1798, or criticism of the government during war, as in the US Sedition Act of 1918.

20. This consideration is, I now think, sufficient to refute an argument for constitutional free exercise exemptions I proposed in an earlier work, namely, that special protection for the cultivation of comprehensive re-presentations is warranted as an aspect of a realistic democratic decision-making procedure (see Gamwell 1995, 155–57). If adherence to a constitutional provision for free exercise exemptions requires an explicit constitutional endorsement of democracy, that provision cannot be explicitly neutral to comprehensive convictions that include or imply a nondemocratic constitution and thus cannot be a formative constitutional provision.

21. Whether Justice Antonin Scalia's opinion for the Court should be credited as an interpretation of US constitutional law is, naturally, another question.

22. Because exemptions stated by a specific law should apply to any comprehensive conviction, reading statutory law through the account of religious freedom proposed earlier implies agreement with the US Supreme Court decision in *United States v. Seeger* (30 U.S. 163 [1965]) finding the exemption within the Universal Military and Service Act of 1948 applicable to Daniel Andrew Seeger, who was an atheist.

23. On my intention, a specific activity is *prescribed* by a comprehensive conviction whenever obligation to engage in that activity specifies the conviction to a particular situation. Given the conviction and whatever is understood by its adherents to be specific to that situation, the activity is obligatory for people in that situation.

24. Writing for the Court in the *Smith* decision, Justice Scalia advanced a similar argument (although he may have confined the meaning of "religion" to conventional religions). "Any society adopting such a system would be courting anarchy," he wrote—and in any event, the contemporary United States "cannot afford the luxury of deeming *presumptively invalid*, as applied to the religious objector, every regulation of conduct that does not protect an interest of the highest order [that is, a compelling state interest]." *Employment Division v. Smith* at 888, see also 888–89.

25. I have discussed this inseparability in Gamwell 2011, 107–15.

26. For instance, a communist organization, persuaded that conventional religion is the "opium of the people" and thus inimical to the pursuit of a classless society, might decide to begin its meetings with the ritual destruction of opium and, therefore, claim exemption from drug laws prohibiting its possession. All claims for such exemptions are, to be repetitious, subject to the compelling state interest test, and even then, a nonspecific right to free exercise exemptions may be politically contentious.

27. Another objection should be considered. Against the present proposal, some may argue as follows: a judge who considers claims for free exercise exemptions could not depend on the distinction between direct and indirect cultivation without defending her or his decision by appeal to the way of reason; with that defense, however, she or he reads the way of reason into the constitutional provision for religious freedom and, thereby, violates it—because comprehensive convictions claiming to be

immune to rational assessment are thereby delegitimized. To the contrary, however, the distinction in question can be sufficiently defended, on my accounting, by asserting (1) the state has a compelling interest in preventing free exercise exemptions for just any activity prescribed by a religious or comprehensive confession, and (2) opposition to a generally applicable law is inconsistent with a claim to be exempt from it because the claim to an exemption does not contest the law's general applicability. Thereby, a judge *implies* the way of reason, because her or his call for circumscribing the relevant activities and thus her or his distinction between exemption from and opposition to a generally applicable law are at least implicitly denied by any comprehensive conviction whose supposed validation depends on some particular historical context. But that is simply to say of this judge that she or he implies the way of reason because it alone makes sense of religious freedom. Nonetheless, defending a decision in the manner suggested remains, as does the constitutional provision for religious freedom, *explicitly* neutral to all comprehensive convictions.

Chapter 8

1. For the present discussion, I will speak of the initial US Constitution as a 1787 document and nonetheless include therein its first ten amendments, which were not ratified until 1791.

2. Naturally, other questions might be asked about the process of ratification stipulated by the Constitutional Convention. For instance, one might ask why conventions rather than state legislatures should be the forums for acceptance or rejection of the Constitution—or again, one might ask why nine ratifying states rather than all thirteen should be sufficient to constitute the "more perfect Union." Here, however, I will confine attention to whether the proposed Constitution consistently seeks ratification in each of the states, separately taken (but see below, note 23).

3. In this chapter, I take "human" to designate a subject, as "subject" is defined in the introduction and chapter 5—so that very small human children, although having the rights characterizing members of the subjective community, are, perhaps, only potentially subjects. Also, I take "we the people" to be adult subjects.

4. Henceforth, in speaking of the Constitution, I will intend the US Constitution.

5. "The Union," Lincoln asserted in his First Inaugural Address, "is much older than the Constitution. It was formed, in fact, by the Articles of Association in 1774" (Lincoln 1946, 582). See note 19 in this chapter.

6. Akil Reed Amar notes the "remarkable centrality and salience of simple majority rule" (Amar 2012, 56; see also 56–63, 357–69).

7. Some thinkers, I recognize, hold that "religion" does designate in something like its conventional sense, and the First Amendment's religion clauses mean only that government should be neutral with respect to differences among religions. Protection for nonreligious convictions is then said to be provided by implication when the First Amendment also affirms "freedom of speech." If so, it follows that government

should also be neutral to the differences between religious (in the conventional sense) and nonreligious convictions. On the extended meaning of "religious," perhaps religious freedom and freedom of speech are, by implication, insofar redundant. In that event, Jefferson's comment in another context seems appropriate: writing from Paris to James Madison about the proposed US Constitution, Jefferson urged the addition of a bill of rights, saying that such a bill "is what the people are entitled to against every government on earth, general or particular, & what no just government should refuse, or *rest on inferences*" (Jefferson, 361, emphasis added). The extended meaning of "religious" in "religious freedom" seeks to make explicit the protection for all convictions about the ultimate terms of evaluation.

8. Indeed, the Revolution was an exercise of power. Without sufficient revolutionary commitment by a large number of colonists, the war could not have succeeded, and given that commitment (see Maier 1997), sufficient power was, as it turned out, present. In effect, members of the Continental Congress in July 1776 declared—having pledged "to each other our lives, our fortunes, and our sacred honor" in so doing—the presence of sufficient power to create political communities or a community.

9. The "opinions of mankind" thereby respected do not themselves constitute a political discussion and debate because there is no worldwide affirmation of self-government or popular sovereignty, that is, government through a full and free political discourse or by the way of reason.

10. Something called the "National Popular Vote Initiative," which seeks to bypass the Electoral College, currently allows states to pass something like the following resolution: "This state shall choose a slate of electors loyal to the presidential candidate who wins the national popular vote, if and only if other states, whose electors taken together with this state's electors total at least 270, also enact laws guaranteeing that they will choose electors loyal to the presidential candidate who wins the national popular vote" (Amar 2012, 457, 459). Perhaps, then, a state ratifying the Constitution asserted, in effect: "this ratifying decision claims moral validity for the new Union if and only if eight other States make a similar claim." But that formulation of the ratifying decision does not erase the presupposition of a prior national public. To the contrary, the new formulation itself expresses a political decision that claims moral validity. In other words, the revised formulation claims moral validity for the following decision: if eight (or any given number of) other states ratify, as this state now does, the Constitution, it has moral validity. The assessment of whether that decision is morally valid is precisely what requires a prior public—just as a prior public is required to assess whether the National Popular Vote Initiative is good.

11. This is especially, although surely not exclusively, so because he shows in such detail how the ideal of popular sovereignty pervades both the written and unwritten Constitution (see Amar 2005, 2012).

12. If Amar thereby reads the Declaration of Independence in accord with the states' rights view, he in no way intends aid and comfort to the Confederacy formed in 1860—because, on his view, the Constitution re-created the states as parts of the

Union; that is, each state, in ratifying the Constitution, gave up its sovereignty (see Amar 2005, 35–39).

13. Asking for the Constitution's authorization assumes its authority, and that assumption may require qualification. The Constitution not only defines but also structures institutionally US politics, and aspects of its institutional structure may be challenged. Even given subsequent amendments, for instance, some may assert that certain stipulations (say, representation in the federal Senate, or the electoral college) are contrary to the ideal of popular sovereignty as stipulated in the document's Preamble, so that one can properly speak of the Constitution's authority only insofar as it articulates a democratic political process. Significant as that issue and possible others are, I will here seek to avoid them by assuming the Constitution's authority (including its provision for constitutional amendment and, therefore, its amendments) to define and structure institutionally subsequent US politics. Indeed, I take the following to be noncontroversial: the assertion that some aspects of the Constitution are not authoritative can be established, if it can, only because they are inconsistent with other aspects of the Constitution—so that, in part or whole, it alone can define and structure institutionally the subsequent US political tradition. In any event, I posit the Constitution's authority as a whole in order to focus on the question of how it is authorized.

14. Accordingly, a person who does affirm the Christian faith but misunderstands it because she or he mistakenly takes some conflicting witness to be authoritative for Christians may be prompted, on learning what is truly authoritative for Christian faith, to reconsider her or his affirmation of it. Similarly, a given patriotic US citizen, who misunderstands the US political tradition's authority (taking its authoritative definition and structure to be determined, say, by a given religion), may have a mistaken understanding of the tradition—and, on learning of the Constitution's authority (including, say, its affirmation of religious freedom), may then be prompted to reconsider her or his affirmation of that tradition.

15. Whether Wilson meant by "in whatever manner" the right of "citizens at large" to assign sovereignty elsewhere than to "we the people," or whether he meant simply that citizens at large remain always the final ruling power, may be debatable. As far as I can see, however, popular sovereignty means that "we the people" have the right to assign sovereignty elsewhere, at least if the decision of some citizens to that effect is not contested.

16. I am inclined to hold, moreover, that commitment to the validation or invalidation of a claim, if it is contested, by the giving of reasons is a pledge issued by making any claim at all, political or otherwise—although here it is sufficient to note how this commitment accompanies a US citizen's every political claim to moral validity. Recognition of this inescapable pledge, whatever the content of one's political claim, is the beginning of a sound argument for the moral validity of popular sovereignty, at least wherever it is possible. Still, the argument cannot be complete without explicating and defending an ultimate principle of evaluation in terms of which democracy is, wherever possible, prescribed.

17. I borrow the terms "primary authority" and "primal *source* of all authority" from Schubert M. Ogden (see Ogden 1986, chapter 3).

18. As it happens, both Ellis and Jensen advance what this chapter has called above the states' rights view. For Jensen: "the reiteration of the idea of the supremacy of the local legislatures . . . militated against the creation of such a centralized government as the conservative elements in American society desired. . . . The constitution which the radicals created, the Articles of Confederation, was a constitutional expression of the philosophy of the Declaration of Independence" (Jensen 1970, 239; see also xxix, 15). With this statement, I judge, Ellis agrees because he writes that "two features of their [the so-called Progressive school, which Jensen represents] story line remain abidingly relevant," the second of which is "the transition from the Articles of Confederation to the Constitution was orchestrated by a political elite that collaborated . . . to replace a state-based confederation with a federal government that claimed to speak for the American people as a collective whole" (Ellis 2015, xiv). Neither historian, I judge, credits the prior presence of a national public to which a ratifying claim for the Articles' relation of states to the central government might be addressed.

19. If we assume that formation of the Union means the beginning of the US political tradition, I am dubious of Abraham Lincoln's assertion: "The Union . . . was formed, in fact, by the Articles of Association in 1774" (Lincoln 1946, 582)—even while he rightly asserts that colonies entered the Union before they "cast off their British colonial dependence" (Lincoln 1946, 603; see note 5 in this chapter). Whether formation in the sense here assumed is what Lincoln meant is, however, itself dubious, given his assertion in the Gettysburg Address: "Four score and seven years ago [1776] our fathers brought forth on this continent a new nation" (Lincoln 1946, 734). In any event, the 1774 Articles of Association did not, to the best of my reading, create an independent political community and did not explicitly commit it to self-government. Not until the Declaration of Independence did these affirmations occur. As mentioned, nonetheless, I take Lincoln to be correct when he writes: "the Declaration of Independence . . . [did not] declare their independence of one another or of the Union" (Lincoln 1946, 603).

20. The 1787 Preamble, unlike the Declaration of Independence, does not explicitly assert its backing by the moral law or by the "laws for nature and of nature's God," as the Declaration has it. "Although the Declaration of Independence, The Articles of Confederation, and several state constitutions had explicitly and prominently invoked God in their opening or closing passages, or both, the federal Constitution conspicuously did not" (Amar 2012, 75). Still, the 1787 Constitution *implies* a claim to consistency with the ultimate terms of evaluation, even if they are rightly understood as divinely given. The Declaration's explicit appeal to a certain understanding of those terms is, if true, only implied by the Constitution because how those terms are rightly understood and thus whether popular sovereignty is good are left entirely to "we the people" and thus the discourse among them.

21. Every version of relativism, even if moral criteria are said to be relative to a certain universal kind or kinds of human decision, contradicts the provision for religious freedom (in the extended sense of "religious") and thus contradicts popular sovereignty—because any such theory must itself be stipulated in the Constitution as something all political participants must explicitly affirm. It is, thereby, a provision with which some possible convictions about the ultimate terms of evaluation disagree (namely, those on which the moral law applies to human decision as such) and thus are not legitimized. In other words, popular sovereignty is compromised by a constitutional constraint—and the political discourse, or political discussion and debate, is not full. Only because the moral law is transcendental is it implied by all convictions about those terms and, thereby, is consistent with religious freedom.

22. To the best of my reasoning, subjectivism as a theory of human decision-making (that is, the theory that no supposed moral utterances are valid or invalid) can be decisively discredited only by argument showing how the moral law is transcendental to human decision as such.

23. As mentioned in note 2, this chapter, other questions might be asked about the process of ratification stipulated by the Constitutional Convention—and while this chapter is confined to why each of the states should hold its own ratifying convention, I wish to note the direction that responses to other questions about Article VII might take. There is (1) the question of why conventions rather than state legislatures should be the forums for acceptance or rejection of the Constitution, notwithstanding the Articles of Confederation stipulation that alterations thereto required the agreement of "Congress" and "the legislatures of every state." Still, this question might be addressed by developing something like the following answer: State legislatures were affirmed by "we the people" by virtue of an institutional structure the proposed Constitution seeks to have renounced, and thus such legislatures have, in effect, a conflict of interest. Accordingly, one-time conventions having ratification as their only purpose better represent "we the people" in each state. There is (2) the question of why nine ratifying states should be sufficient to constitute the "more perfect Union" when the Articles of Confederation stipulated unanimity among the thirteen for amendments thereto. This question is, I judge, more difficult—but might be addressed by developing something like the following answer: Because acceptance or rejection through a convention in each state was, as was ratification of the Articles of Confederation, the act of "we the people" of the United States, to insist on acceptance by all thirteen would allow a minority of people to veto the judgment of the majority thereof—and thus a majority principle was substituted for the unanimity principle. To be sure, this change may be criticized for violating the prior ratification of unanimity, but recognition that a single people was the agent of ratification (of both the Articles and the Constitution) perhaps allowed the 1787 Convention to consider unanimity simply an excessive kind of majority—affirmed by the Articles because, in the institutional structure they articulated, "we the people" sought so to institutionalize "perpetual Union" that it would be largely consistent with the freedom and independence

of each state. Insistence on unanimity rather than a majority would, in other words, imply creation of the Union by thirteen separate peoples—in contrast to the single people that was throughout sovereign over the kind of Union effected. At the same time, ratification through the several states does imply that states in which the new Union was denied should not be forced to join it. Nine ratifying states, then, seemed to be a proper number because any nine would include a majority of "we the people" (at least according to the Convention's allocation of seats in the proposed House of Representatives), without which, Madison insisted, there could be no ratification.

WORKS CITED

Alston, William. 1984. "Hartshorne and Aquinas: A Via Media." In *Existence and Actuality: Conversations with Charles Hartshorne*, edited by John B. Cobb Jr. and Franklin I. Gamwell, 78–98. Chicago: University of Chicago Press.
———. 1993. "Aquinas on Theological Predication: A Look Backward and a Look Forward." In *Reasoned Faith: Essays in Honor of Norman Kretzman*, edited by Eleonore Stump. Ithaca, NY: Cornell University Press.
Amar, Akil Reed. 1987. "Of Sovereignty and Federalism." *Yale Law Journal* 96/97 (June): 1425–1520.
———. 2005. *America's Constitution: A Biography*. New York: Random House.
———. 2012. *America's Unwritten Constitution: The Precedents and Principles We Live By*. New York: Basic Books.
Apel, Karl Otto. 1979. "Types of Rationality Today: The Continuum of Reason between Science and Ethics." In *Rationality Today*, edited by Theodore Gereats, 307–50. Ottawa: University Press.
———. 1980. *Toward a Transformation of Philosophy*. London: Routledge and Kegan Paul.
———. 1984. *Understanding and Explanation: A Transcendental-Pragmatic Perspective*. Cambridge, MA: MIT Press.
———. 1994. *Selected Essays: Volume I: Toward a Transcendental Semiotics*. Edited and translated by Edwardo Mendieta. Atlantic Highlands, NJ: Humanities Press.
———. 1996. *Selected Essays, Volume Two: Ethics and the Theology of Rationality*. Edited and translated by Eduardo Mendieta. Atlantic Highlands, NJ: Humanities Press.
———. 1998. *From a Transcendental-Semiotic Point of View*. Edited by Marianna Papastephanou. Manchester: Manchester University Press.
Aquinas, Saint Thomas. 1973. *Basic Writings of Saint Thomas Aquinas: Volume One: God and the Order of Creation*. Edited by Anton C. Pegis. Indianapolis: Hackett Publishing.
———. 1975. *Summa Contra Gentiles, Book Three: Providence, Part I*. Translated by Vernon J. Bourke. Indianapolis: Hackett Publishing.
Aristotle. 1962. *Nicomachean Ethics*. Indianapolis: Bobbs-Merrill.

Ashworth, E. J. 1992. "Analogy and Equivocation in Thirteenth-Century Logic: Aquinas in Context." *Medieval Studies* 54: 94–135.
Augustine, St. 1955. *The Spirit and the Letter*. Edited by John Burnaby. Philadelphia: Westminster Press, 182–250.
———. 1985. *City of God*. New York: Penguin Books.
———. 1993. *On Free Choice of the Will*. Indianapolis: Hackett Publishing.
Barry, Brian. 1995. *Justice as Impartiality*. Oxford: Clarendon Press.
Beer, Samuel H. 1993. *To Make a Nation: The Rediscovery of American Federalism*. Cambridge, MA: Belknap Press of Harvard University Press.
Burrell, David B. 1973. *Analogy and Philosophical Language*. New Haven, CT: Yale University Press.
———. 1979. *Aquinas: God and Action*. Notre Dame, IN: University of Notre Dame Press.
DeGeorge, Richard T. 1985. *The Nature and Limits of Authority*. Lawrence: University Press of Kansas.
Dewey, John. 1957. *Reconstruction in Philosophy*. Boston: Beacon Press.
———. 1958. *Experience and Nature*. New York: Dover Publications.
Dworkin, Ronald. 1986. *Law's Empire*. Cambridge, MA: Harvard University Press.
———. 1996. *Freedom's Law: The Moral Reading of the American Constitution*. Cambridge, MA: Harvard University Press.
———. 2000. *Sovereign Virtue: The Theory and Practice of Equality*. Cambridge, MA: Harvard University Press.
———. 2006. *Is Democracy Possible Here? Principles for a New Political Debate*. Princeton, NJ: Princeton University Press.
———. 2011. *Justice for Hedgehogs*. Cambridge, MA: Harvard University Press.
———. 2013. *Religion without God*. Cambridge, MA: Harvard University Press.
Ellis, Joseph J. 2015. *The Quartet: Orchestrating the Second American Revolution, 1783–1789*. New York: Random House (Vintage Books).
Ford, Lewis. 1966. "Tillich and Thomas: The Analogy of Being." *Journal of Religion* 66, no. 2: 29–45.
Gamwell, Franklin I. 1990. *The Divine Good: Modern Moral Theory and the Necessity of God*. San Francisco: HarperCollins.
———. 1995. *The Meaning of Religious Freedom: Modern Politics and the Democratic Resolution*. Albany: State University of New York Press.
———. 2000. *Democracy on Purpose: Justice and the Reality of God*. Washington, DC: Georgetown University Press.
———. 2005. *Politics as a Christian Vocation: Faith and Democracy Today*. New York: Cambridge University Press.
———. 2011. *Existence and the Good: Metaphysical Necessity in Morals and Politics*. Albany: State University of New York Press.
———. 2015. *Religion among We the People: Conversations on Democracy and the Divine Good*. Albany: State University of New York Press.
Geertz, Clifford. 1973. *The Interpretation of Cultures: Selected Essay*. New York: Basic Books.

Gewirth, Alan. 1978. *Reason and Morality*. Chicago: University of Chicago Press.
———. 1996. *The Community of Rights*. Chicago: University of Chicago Press.
Habermas, Jürgen. 1990. *Moral Consciousness and Communicative Action*. Cambridge, MA: MIT Press.
———. 1992. *Postmetaphysical Thinking: Philosophical Essays*. Cambridge, MA: MIT Press
———. 1993. *Justification and Application: Remarks on Discourse Ethics*. Cambridge, MA: MIT Press.
———. 2008. *Between Naturalism and Religion*. Cambridge: Polity Press.
Hamilton, Alexander, James Madison, and John Jay. 1998. *The Federalist with Letters of "Brutus."* Edited by Terence Ball. New York: Cambridge University Press.
Hartshorne, Charles. 1948. *The Divine Relativity*. New Haven, CT: Yale University Press.
———. 1962a. *The Logic of Perfection and Other Essays in Neoclassical Metaphysics*. LaSalle, IL: Open Court.
———. 1962b. "What Did Anselm Discover?" In *Union Seminary Quarterly Review*, 17, no. 3 (March 1962): 213–222.
———. 1970. *Creative Synthesis and Philosophic Method*. LaSalle, IL: Open Court Press.
Heidegger, Martin. 1993. *Basic Writings*. Edited by David Farrell Krell. San Francisco: Harper San Francisco.
Hobbes, Thomas. 1962. *Leviathan: Or the Matter, Forme and Power of a Commonwealth Ecclesiastical and Civil*. New York: Collier Macmillan.
Hume, David. 1955. *Dialogues Concerning Natural Religion*. New York: Hafner Publishing.
———. 1975. *Enquiries Concerning Human Understanding and Concerning the Principles of Morals*. Oxford: Clarendon Press.
Jaffa, Harry V. 1999. *Storm over the Constitution*. Lanham, MD: Lexington Books.
———. 2000. *A New Birth of Freedom: Abraham Lincoln and the Coming of the Civil War*. New York: Rowman and Littlefield.
Jefferson, Thomas. 1999. *Political Writings*. Edited by Joyce Appleby and Terence Ball. New York: Cambridge University Press.
Jensen, Merrill. (1940) 1970. *The Articles of Confederation: An Interpretation of the Social-Constitutional History of the American Revolution, 1774–1781*. Madison: University of Wisconsin Press.
Kant, Immanuel. 1949. *Fundamental Principles of the Metaphysic of Morals*. Indianapolis: Bobbs-Merrill.
———. 1956. *Critique of Practical Reason*. Indianapolis: Bobbs-Merrill.
———. 1965. *Critique of Pure Reason*. New York: St. Martin's Press.
Körner, Stephan. 1969. *Fundamental Problems of Philosophy: One Philosopher's Answers*. Sussex, UK: Harvester Press.
Kretzman, Norman. 1997. *The Metaphysics of Theism: Aquinas's Natural Theology in Summa Contra Gentiles II*. Oxford: Clarendon Press.
Lincoln, Abraham. 1946. *Abraham Lincoln: His Speeches and Writings*. Edited by Roy P. Basler. Cleveland, OH: World Publishing.

MacIntyre, Alasdair. 1988. *Whose Justice? Which Rationality?* Notre Dame, IN: University of Notre Dame Press.
Maier, Pauline. 1997. *American Scripture: Making the Declaration of Independence*. New York: Random House.
———. 2010. *Ratification: The People Debate the Constitution, 1787–88*. New York: Simon & Schuster.
McInerny, Ralph. 1996. *Aquinas and Analogy*. Washington, DC: Catholic University of America Press.
McPherson, James. 1991. *Abraham Lincoln and the Second American Revolution*. New York: Oxford University Press.
Morgan, Edmund S. 1988. *Inventing the People: The Rise of Popular Sovereignty in England and America*. New York: W. W. Norton.
Murray, John Courtney, S.J. 1960. *We Hold These Truths: Catholic Reflections on the American Proposition*. Kansas City: Sheed and Ward.
Nagel, Thomas. 1986. *The View from Nowhere*. New York: Oxford University Press.
———. 2010. *Secular Philosophy and the Religious Temperament: Essays 2002–2008*. New York: Oxford University Press.
Niebuhr, Reinhold. 1941–43. *The Nature and Destiny of Man*. 2 vols. New York: Charles Scribner's Sons.
———. 1942. "Religion and Action." In *Science and Man*, edited by Ruth Nada Anshen, 44–64. New York: Harcourt, Brace, and Co.
Ogden, Schubert M. 1966. *The Reality of God and Other Essays*. New York: Harper & Row.
———. 1984. "The Experience of God: Critical Reflections on Hartshorne's Theory of Analogy." In *Existence and Actuality: Conversations with Charles Hartshorne*, edited by John B. Cobb Jr. and Franklin I. Gamwell, 16–37. Chicago: University of Chicago Press.
———. 1986. *On Theology*. San Francisco: Harper and Row.
———. 1991. "Must God Be Really Related to Creatures?" *Process Studies* 20, no. 1: 54–56.
———. 2018. *Notebooks*. Eugene, OR: Wipf and Stock.
Parkinson, Robert G. 2016. *The Common Cause: Creating Race and Nation in the American Revolution*. Chapel Hill: University of North Carolina Press.
Proudfoot, Wayne. 1985. *Religious Experience*. Berkeley: University of California Press.
Rawls, John. 2005. *Political Liberalism*. Expanded edition. New York: Columbia University Press.
Rorty, Richard. 1979. "Transcendental Arguments, Self-Reference, and Pragmatism." In *Transcendental Arguments and Science*, edited by Peter Bieri, Rolf Horstman, and Lorenz Kreuger, 77–103. Dordrect, Holland: D. Reidel.
Rundle, Bede. 2004. *Why there is Something rather than Nothing*. Oxford: Oxford University Press.
Stout, Jeffrey. 2004. *Democracy and Tradition*. Princeton, NJ: Princeton University Press.
Schleiermacher, Friedrich. 1958. *On Religion: Speeches to Its Cultured Despisers*. Translated by John Oman. New York: Harper & Row.
———. 1989. *The Christian Faith*. Edinburgh: T. and T. Clark.

Sunstein, Cass R. 1993. *Democracy and the Problem of Free Speech*. New York: Free Press.
Tillich, Paul. 1951. *Systematic Theology*. Vol. 1. Chicago: University of Chicago Press.
Whitehead, Alfred North. 1925. *Science and the Modern World*. New York: Free Press.
———. 1927. *Symbolism: Its Meaning and Effect*. New York: Capricorn Books.
———. 1938. *Modes of Thought*. New York: Capricorn Books.
———. 1958. *The Function of Reason*. Boston: Beacon Press.
———. 1961. *Adventures of Ideas*. New York: Free Press.
———. 1978. *Process and Reality: An Essay in Cosmology*. Corrected edition. Edited by David Ray Griffin and Donald W. Sherburne. New York: Free Press.
Wilson, James. 2007. *Collected Works of James Wilson*. 2 vols. Edited by Kermit L. Hall and Mark David Hall. Indianapolis: Liberty Fund.
Wippel, John F. 1984. *Metaphysical Themes in Thomas Aquinas*. Washington, DC: Catholic University of America Press.
———. 1992. "Thomas Aquinas on What Philosophers Can Know about God." *American Catholic Theological Quarterly* 66, no. 3: 290–97.

INDEX

Activity, defined, 7, 130, 132–39 passim
Actual vs. virtual consent, 196–97
Actuality, defined, 6, 116, 122, 135
Adam, 88, 92–94 *passim*, 96, 102, 135, 23
Adhere vs. profess, defined, 209–10
Affordable Care Act, 170, 190
Aggregates, defined, 116–17
Alston, William, 66–67, 226–27
    his concept of God, 229
Amar, Akhil Reed, 200, 201, 205, 206, 211, 244, 245–46
Amoralism, defined, 124–25
Analogical speaking of God's essence:
    criticized, 47–70
    cannot avoid pure equivocity, 53–58
Apel, Karl-Otto, 74, 26–27, 138, 216
    denies strict metaphysics, 39
    "dialectical strategic rationality," 222
    Kant, relation to, 37
    moral naturalism, 27
Apostolic witness, 48, 208, 209
Aquinas, St. Thomas, 2, 13–14, 31, 114, 222, 223, 231
    analogical speaking of God, 47–70
    "being" as analogous, 60, 227
    difference of metaphor and analogy, 51–52, 228
    essence and existence of God, 29–30
    "healthy" as analogous, 52–54, 226–27
    his vicious circle, 49, 62
    his theistic arguments, 33, 58–62

    res significata and *modus significandi*, 227
    species, 233
    teleology, 160
Aristotle, 114, 131, 151, 160
Articles of Association, 244, 247
Articles of Confederation, 195, 196, 202, 206, 211–13 passim, 218, 219, 247, 248
Ashworth, E. J., 227
Augustine, 2, 14, 99, 100, 104, 106, 113
    christology, 88
    City of God, 93
    ignorance and difficulty, 88
    On Free Choice of the Will, 87–90 *passim*
    Pelagian controversy, 88
    primal vs. specific freedom, 89
    source of temptation, 87–94 (and notes thereto)
    Spirit and the Letter, The, 88
Authority, defined, 208
Autocratic or aristocratic, 204

Barry, Brian, 234
Beer, Samuel H., 193, 194, 196–198 *passim*
Being and Time, 231
Boerne v. Flores, 180
Bultmann, Rudolf, 47
Burke, Thomas, 212
Burrell, David, 49, 228–29
    Aquinas's circularity, 49, 62
    his account of analogy, 62–65
Burwell v. Hobby Lobby, 179, 191

Cajetan, 227
Calhoun, John C., 194, 195, 206
Chapter outline, 13–17
Children, 234
Christian faith, 47, 72–74 passim, 76, 78, 85, 86, 97, 209, 230, 246
Christian Faith, The, 230
Citizen, defined, 240
City of God, 93
Civil war, 194, 206, 218
Classical metaphysics, 6–7, 13
Classical theism, 6–7, 85, 106
Clinton, William, 170
Co-determinant, 75–78 passim, 80–82 passim, 85
Common human experience, defined, 240
Communist organization, 243
Comprehensive conviction, defined, 16, 26, 170, 183
Comprehensive purpose, 2, 15, 128–30 passim, 133, 134, 137–39 passim, 239
Comprehensive reservation, 187, 189
Confederacy, 206, 245
Consciousness, defined, 119–20
Constitutional authority, 194, 207, 217, 246
Constitutional Convention, 193, 211, 213, 244, 248
Continental Congress, 195, 198, 212, 213, 245
Convictions and confessions, defined, 184–85
illustrated, 186
Critical reflection, defined, 1, 4
Critique of complete negation, 21–46, 81–82

Declaration of Independence, 195, 196, 201, 203, 207, 212–214 passim, 245, 247
Defect, 88, 97, 98, 105, 232
Deficient cause, 93
Democracy, defined, 17
Democratic constitution, defined, 162, 176
Developed understanding, defined, 8
Devenish, Philip, 3
Devil, 92–94 passim, 96, 99
Dewey, John, 21, 128
Direct and indirect cultivation, 185, 187–88
Divine individual, defined, 117–18
Dualism, 67
Duplicitous, 85, 91, 96, 97, 102–5 passim

Duplicity, 11, 95–97, 101–3 passim, 107, 134, 174
Dworkin, Ronald, 2, 15, 25–26, 36–37, 141–67 passim (and notes thereto), 172–73
broadly Kantian, 157–67
circularity, 36, 37, 145, 146, 153, 155, 156, 238
denial of transcendental moral law, 153
embracing dualism of understanding, 26, 37, 144, 153, 237
ethics, 146–47
ethics and morality, 146, 156–57, 160–61
external skepticism, defined, 150
functional vs. substantive views of religion, 142
Hume's principle, defined, 143–44
Is Democracy Possible Here? Principles for a New Political Debate, 142
Justice for Hedgehogs, 142
Kant's principle, defined, 147
moral naturalism as fallacious, 25–26
morality as implicitly transcendental, 152–53
political and legal rights, 148
and Rawls, 146
reflective equilibrium, 146
religion as special case, 161
Religion without God, 142
religious freedom, 148–67
scientific and interpretive judgments, 144–45, 155–56

Ellis, Joseph J., 212, 247
Emotivism, 124
Employment Division v. Smith, 179, 182, 188, 243
"Existence" is not a predicate, 59, 221
Existential denials as nonmetaphysical, 222
Existential necessities, defined, 3–4
Existentialist, 89, 94, 96, 97, 99
Existential statement, defined, 11, 32

First Amendment, 142, 171, 178–80 passim, 182, 197, 198, 200, 215, 218, 238, 244
First cause, 56–60 passim, 62, 226, 228
Formative, defined, 163–164, 242
Fragmentariness, 7, 15, 98, 103, 105–7 passim
Freedom's Law: The Moral Reading of the United States Constitution, 235

INDEX

Free exercise exemptions, 16, 178–91
Full and free political discourse, defined, 175, 197
Function of religion, 86

Gamwell, Franklin I., 234, 243.
Geertz, Clifford, 26
Gewirth, Alan, 126
Good, defined, 135
    a variable, 129, 135
Great Britain, 203
Great debate, 206, 211

Habermas, Jürgen, 126–27, 169, 170, 172–73, 239
Hamilton, Alexander, 201
Hartshorne, Charles, 32, 42–44 *passim*, 65, 66, 68, 70, 85, 106, 113, 224, 25
    analogy, 229
    concept of God, 60, 68, 106, 222, 229
    existence as a predicate, 222
    freedom as metaphysical, 114–15
Heidegger, Martin, 38, 95, 231
Hobbes, Thomas, 124–25, 217
Hobby Lobby, 170, 179, 190, 191
House of Representatives, 193, 194, 249
Hume, David, 37, 83, 124–25, 215
    morality as fact, 150, 151–52
    "'nothing exists' is possibly true, 222

Ideal, defined, 200
Ideal possibility, 98
Immorality, defined, 130–31, 132–33
Implicit understandings, defined, 12, 119–20, 122–23
Individual, defined, 6, 22, 116–17, 130

Jefferson, Thomas, 240, 242, 245
Jensen, Merrill, 212, 247
Jesus, 48, 74, 78, 88, 95, 186, 230
Justice as Impartiality, 234

Kantian tradition, defined, 126
Kant, Immanuel, 2, 5, 13, 15, 23, 27
    better and worse, 242
    "existence" as a predicate, 221

good will, 123
    his influence, 29
    his insight, 152, 157, 167
    implied agreement with teleology, 129
    intuitions, 76, 77
    Kantian tradition, 126, 127
    moral law, 15, 71–72, 130
    noumena, 30, 31, 33, 77, 231
    noumena and phenomena, 30, 31, 33–34, 231
    "ought implies can," 91, 118–19, 124, 130, 138
    practical reason as moral theory, 124–25, 152, 157, 167, 215
    rational creatures generally, 4, 11
    significance of temptation, 91–92
    transcendental illusion, 85
    use of "transcendental," 4, 11
Kierkegaard, Søren, 96, 97
King of Great Britain, 196
Knowing defined, 24, 32
Körner, Steven, 227
Kretzman, Norman, 228

Law's Empire, 235
Laws of nature and nature's God, 198
Liberal theological tradition, 94
Lincoln, Abraham, 194, 196, 197, 201, 244, 247
Logic, kinds of, defined, 4–5, 22–23

MacIntyre, Alasdair, 90
Madison, James, 201, 211, 240, 245, 249
"Many become one, and are increased by one," 16, 122, 135
Meta-ethics, 111, 130, 146, 154, 237
Metaphor, 240
Metaphorical, 14, 24, 47, 48, 51, 52, 63, 228
Metaphysical features, 4, 9, 10–11, 23, 113, 221, 224–25, 234
Metaphysical good, 123–30 *passim*
Metaphysics:
    two senses, 1–17 *passim*, 23, 49, 72, 111–12
    as systematic, 6, 8, 44, 46, 85, 112
Modus vivendi, 164, 175, 218
Monarchical or aristocratic, 181, 209
Moral and nonmoral, 15, 111–39 *passim*

Morgan, Edward S., 211
Morris, Gouverneur, 193
Murray, John Courtney, 172–73, 242

Nagel, Thomas, 28, 39–40, 42, 222, 223
National Popular Vote Initiative, 245
Native American Church, 179
Negative vs. positive designation, 23, 32–36
Neoclassical metaphysics, defined, 1, 6, 7, 13, 44–45, 113–18 *passim*
Niebuhr, Reinhold, 2, 14, 47, 99, 104–5 *passim*, 106, 232–33, 240
  account of revelation, 95
  bias toward sin, 97, 232
  collective egoism, 104–5
  existential vs. explicit consciousness, 95
  Gifford Lectures, 87
  God as completely eternal reality, 100, 232–33
  modern theology, 94, 96
  self-contradiction, 97–98
  self-deception, 95
  "sin posits itself," 94–98 *passim*
Nonhuman animals, 7, 132, 230, 234
Nonteleology, defined, 126–27, 137, 189
  critique of, 127, 129
  theories of, 111
Normative ethics, 111, 130
"Nothing exists," 13, 21–46 *passim*, 72, 84, 112, 115, 222–24 *passim*

Ogden, Schubert M., 3, 44, 47, 113, 118, 225
On Free Choice of the Will, 87–90 *passim*
Original decision, 93, 96, 98, 100, 106, 133, 134, 234
Original freedom, 89, 90, 91, 94, 97, 98, 99, 100, 102, 233
Original sin, 94, 97, 98

Partially positive, 42
Patriotic citizens, 182, 208–11 *passim*, 214, 218, 246
Paul, 89
Persuasive power, 93, 94, 96, 101, 102–6 *passim*
Popular sovereignty, defined, 17, 163, 175, 183, 195–202

Pragmatic self-refutation, defined, 22, 71–72
Preamble, US Constitution, 193, 202, 204, 218, 220, 238, 246, 247
Primal and specific freedom, 101
Primal authorizing source, 211, 247
Primal freedom, 89, 90, 95, 101–3 *passim*, 133
Prime matter, 114
Principle of prior actuality, 14, 58–59, 65–67 *passim*, 69, 70, 229
Progressive school, 247
Promise of the Revolution, 193–220
  consequences of, 213–220
Proudfoot, Wayne, 76, 82, 231
Pure act, 56, 59, 67

Ratification:
  alone the only source of authority, 206–8
  necessary condition of authority, 210–11
Rawls, John, 146, 169, 174, 239
  overlapping consensus, 171–73, 239–40
Religion, defined, 26, 185–86, 88
  conventional meaning, defined, 161, 170
  extended meaning, defined, 162, 174
  function of, 86
  Schleiermacher's view of, 78–79
Religious emotion, 78–79, 81, 86
Religious freedom, defined, 162–64, 174–78
Religious Freedom Restoration Act, 170, 171, 179, 183, 190
Religious liberty, 2, 238, 240
Religious symbolism, 23, 14–15, 47–48, 51–52, 63, 228
Res significata and *modus significandi*, 52–53, 227
Revolution, the, 199, 201, 211–13 *passim*, 218, 219, 245
Rorty, Richard, 227

Scalia, Antonin, Justice, 188, 243
Schleiermacher, Friedrich, 2, 14, 47, 71–80 (and notes thereto)
  account of objects, 76–77
  arresting statement, 73, 79
  Christian Faith, The, 230
  "indispensable third," 78
  meaning of philosophy, 73, 79–80
  metaphysical and moral content, 77–78, 84

INDEX

Scholastic use of "transcendental, 4
Seeger, Daniel Andres, 142, 243
Self-abasement, 105
Self-assertion, 104–5
Self-differentiating, 45, 69, 115, 117
Self-government, 196–99 *passim*, 201, 245, 247
Self-understanding, defined, 121–22
Semantic self-contradiction, defined, 22
Shelby v. Holder, 123
Slavery, 199, 201, 206
Social character of temptation, 96, 97, 103–4, 105
Social practices, 136–39, 145, 241
Sockness, Brent, 3
Space, 30, 34, 115–16, 223, 233
Specific freedom, 89, 101
Spirit and the Letter, The, 88
State's rights and national views, defined, 195–96
Stevens, John Paul, Justice, 180
Stout, Jeffrey, 239–40
Subjective necessities, defined, 3–4
Subjectivism, 16, 195, 217, 218, 248
Subjectivity, defined, 7, 8, 22, 130–34
Subjects, defined, 7–8, 130–39
Summa Contra Gentiles, 48, 58, 222, 226, 228, 231
Summa Theologiae, 48, 58, 223, 225, 231

Teleology, defined, 127
    usual critique of, 128, 136–39

Tillich, Paul, 47, 80, 89, 228, 231
Time, 30, 34, 38, 74, 113, 116, 117, 223, 230, 231
Transcategorical, 63, 64
Transcendental metaphysics, defended, 21–46
    broad and strict, defined, 1–2, 3, 72, 83
    defined, 8–12
    part of philosophy, 11
    and Schleiermacher, 71–75
Treaty, defined, 195

Ultimate terms of evaluation, defined, 162
Unconditionally necessary, 13, 112
Understanding, defined, 119, 120–21
Universalism, defined, 126–28
United States v. Seeger, 243
US Sedition Act of 1798, 243
US Sedition Act of 1918, 243

Vishio, Alex, 3

Way of reason, defined, 163, 173–78
Whitehead, Alfred North, 10–11, 12, 44, 68, 85, 113, 116, 214, 225
    coherent and adequate, defined, 43
    creativity, 116–17, 122, 135
    creativity in present actuality, 136
    implicit awareness, 12, 120
Wiecek, William M., 201
Wilson, James, 196, 201, 202, 209, 212, 246
Why there is Something rather than Nothing, 223

www.ingramcontent.com/pod-product-compliance
Lightning Source LLC
Chambersburg PA
CBHW020644230426
43665CB00008B/310